STAYING MARRIED

Also By Anita Doreen Diggs

Talking Drums: An African American Quote Collection
The African American Resource Guide
Success At Work: A Guide For African Americans

STAYING MARRIED:
A Guide For African American Couples

Anita Doreen Diggs
and
Vera S. Paster, Ph.D.

Kensington Books
http://www.kensingtonbooks.com

KENSINGTON BOOKS are published by

Kensington Publishing Corp.
850 Third Avenue
New York, NY 10022

Library of Congress Card Catalog Number: 98-065137
ISBN 1-57566-248-5

First Printing: September, 1998
10 9 8 7 6 5 4 3 2 1

Printed in the United States of America

ACKNOWLEDGMENTS

To my parents, Gertrude E. Simpkins and Thomas V. Simpkins, who emerged from the struggles with victory and grace.

To my husband, G. Nicholas Paster, Ph.D., for our love and for his unlimited support through the years.

To our children and grandchildren, for their inspiration, and to my sister, Peggy Johnson. To our special friends who generously enrich our lives.

I dedicate this effort to help those who love.

Vera

* * *

To my daughters, Temica Johnson, Lateshia Johnson and Tayannah McQuillar, in the hope that all three of them will have happy, healthy and productive marriages.

Anita

AUTHORS' NOTE

We'd like to thank Monica Harris, our first editor at Kensington for believing in this book from the start, and Elise Donner Smith for helping us whittle it into shape.

For all the brothers and sisters out there
who are trying so hard to stay married.

Contents

PART THREE: Home Life & Leisure Time

PART FOUR: Mental Health

PART FIVE: Career Conflicts

PART SIX: Money Matters

After the First Dance

by Anita Doreen Diggs

A fancy wedding does not necessarily lead to a happy marriage. Matthew and I were married on June 11, 1994. It was a gorgeous spring day. I had fallen in love with Matthew's intellect, sense of humor, his way of looking at the world and the way he seemed to need me in his life. We shared a love of live entertainment, movies and *The History Channel* on cable TV.

My dress was a traditional white bridal gown with a seven-foot train and a headpiece with a ten-foot veil attached to it. I had ten bridesmaids, all dressed in slim-fitting, teal-colored, ankle-length dresses and teal pumps. The invitations and matching programs were printed in teal ink on heavy white paper. The groom and his men were dressed in gray. Our little flower girl wore ringlets in her hair and a frothy white dress. The ring boy was adorable in an outfit that matched Matthew's and he carried the rings on a white silk pillow. Six white stretch limousines carried us all to the famed Canaan Baptist Church on 116th Street in Harlem.

Reverend Wyatt Tee Walker performed the ceremony and off we went to Riccardo's, where a sumptuous feast, two bars and music from the '60s and '70s awaited our two hundred guests.

As our wedding video shows, I couldn't keep the grin off my face as we bobbed and swayed in our first dance as man and wife. The song was *Let's Stay Together* by Al Green. We honeymooned in the Poconos.

One year later, my life was in a shambles and I wanted to get as far away from Matthew as possible. That is when I came up with the idea of studying other African Americans and the way they were handling married life. It is true that all marriages are difficult, but I wanted to focus on the married world of the Black American. I wanted to focus on ways to improve the success rate of marriage between African American men and women.

After doing extensive research on the subject of African American marriages, I decided that by using the expertise of a trained professional I could get stories about real life couples. After interviewing many black psychologists, I was lucky enough to meet Dr. Vera S. Paster. She has been a marriage counselor to African American couples exclusively for over twenty years. *Staying Married: A Guide For African American Couples* evolved out of her formal education and voluminous files of case histories, my research, as well as the experiences of my married friends and family members. In 1970, the total number (includes all 50 states) of African American couples who filed for divorce was 27,320. By 1990, the number had increased to 56,267. Obviously, healing is not easy, but Dr. Paster has seen many healthy marriages made stronger and sick marriages healed.

One explanation as to why so many African American couples find it so hard to stay married is that one or both parties is functioning with no model of a healthy marriage to imitate. If neither of you grew up in a healthy marriage, you need to be aware that you have no example to follow. It's like trying to sew a dress without a sample or a pattern. It's hard, but it can be done.

Another explanation for our staggering divorce rate is that in the absence of real life models, we form our opinions of what marriage is all about from movies and television. These screen tales mainly portray enchanting beginnings followed by a main problem that is easily or rapidly resolved. The couple then rides off into the sunset to live happily ever after. These stories have nothing in common with reality.

In real life, the principal difference between happy partners and distressed ones is that happy partners are willing and able to make the marriage a top priority in their lives. They think in terms of "We" not "Me."

We have provided examples of strong, successful Black married couples, as well as examples of Black married couples who were in distress and the practical solutions they adopted to strengthen their marriages. We discuss the most common and surmountable problems Black married couples face.

Matthew and I separated for a while but we are now back together. So far, he and I are happy with our decision to reconcile.

If Doctor Paster and I can help even one other Black couple to stay married, then our labor will have been worthwhile.

Anita Doreen Diggs
New York City
September 1998

Happily Ever After

by Vera S. Paster, Ph.D.

There is much research that demonstrates that the intimate connection with a loving mate helps prevent mental breakdown and promotes well-being in all areas of life. There is also much evidence that, other things being equal, a basically harmonious, two-parent family life, preferably buttressed by supportive extended family and community members, is the best circumstance in which to raise children to be healthy, productive adults. A gratifying marriage is nourishment for the heart, body and soul. When marriages break down, the whole family suffers, so a healthy, enduring marriage is worth fighting for.

During slavery hunger for family cohesion developed into fierce allegiance to family ties after emancipation. It is our tradition for family (nuclear and extended) to cling together, to stay close. Even those not related by blood or marriage are enfolded into "our family." Black people have developed institutional supports to help maintain equilibrium, supports like the church, clubs and lodges. There's a sense of shared danger that keeps our people, including family, together. We have learned to make do with little or nothing and have generations of practice maintaining our balance, despite the worst troubles.

We have always told ourselves that we must be strong and follow our goals, whether it means going under, around or over barriers put in our way. We know how to laugh in the midst of despair and find the joke in the antics of those we believe to be our oppressors. These are our strengths which have been honed through over three hundred years of oppression.

The problem of marital breakup has dramatically worsened during the last twenty years. According to the U.S. Census, in

1970, 87 percent of all families consisted of two married-to-each-other parents. By 1991, this had dropped to 79 percent. The situation has been worse for Black families. Caucasian intact families dropped from 89 percent in 1970 to 83 percent in 1991. Black intact families, however, dropped from 68 percent in 1970 to less than half in 1991. According to the 1991 Census report, only 48 percent of Black families had two married parents in the household.

Why this plunge in the longevity of marriages? There are many factors, none of which probably causes breakups, but all of which accumulate to create too many assaults on a modern marriage for some to survive. For example, years ago, stability was maintained because of the acceptance of shared and largely unquestioned values. During current times of social transition there is an absence of consensus about rules for living. When women were handed from father to husband, it was with the understanding that the men were responsible for their daughters' and wives' well-being in exchange for their sexual innocence and fidelity, their respect for a father's or husband's leadership, and their loyalty in putting the man's welfare first. For a wife, this included her seeing to her husband's well-being, health, and daily care and feeding; her provision of a clean, comfortable home and well-brought up children. When this contract was fulfilled, it was easier for all to go well. Or, well enough. But these rules have changed or been challenged but have not been replaced. In addition to the old expectations which some women and men still hold, they also seek freedom from the burdens and restrictions that those rules impose. Women feel pushed by their own self-expectations and the general social pressures, to say nothing of current economic necessity, to experience the full measure of life. We want success in the marketplace outside of home, and we want to be our own master. Guilt, pressure, fatigue, a sense of failure caused by not being able to "do it all" or, if we manage to do much, feeling insufficiently appreciated for our struggles and accomplishments, strain women and their marriages. Men feel constantly challenged by their responsibilities and by wives who are demanding to be confided in and brought to orgasm, to be both more manly, "sensitive" and successful. The American values of being "happy," gratified, doing and having it *now,* also hinder overcoming the inevitable problems encountered in all marriages. The social acceptance of divorce and the easy access to it, with the more widespread capability of women to attain some kind of economic survival without a husband, help make divorce a first rather than a last resort. Of course, many of these societal changes are welcomed progress, but all changes have negative effects, too.

It cannot be a surprise that Black families in this country are more vulnerable to destabilization. In addition to all of the above societal factors that affect everyone in our culture, there are special hazards for the marriages of African Americans, just as there are special hazards in all areas of living. Our health is worse; we die earlier. Many of us, whether or not we have jobs, live in poverty, a condition of peril for marriages. We are the last hired and first fired, and whether professional, white collar workers or laborers, we are economically insecure. It has been found that financial insecurity is more debilitating than being without a job. Black men and boys bring home the stress of coping in a society where they are feared by strangers, demeaned and even gratuitously abused. There is an ongoing effect, if not effort, to undermine the esteem of Black young people and adults who are constantly confronted with efforts to prove that they are not able to compete, indeed not entitled to try to achieve, be educated or even be counted in the census or to vote. Campaigns against negatively defined Affirmative Action programs are succeeding in overturning gains that both Black and white people died for in the '60s and '70s. The pressures from an accumulated exposure to these assaults overtax our marriages. The situation is compounded by the lack of models of people in long-term marriages, people who can support the efforts of other families to stick it out through thick and thin. No more network of family, kin, neighbors and church, comembers in close-knit Southern or Caribbean villages who support or push couples to remain together. Like the rest of our transient society, we do not even live near our family and we barely know our neighbors. In fact, we characteristically try our best to avoid exposing the troubles in our families to "outsiders." Yes, it is no wonder that a disproportionate number of Black families break down under these burdens. And it is not surprising that we and large numbers of our children— suffer from the consequences—to say nothing of what will happen to the generations to come.

Throughout our beleaguered history in this country, the strengths of the African American family have fortified and sustained us. We have been afflicted by so many accumulated blows from so many systems (economic, educational, health, political), and yet we lack the practicality of mass mobilization for direct action against identifiable oppressors that "keeps hope alive." Now, more than ever, we must work collectively and individually to regain the strengths of stable, positive family life.

Just as an increasing number of us can be considered casualties because we are in the criminal justice system, are addicts or have AIDS or some other chronic disease, so also, there are increasing numbers of us who are survivors. We are seeing to the education of our children, serving in hard-earned executive positions in major corporations, earning advanced professional degrees, heading our own businesses and agencies, becoming recognized stars in public arenas, running cities, being active in congress, even running for president of our nation. Yes, more than ever, many of us are doing very well. And the majority of us are getting by, living our lives as best we can, working every day to make ends meet, take care of our families and find a little enjoyment in the process. Regardless of where we fit within this continuum, however, it is clear that all of us need help in keeping our marriages together.

My years of work in a variety of settings have continually confirmed that all kinds of troubles, both expected and surprising, result from marriages that fail. Countless numbers of children learn how to be women and how to be men from the examples set by parents who are at war with each other. The most tragic are the psychological and social injuries suffered by the children of those families. Their special problems are evident to me every time I meet with troubled children. When I started out as a young, newly trained psychologist in the Family Court and in juvenile correctional institutions, I examined children who had committed serious assaults, runaways who had exposed themselves to and found the perils of the streets, and frustrated parents who had given up on children who were out of their control. Almost none of these youths had two parents at home. When I asked them about their missing parent (the separated parent usually had disappeared), erstwhile "toughies" would often be overcome with tears of sadness.

Separation of their parents leaves many children feeling betrayed by their remaining parent and abandoned by the one who left. Children react with hurt and rage, compounded by fear and guilt. They lose their childhood faith in being important enough always to be loved and protected in a good world.

I served the New York City school system for over twenty years, first as a school psychologist, then, in the capacity of a Supervisor of School Psychologists, and finally, as the director of the school system's entire mental health agency. In those roles I have been in most of the over one thousand schools in the city on behalf of providing help to troubled children, as well as to their parents and teachers. Again, those children who were worse off are those who had already, or were currently witnessing their parents' marriages crumble. Later, when I developed and served as the director of a community sponsored and community responsive mental health center in a hard pressed but caring area of upper Manhattan, and later, as the Commissioner for Child and Adolescent Mental Health Services for the State of Massachusetts, I found the same plights. Of the children who showed distresses of the kind that brought them to the attention of agencies like ours, those without two parents seemed to be worse off and more difficult to turn around.

I am writing now as the Director for City University's City College Mental Health Clinic for child, adolescent and family treatment. In all of these settings, the most injured children are those from fractured families. The only worse off group are those in foster homes, children who have no functional parenting relative at all.

Why are children so victimized by their parents' divorce? One reason is because children are dependent on parents for many things, for example, their view of the world as safe and predictable, where they have a place and will be protected and loved no matter what. When one of the parents deserts them (and the most peaceful separation is experienced by the children as a desertion), the children lose their trust in others. Children also see themselves as the center of their world. They believe themselves to be responsible for the good and the bad things that happen to them and to those they love. If their parents fight or separate, the children believe themselves to be the cause. "If I didn't do that bad thing, or have that bad thought, my father would not have left us." This guilt often pushes children towards punishable or other self-endangering behaviors because they feel unloved and unlovable. No matter how unresponsive some may seem to be, children do mourn the disruption of their home.

Many children do not have the resources to overcome this grief. Nor do they know what to do with their rage—rage at the abandoning parent, even if the child has regular visits with him, and rage at the parent who remains, for not having held things together.

Anger at parents who are ever more precious because they have demonstrated that they may disappear at any time is not easy for a child to manage. If they thrash out against the world, they cause themselves and others a lot of trouble. If they swallow their pain, they prolong their suffering, which interferes with the normal developmental tasks of childhood.

No matter how welcome the separation might be when it finally comes, the adults involved must also cope with their own sense of disappointment, failure, rejection, anger, depression and guilt.

The parents suffer an immediate drop in standard of living. This adds to their peril, especially if the couple's combined income was already marginal.

Yes, some children and adults do thrive better after the ending of a cruel or a coldly, psychologically disinvested marital arrangement, but even then, they all pay a price and must overcome the inevitable injuries.

I am convinced that much of the anguish I have encountered could be avoided if couples were exposed to knowledge about marital relationships early on, and were guided in ways to understand and constructively deal with the unavoidable conflicts and the social pressures that stress all marriages.

Because I am a therapist who specializes in healing the wounded, I am very interested in Primary Prevention. The Primary Prevention movement recognizes that we cannot rely on remedying the suffering of individuals to achieve real wide-ranging improvements. There are not enough healers and there are no guarantees that the treatments will succeed. It is better to attack the sources of suffering—better to prevent than to fix. That means, we must figure out the causes of the trouble and either eliminate them or strengthen potential victims against their negative effects.

The psychologist George Albee has been the leader of establishing this approach in the field of mental health. When I was appointed by President Carter to the President's Commission on Mental Health, the task force on which I served was headed by Dr. Albee and consisted of the nation's preeminent psychologists, psychiatrists and mental health advocates, whose work demonstrated the effectiveness of primary prevention approaches. That panel recommended that all government funding of mental health research and services include a proportionate amount to be set aside for primary prevention activities. Unfortunately, this has not yet happened.

This book is written in the context of primary prevention. Our purpose is to provide specific guidance in keeping marriages going in positive, loving support. Ms. Diggs and I hope that African American couples will find support and guidance within its covers. Its purpose is to point the way to hope for faltering marriages, to strengthen those that are vulnerable to breakdown and to enable the binding joys of intimacy for all who are fortunate enough to have joined hands with a life partner. We know that people do thrive living an independent, positive single life. We know that it is better for children and adults if partners live divorced rather than feel stuck in a miserable, demeaning legal union. But we also know that, other things being equal, our souls can soar in the deepening intimacy of a stable, secure marriage.

We want to disseminate what we have learned. Damaged children, their parents, teachers, caretakers and child advocates, my students, colleagues and especially my patients, have taught me well about these matters. My fortunate endowment of loving, sturdy family members and dear friends, and a remarkable, sustaining husband have shaped the lessons I have learned, leading to what is now shared with you.

We want to spread our philosophy that a stable, positive marriage can be a wonderfully enriching institution within which to raise thriving children; that stable marriages strengthen our survival as an oppressed people, and enable our progress within the larger society.

We hope that a word, a concept, an example within these pages will uplift a faltering marriage or add zest to one that is ongoing. We want you to find understanding of some of the underlying forces that may lead to the reactions that you find in yourself and in your spouse.

To live happily ever after the wedding does not happen magically. But to live happily is worth all the effort and help required. We offer this help.

Please note: All case studies are disguised, no original names or facts have been used and some situations are combinations of actual experiences. Any other similarities are purely coincidental.

Vera S. Paster, Ph.D.
New York City
September 1998

PART ONE:

The Marriage

CHAPTER ONE

Intimacy

"My father could just break my mother's concentration with some of the funny, romantic things he used to say or do."
—Attallah Shabazz
Ebony magazine, February 1992

Every bride and groom hears it. It's a cliché, but it's true. Marriage takes work. The foundation of marriage is intimacy which can only be achieved through mutual acceptance, communication, honesty, sharing and trust. This "work" should be gratifying, even fun. And it can be, especially if it starts before the wedding bells begin to sound. The later the work starts, the more difficult it will seem but as long as you consider yourselves a couple, it is never too late to begin.

Take another look at the quotation which opens this chapter. We remember Malcolm X as our "shining Black prince," a man who spoke the truth as he saw it and never allowed the dominant culture to bring him to his knees. His daughter, Attallah Shabazz, remembers her daddy as a romantic man who, in spite of his busy schedule and heavy workload, always took the time to be romantic and intimate with his wife.

Intimacy is the great gift of marriage. It is that warm, loving sense of being as close to your spouse as any human being can be to another. It is knowing your mate's needs, goals, opinions and sensitivities. It is knowing that the two of you can share joy, pain and disappointment while still feeling safe in the relationship. It is knowing that you and your partner can spend time apart without losing your closeness.

Happiness Is Not a Goal

It is not enough to say "we just plan to be happy." This statement is vague. You are each individuals and have different needs that must be met in order for both of you to be "happy." If "being happy" is as far as the two of you have gotten in terms of goal setting, the marriage is jeopardized at the starting gate. When two people try to share the same space, and are working with two different, unarticulated agendas, there are bound to be some nasty surprises.

If you haven't already done so, now is the time to start talking about your goals and dreams and planning what the two of you will accomplish as a couple. "Happiness" can never be the goal. Working on shared goals and dreams leads to happiness.

The Hidden Self

Fatima, 30, was a big woman. Tall and hefty. What a lot of people call full-figured. A kind and considerate person, she was a good storyteller who attracted lots of people to the home she shared with her husband, Lonnie. Since Lonnie was a quiet fellow who was content to let Fatima do all the talking, it took him three years to realize that although he enjoyed his wife's company immensely, he really didn't know her at all. This bothered him, but when he brought the subject up, Fatima dismissed it by saying "I don't really have anything to tell you, honey." Well, Lonnie was smart enough to realize that anyone who has lived more than three decades has experienced joy, heartbreak and everything in between.

He mulled this over for another six months and, during this time, his imagination filled in the gaps left by Fatima's silence. Could there be another husband and six lonely kids living in another state? After all, she was cagey on the subject of starting a family. Suppose Fatima was really an escaped convict? After all, she claimed to have no blood relatives.

Naturally, Lonnie became uncomfortable in his wife's presence. Fatima ignored the tension at first but soon, the silent times in their house were occurring with greater frequency and lasting longer. They went for counseling. It didn't take the couple long to trace Fatima's secretive nature back to the household she grew up in. Her parents had been remarkably uncommunicative. During Fatima's childhood, her days were numbing in their sameness. Her mother got the children ready for school without saying a word, unless a scolding was called for. After school, the children went to their rooms until Daddy came home for dinner. The parents and children ate quietly and then everyone sat in the living room and watched television until bedtime. The only time conversation eddied about them was when company came over. Then, Fatima's mother swapped stories with her sisters. Her father was the life of each party, drinking, laughing and telling jokes. Now, Fatima didn't know any other way to be.

It took over a year of counseling but she learned to share her ideas, dreams and inner feelings with Lonnie and they are still together.

Each of us has an open side. That is the side of yourself that you allow your friends, neighbors, acquaintances and colleagues to see. Then, there is the hidden self. Perhaps your mother and best friend have seen that side of you. Or, you could be an extremely guarded individual who has let no one catch a glimpse of it.

Whatever the case, your partner has to know your hidden self.

This does not mean you have to have a marathon talking session that leaves him or her reeling or confused. Intimacy does not mean you must tell your partner every thought or idea that comes into your head. There is a big difference between sharing who you are today and confessing every deed you've ever done. Sharing yourself will enhance the marriage; dumping unnecessary baggage on a spouse early in the marriage is not a good idea.

But over time, you must reveal who you really are deep down inside. In order to have true intimacy with your spouse, you need to be loved for who you really are.

You both need to feel secure in the knowledge that your partner accepts the real you and is just as committed to that hidden self as to that self you present to the world.

Acceptance

He likes to get to the airport at least an hour before passengers are advised to be there; she likes to arrive at the time of boarding. He is an early riser, has lots of energy, is quick and hates to wait. She does not feel awake until almost noon and hates to rush; in fact, she is slow-paced and often late.

We are born with a disposition towards basic styles such as these. We can even see it in babies. Some are placid, sleepy and gurgle happily between naps. Others enter the world screaming and remain high strung and actively responsive. These basic dispositions stick with us. Try as we might, we cannot really change our basic nature. And why should we? They are all good. Accept your nature and that of the person you married.

If you find yourself married to someone who seems to be everything that you are not, there are two basic choices:

1. Let your lives be enhanced by the differences. In other words, when working toward a specific objective, use the best of each of you to achieve it.
2. Spend your time together criticizing and otherwise trying to reform the other to your "correct" way of being. This rarely leads to a lasting marriage. At least, not a happy one.

Actually some partners (usually the wife) find a third choice. They try to change who they are in order to please the spouse. Many times, the partner who does this is already feeling shaky about who she is. Often, she already has started to worry that she is not as good, smart or physically attractive as her mate. Whatever the reason, trying to change your basic nature can lead to rage, self-alienation or a severe case of depression.

Celebrate and accept your differences. Laugh at them when you can.

Patience

Learning how to stay married takes time. Be patient with yourself and your spouse. Remind yourselves that you are trying to learn new ways of relating to someone you love. The habits that you brought to the marriage were developed over many years. It will take almost that long to adjust those habits in order to protect your marriage.

Patience also means not becoming angry or discouraged when your partner is not working on some agreed-upon idea in the style or at the pace you would choose. Accept your partners methods and any setbacks that occur.

During times of stress, whether caused by problems in or outside of the marriage, you will have to remind yourself of your commitment to the marriage. There will be hard times. There will be times when you don't like each other very much. But through it all, if you cultivate patience and optimism, your resilience eventually will take you back to the positive side of your life together.

Communication

Reggie Jackson said it best: "You work to make a successful marriage. It isn't just enough to be the breadwinner and for your wife to be a caring and supportive helpmate. You have to talk: husband to wife, man to woman, human being to human being." Not communicating or misinterpreting the communication is the basis of many marital problems.

Learn to view each conversation you have with your spouse as a gift. Even if you don't like what is being said, communication is still taking place. Issues are being aired which means they can be handled, rather than kept inside to gnaw away at the fabric of your marriage. Even if you don't like the things you hear, think of the conversation as a gift. Communication has taken place and now issues that might have been the eventual seeds of destruction for your marriage can be addressed.

Learn to listen. Quietly practicing what you are going to say when it is your turn to speak does not count as listening. Doing something else (such as washing dishes, replacing tiles, fixing the toaster, hanging a picture) while your mate is trying to communicate with you does not count as listening, either. Give your mate your full attention. Hear what your spouse is saying and try to understand why he is saying it.

If you're talking out problems, it can be hard to sit there with your mouth shut when you feel the other is wrong. But listen until the other stops speaking before you respond. Try not to disagree with everything you hear. We show that we value our mate when we hear her out, instead of waiting for her to stop talking so that we can fling a zinger of a rebuttal.

Your response should indicate your desire to work things out.

Aim for honesty when necessary. *When Lalla married, she decided that she wanted to start married life with complete trust between herself and her new husband, Abdul. As time went on, she never found the right time and situation for this mutually disclosing session. She'd had a wild life when she was in school and during her single years. Now, she felt she had settled down and wanted to put all of that behind her.*

She worried about her procrastination. She felt she had to be

*honest and give her all to Abdul. She also thought that he might
lose respect for her, even leave her if she delayed too long in telling
the truth.*

*Lalla decided that she would talk over her dilemma with her
best friend. She'd always found Beth to be honest and levelheaded.
And besides, Beth had done most of the same things Lalla had.*

*When she and Beth got together, Lalla explained the situation.
Beth listened carefully and then answered the way many women
do. She told her own story. Beth had decided long ago that her
past was her own business and had not informed her husband of
many things. Beth was at peace with her decision.*

*Lalla understood her friend's decision but she was still unsure
of how to act. Finally, she decided to tell Abdul everything. One
night, when they got into bed, she began to discuss a drug-oriented
film they had seen that evening. Lalla started talking about her
party years, about the sex and the drugs. There was no answer
from Abdul and Lalla was afraid to turn over and face him. When
she finally summoned the nerve to twist herself around in the bed,
there were tears streaming down her face—until she realized that
Abdul was sound asleep.*

*The next morning, Lalla casually asked her husband what he
had heard her say. All he could recall was the soothing sound of
her voice talking about the movie. Lalla felt that this was a sign
which was telling her to leave well enough alone.*

It is hard to determine whether you should communicate all
your concerns to your mate. What is the difference between honesty
and throwing destructive land mines into your marital bed by
bringing up issues neither of you can change and which do not
affect the other partner? In this case, Lalla's friend Beth was right.

TIPS FOR HONEST COMMUNICATION

♦ Don't pretend to go along with the program just to keep the
peace.
♦ Don't be afraid to admit it, if you've promised to do something
and find out you really can't.
♦ Don't be afraid to ask your mate for help when you need it.
♦ Honesty does not mean cruelty. Whatever you have to say
can be said without stabbing your mate in the heart.

Eliminate sentences that begin with "if you really loved me." *When Boyd and Jilly entered counseling, they were both simmering with unexpressed anger.*

JILLY: *When Boyd and I walk the streets, he never holds my hand. When a man really loves his wife, he holds her with pride in public places.*

BOYD *(surprised): We've been married six years and you've never shown affection toward me in public. I thought you didn't like that sort of thing. Since we're on the subject of true love, I have something to say, too.*

COUNSELOR: *Go ahead. . . .*

BOYD: *If Jilly really cared, she would watch old Westerns with me sometimes, even though she doesn't like them.*

JILLY: *When did you ever ask me?*

BOYD *(bitterly): Why bother? I figured you'd say no.*

Your mate is not a mind reader. "If he (or she) really loved me, he (or she) would know what I need" is a dangerous assumption to make. It is unreasonable to expect your spouse to magically discern what you want. It is absurd to expect your spouse somehow to forsee what you expect without being warned. If you could gain psychic ability and read your spouse's mind, would that prove your love?

A word about timing. When you need to discuss something serious with your partner, make sure the time is right.

For example, she is trying to soothe a colicky baby. Perhaps you could wait until later to mention how tired you are of having chicken for dinner.

If he is furious with his boss and circling job ads in the newspaper, maybe that is not the best time to remind him of his promise to buy you a fur coat on your third anniversary.

Ask yourself if the timing seems right before starting a serious talk.

Share the Joy of Being Alive

Every day that you wake up is a good day. Try to experience a little beauty, adventure or joy on a regular basis. Have you ever:

♦ watched the sun rise or set?

- ♦ walked in the woods?
- ♦ spent time on a real farm?
- ♦ watched the tide come in?

Once in a while, you just have to leave your challenges and goals behind. Get back to the basics and marvel at the way Mother Nature works. Run. Racewalk. No matter what is going on in your marriage, once in a while just hug each other and be glad that your time is not yet up.

Be Generous

Crawford spent a lot of money on himself. He needed to visit the barbershop twice a week, dressed in the best suits and bought state-of-the-art stereo equipment on which to play his jazz CDs. When Linni complained that he never gave her anything, he wisely cleaned up his act. However, every gift he gave his wife came with a price tag. If he came home with a new dress for Linni, he casually asked if she'd take over his chores the next day. If she asked for extra money, Crawford nonchalantly inquired where the dollars from the previous week had gone.

It was infuriating and Linni finally put a stop to it. She calmly reminded him that they were partners and she wasn't out to get over him. It took some practice but Crawford finally was able to give without the fear of seeming gullible. He learned that a good marriage means never having to "watch your back."

A particular loss in the Black community during these last days of the twentieth century is the spirit of giving without expecting anything in return. We tend to think in terms of "I've got to get mine." When we are not thinking selfishly, we still hesitate to give freely out of a fear of being viewed as weak. No one wants to take a chance on being used so we guard our turf and feel that others should do the same or get swallowed up by the ways of life.

Try not to act this way toward your life partner.

Operate from a base of goodwill rather than one of suspicion or fear. Think of ways to surprise your spouse. Gifts that are not expected are usually appreciated the most.

A Sense of Humor

Sometimes, life isn't very amusing. The rent is due and you don't have it. Your wife and kids are laid up with the chicken pox and the boss is bugging the staff to do more overtime. The list is endless but things always get better. Don't let the down times keep you from laughing. Always look for the bit of humor in any situation.

Humor also comes when we don't take ourselves too seriously. That means that we accept the fact that we could be wrong now and then, and our mate's view of a situation might be correct. We help establish and preserve our intimacy with laughter.

Think of the relative shortness of the longest span of married life, no matter how old we are when one of us meets that final parting.

Think of the tragedies of life that cannot be avoided.

Think of the enduring intimacy of mutual caring which is our goal.

Think first, and then it is easy to laugh at some part of our challenges as well as at the minor differences in our individual way of doing things.

A good laugh cures many ills. Shared laughter prevents them.

Admit It When You're Wrong

For just a moment, stop and pretend that you are the husband in the following imaginary conversation.

HUSBAND: *I'm upset that you invited our families and friends over for Kwaanza without consulting me.*

WIFE: *We're always going over to everyone else's house. Do you want us to look like users?*

HUSBAND: *What I'm saying is that I was surprised when several people called today to accept an invitation that I knew nothing about. I felt like a fool.*

WIFE: *You're getting upset about nothing. Everyone is going to have a good time.*

HUSBAND: *You are deliberately missing my point. Why didn't you discuss this with me?*

WIFE: *Are you going to turn into a control freak?*

HUSBAND: *This is getting out of hand. I just want you to apologize for not discussing it with me. That's all. Once I get past that, I can start looking forward to the celebration.*

WIFE: *I'm not going to start checking in with you everytime I get ready to do something.*

HUSBAND: *Why are you fighting me on this when we both know you were wrong not to tell me?*
WIFE *(mumbling)*: *Yeah. Okay.*

How do you feel as the husband in this case? Probably angry and frustrated.

Have you ever found yourself fighting ardently over an issue that did *not* mean that much to you? The humility of allowing yourself to be wrong is based on self-acceptance, and secure self-love. If you are wrong, say so. Tell your spouse what your behavior was all about and apologize. Also explain how you hope to handle such an incident in the future.

When we are comfortable with ourselves we don't have to seize every opportunity to prove to others that we are right.

When we are comfortable with ourselves, we can afford to support the sense of well-being and self-respect of the one we love.

We, Not Me

Once you get married, you must take what is best for the marriage into account whenever you are making a major decision. If you approach situations by basing yourselves on a "me" agenda, there can never be true intimacy. When you find yourself automatically thinking in "we" terms on a regular basis, it is a sure sign that oneness is being achieved.

Being Married Does Not Mean Losing Your Identity

Both men and women can be better satisfied with marriage if they redefine what it means to be married. It doesn't mean that you lose control over your life or have to let go of all your dreams. It doesn't mean that pursuit of any individual goal takes away from your "commitment to the marriage." Quite the contrary.

There has to be a degree of balance worked out between husband and wife. If you fail to bring a degree of balance to your marriage, the day will almost surely come when you feel resentful at having given up so much. Then, you'll either leave the marriage or resign yourself to a deadened relationship.

Love means being fair. Each of you has to know when to step back and let the other partner take the ball and run as far as his or her talent and discipline will take them.

LITTLE THINGS MEAN A LOT

Be thoughtful.
Be polite.
Romance each other.
Back up loving words with loving deeds.

Empathy

If your spouse fails to achieve a desired goal you didn't think was worth pursuing in the first place, try to remember what your own disappointments have felt like. If your mate's friend, whom you never liked, moves out of the country, don't breathe a sigh of relief in front of your mate. Empathy is the ability to put yourself in another's shoes, walk around in them a little bit, see how they feel and act accordingly.

Secrets

Generally speaking, there shouldn't be any deep, dark secrets between the two of you. Yet, there are times when keeping quiet is the best idea. Here is a sample of thoughts that are better left unshared:

- ♦ You had an erotic dream about her best friend.
- ♦ You hate the Christmas present he gave you and can't imagine wearing it in public.
- ♦ Your mother hates her and is only being nice because it is the right thing to do.
- ♦ You loathe his old college chum without good reason.

Watch Happily Married Couples

If you are lucky enough to know any couple that has been married for twenty years or more, pay attention to them.

Do you notice how they finish each other's sentences because they are so familiar with each other's thinking?

Do you notice how they have settled into a way of being with each other—whether in agreeable companionship or bickering interaction—with no threat of parting?

Do you notice that they are good friends, bound by romantic love? Observe these long-married couples. Talk to them. They have found their way to the prize we all seek.

CHAPTER TWO

Did I Really Marry This Person?

"One marries many times at many levels within a marriage. If you have more marriages than you have divorces within the marriage, you're lucky . . ."

—Ruby Dee
I Dream A World, 1989

The years of courtship and preparation for the wedding are a heady and exciting phases of a couple's relationship. However, true intimacy develops long after the ceremonies and celebrations have come to a close. Once the honeymoon ends (it can be a week or seven years), the other person's habits and human weaknesses become visible and glaring. This is called disenchantment and it is just a normal stage that all married couples go through. A lot of couples let the small signs of affection dwindle because they link those actions with the start of a relationship. They feel self-conscious about pet names and romantic jokes because they see these things as a groundwork to beginning an alliance and feel they are supposed to be way beyond that. The reality is just the opposite. These small signs of affection help keep a marriage together.

It is usually during the disenchantment phase that you start to have doubts about your choice of a mate and become convinced that you made a mistake. You start wondering why you married at all. I mean, you had a great job, wonderful friends and a beautiful studio apartment. And, you had good times with the person with whom you've now exchanged vows. "Why oh why," you moan, "did I go and mess everything up?" "Marry in haste, repent in leisure" you gloomily remember hearing someone say. Never mind that the two of you dated for six years before marrying.

One young couple had been married for three years without once having a serious disagreement. Their first fight was an eye-opening experience for both of them.

May ran into an old boyfriend from Fisk University and had lunch with him. A friend of her husband's saw them and told Jonathan. He was furious and after the initial argument, Jonathan stalked about the house with a tight jaw and said nothing. May was very uncomfortable. After a week of this treatment, she became defensive. Jonathan was being unfair. She told him off and the incident accelerated into a huge fight with screaming and name calling flying back and forth. May says, "We've been married for three years and this is our first fight. I don't want our lives to be this way . . . screaming insults at each other whenever there is a serious disagreement. It was only a lunch and if Jonathan hadn't quit his job two months ago because of some insignificant racial slight, we would still be going out to restaurants and maybe I wouldn't have accepted the lunch invitation."

Whoa! There is a lot going on here. First of all, May obviously had no intention of telling Jonathan about her encounter. There are many different ways of lying and she needs to get in touch with the need for honesty if this marriage is going to work. Jonathan may have looked at the innocent meal as exactly that if he had heard about it from her own lips.

And what about this "friend"? This couple needs to talk about his motives for running back to Jonathan with what he "saw." If he is operating out of jealousy, or because he initially disapproved of Jonathan's choice of a bride, he is going to be a disruptive influence in their lives.

Jonathan must have been deeply saddened by May's cavalier dismissal of what happened on his job. There is no indication that he is irresponsible, so whatever happened must have been very hurtful. She should not get into the habit of dismissing his pain as "insignificant."

Instead of "telling Jonathan off" when she got fed up with his sulking, May could have handled the situation more effectively since it was she who disappointed her spouse in two different ways. May would do well to remember these hints.

1. Avoid name calling.
2. Avoid blaming. Jonathan did not cause tension in the household. May could have taken responsibility for not considering Jonathan's feelings. What if the situation had been reversed?
3. Call a time-out . Once the yelling started, it was time to call a time-out. Jonathan and May should have avoided each other for at least an hour of cool-down time and focused on other activities.
4. Focus on the true cause of the argument. After the hour was up, Jonathan and May should have focused on the true cause of the lunch date, namely, that May was acting out her resentment over Jonathan's unemployment.
5. Talk to discover a resolution. May and Jonathan should have sat down and talked about Jonathan's career issues, the importance of making major decisions together (such as leaving a place of employment), and what their feelings are about spending time with lovers from their respective pasts.

Each of you has preconceived notions of what your marriage will be like. One of the most harmful preconceived notions you may have is that friction and disharmony are to be expected in any love relationship between a Black man and woman. Unlike whites, African American partners cannot automatically click the remote control or go to the movies and find loving couples to emulate. Television producers and Hollywood filmmakers haven't done much to show that loving relationships between Black men and women even exist at all. A rare exception is *The Cosby Show*. Traditionally, Black love has been depicted as something far removed from white relationships. During the past fifty years, filmmakers and producers have portrayed Black couples fighting each other or fighting the system. The man is shown as running away and leaving the family for the welfare system to support. The couple is portrayed as in lust, not in love. There is no romance, no affection, no devotion. There is none of the passion, tenderness and individual respect that are so prominent in the love stories played out every day by millions of Black men and women in the real world. One way to overcome this preconceived notion is to spend lots of time with other happily married African American couples while engaged in activities that do not include viewing the endless stream of harmful propaganda that continues to pour out of Hollywood.

Whether the preconceived notions come from mass media or family experiences, they are with you and firmly in place even before the marriage gets under way. These notions were shaped over many years by family, friends, books, songs and the dreams you had as children. With each of these notions working in the background, much is expected of your new partner. If you realize this in time, these notions can be discussed. If the marriage isn't honest, disappointment is inevitable. Accumulated disappointments are usually fatal.

Some men, who may have been very open with their feelings before marriage, seem to go on a permanent emotional vacation once they get comfortable.

When you first married, he would sit for hours and have long, even philosophical conversations with you. But once things settled, he seemed to retreat into an "old married man" attitude. Dahlia gives us an example of what happened between her and Ray.

Ray and I have been married a year. I get home before he does, so I have time to pretty up, straighten out the house, and get a romantic dinner going.

Most nights I set the table with flower buds and candles, take a shower, fix my makeup, redo my hair and fuss around in the closet to find an alluring outfit.

For the last month or two, when he comes in he barely grunts a hello. He heads for the bathroom and then sits on the couch and puts on the TV or he flips through the newspaper. It depends upon which is more exciting at the moment, but in a matter of minutes, he's either glued to one or the other—the TV or the paper.

Staying happily married is a long process. The initial excitement of falling in love should change to a sense of being in a close, warm, nurturing relationship. Determination to hold on to the thrill will only result in disappointment. Those intense, early emotions are partially caused by the newness of the relationship. Gimmicks are fun but they don't replace patience or the day-to-day work of building a lasting marriage

Let's get real. How many times can Roy "ooh" and "aah" over Dahlia's inviting outfits. He deserves praise for having managed to summon up enthusiasm for such an extended period of time. Roy may beat a hasty retreat because it may seem that Dahlia expects a romantic response to those outfits . . . EVERY SINGLE

DAY. On the way home, Roy probably worries about having to perform once he gets there and so becomes even more exhausted.

Dahlia also needs to give herself a break. After toiling all day, she comes home, reapplies makeup and expends her remaining energy doing a second shift. Dahlia must ask herself if she is desperately afraid of losing her husband. She needs to slip into something comfortable and talk to Ray . . . while he prepares dinner, on occasion.

It is true that a lot of men unwind by reading the paper or watching the evening news when they get home from work. What's wrong with that? Instead of stewing and grumbling about it, figure out what your own needs are at the end of the day and find ways in which to meet those needs.

Ask your spouse to do the following exercise with you.

GETTING TOGETHER

1. Each of you take a separate piece of paper and jot down what you think is the ideal way to spend the after work/before bedtime hours.
2. On another slip of paper each of you should state the time when you are most amenable to discussing serious issues. During breakfast? On the weekend? After dinner? Everyone is different.
3. Compare your ideas and then combine them on one single sheet of paper.
4. Try the plan for two weeks, making changes as necessary.

Marriage is not a magical state of being that will bring eternal happiness.

People don't actually change when the honeymoon is over. They just feel secure enough in the relationship to show more of themselves, which includes the blemishes. In short, the two of you no longer wear company manners.

Partners and the marriage itself will go through many stages. If these stages are to be traveled successfully there has to be unwavering commitment on both sides. Each of you is an individual and one cannot change the other. Talk a lot and share ideas. The goal is to enjoy each other's differences. Couples who have stayed married for a long period of time aren't just lucky. Staying married requires an infinite amount of patience—certainly more than you've ever needed before.

Gertrude had only been married a month when she said angrily, "We missed my parents fiftieth anniversary party because he was too stubborn to listen to me. I told him that the car was making funny noises. We ended up stranded on the New Jersey Turnpike for hours until the auto club came for us. By then it was too late, so we just went back home. I told him that if this is the way he's going to act, he'll find himself in divorce court before the year is out."

Of course, Gertrude was unhappy at missing such an important event but threatening her new husband with divorce was unconscionable. If something like this makes Gertrude consider divorce, what happens five years from now if the house burns down and her husband loses his job—all in the same day? Gertrude needs to grow up. This is not Wedding Day Barbie. It is real life, shared with an imperfect human being just like herself.

PATIENCE IS ALL

♦ Refrain from showing impatience while waiting for your spouse to work through old and unproductive patterns.
♦ Refrain from looking at one inconsequential event during the early days and asking yourself, "Is this what I have to put up with for the rest of my life?"
♦ Refrain from taking over when your partner is working at something and insisting on demonstrating a faster or "better" way of doing it.

There is one thing that is 100% certain about husbands, wives and marriage: Change will occur in all three and this will happen many, many times. Look at every change as an opportunity to learn and grow together.

When a couple is dating, they show each other their good sides and reinforce their love for the other through joking, kissing, holding hands and going out of their way for each other. After the marriage, each person tends to express love in the way which feels most comfortable.

What Kind of Love Does Your Spouse Need?

If you lived alone for a long time before getting married, it won't take long before you start grumbling about your lack of privacy.

Everyone can and should have their private moments, but you voluntarily gave up your right to complete privacy on your wedding day. Soon after that you begin to see that the person you married is a real human being with real faults, and some irritating habits. After the first real fight, you understand that your married life isn't all sparkle and glitter.

Marriage can be quite mundane at times. Suddenly, you start to wonder if you made a mistake. It is important to understand that this is a common feeling. It is not a time to think about filing for divorce.

It is the time the two of you should start adjusting your expectations of what the marriage will be like. It is also a good time to talk about what kind of love you need from each other and set common goals.

Gilbert and Selena had been married for two years before the honeymoon ended.

SELENA: *I'm always saying nice things to my husband. I tell him how good he looks when he gets home. I let him know that I've missed him and how much I love him.*

GILBERT *(interrupting): Yeah, she says things like that. But talk is just that—talk. All I've asked her for is home-cooked meals but she always orders take-out.*

SELENA: *I bet he can't remember the last time he complimented me or said "I love you."*

GILBERT: *Maybe I haven't said it in a while but whenever I have extra money, I buy Selena something nice. The bills are always paid on time and Selena never has to worry about me fooling around with other women because she always knows where I am. When we were dating, Selena always gave me the down home cooking I'm used to.*

SELENA: *Yes, I cooked for him when we were dating but I lived at home then and I wasn't working. Did he expect me to keep that up for the next twenty years?*

GILBERT: *Yes. Selena was the first woman I'd ever met who cooked better than my mother.*

Gilbert and Selena still love each other. They are just expressing it in different ways. Selena needs Gil actually to say the words more than she needs the gifts that he buys. Gil needs the smell, sounds and tastes of a busy kitchen to feel loved. There is no problem here at all.

Give your partner the kind of love he or she needs, not the kind you think he or she should have.

CHAPTER THREE

Making Decisions

All of us make small decisions daily without giving them a second thought. When you dress for work in the morning, you've made several separate decisions about the different articles of clothing that make up your ensemble. When you start your car, you've made several separate decisions concerning where to place your feet and how to start the ignition. These decisions are relatively easy because they happen through force of habit and are made on your own.

There are constant tests of couple cohesion that we pass and fail almost daily without even knowing what it is we are doing. These are bricks in the foundation of our marriage. As the years go by, we either add bricks that strengthen our alliance, or create cracks in the wall which eventually destroy it. One of the keystones of marriage is the way we handle decisions.

Throughout the day, we make many decisions that only affect us as individuals such as, "Shall I walk for the exercise or take the bus and enjoy the leisurely ride?" Other decisions involve both members of the couple. It is when we try to reach a major decision along with someone else that things can get complicated. Some decisions are of relatively minor importance. Do we bring home take-out or cook tonight? Which movie do we see this afternoon?

Some of the trouble with positive decision making by couples reflect gender differences.

"Either do something to take care of the situation or shut up," is a typical male reaction. Men are conditioned to master problems, their own and those of family members. Men are also conditioned to rescue. It is no surprise that many a husband's first response to hearing his wife's problem is to provide the answer. Many women like this, but most do not. They feel that they are misunderstood and that they are regarded as incapable of coming up with their own answers. Neither husband or wife recognizes that they are acting out a gender difference.

In the area of decision making, differences are often sex-determined and as such, allowances should be made for them. For example, shopping. Typically, men will go into a store with the notion of what they need, get it or not, then leave. Some men can buy a suit in five minutes. In contrast, women like to look around first, perhaps explore several stores, try on many different choices, and finally, after one or more days of such shopping, settle on the dress. When these differences are deeply ingrained and highly charged, husbands and wives should avoid shopping together for personal items.

There are times when you need to decide together about certain purchases, for example, about furniture for your home. Your home should reflect the taste of both of you. Gender differences are relevant in this case too, however. Men tend to zero in on the main focus; women tend to have a broad view that encompasses details. This frequently leads to impatient disputes as to whether an item fits. It is more constructive for the woman to point out the details upon which her preferences are based, instead of scolding her husband's choices.

Other decisions are of major significance. Do I take a second job in order to send our child to private school?

The *type* of decision isn't important. The way couples handle it, is.

On the way home from a lovely evening at the beautiful new suburban home of some good friends, Peggy announced to Rufus that she would like to live in the same town. They certainly could afford it but Rufus didn't like the idea and dismissed it outright. Peggy left it alone that night, but a few weeks later she raised the issue again. Rufus still didn't like the idea.

As he and Peggy explored the idea, it was clear they had major differences.

Peggy liked the greenery, the lack of crowded, noisy streets, the idea of living in a spacious home with her own washing machine near at hand, and the perception of wealth that suburban life provided. She and Rufus both had worked very hard for the past five years. She felt that they had earned it.

Rufus did not want to live in a white suburb. He felt that Black people who "deserted their communities as soon as they had something to offer it" were contemptible. Rufus also felt strongly that their children would lose pride in their heritage if they went to a predominantly white school.

Peggy understood her husband's concerns. She countered his comments about the children with the observation that "what we do teach at home is more important than what they don't get taught at school. If the children see that we have Black friends and keep up the cultural traditions at home, they will imitate this behavior as adults."

Rufus listened carefully, but he still wasn't willing to make the move.

Here is how this couple worked out a decision. Each of them wrote a list they understood the other was looking for.

Rufus wrote:

♦ giving back to the community
♦ insuring positive Black identification in the children
♦ preventing the children from looking down on Blacks with less money

Peggy wrote:

♦ more space to live in
♦ less noise from outside
♦ a washing machine at home
♦ better schools

Then, they shared what they had written.

This demonstrated that each had really heard and understood the other. Then they discussed each of the items on the lists many times. All of this took several months of discussion, advocating, exploring reactions and then, going over the whole thing again.

Now that the lines of strict segregation have blurred and some African American families have a toe-hold in the middle class, many couples are struggling with a decision their parents never dreamed of facing. In the end, Rufus and Peggy realized that their issue was not race, it was class, and they ended up moving to an affluent suburb that was racially mixed so the children could experience living in a diverse environment, which both agreed was a healthy choice. Their solution was right for them, but the important thing is that they were able to reach a decision in a manner which was good for their marriage. Neither just gave in to end the debate. They were able to think of the long-term consequences of their major decision and they treated each other with respect during the entire process.

One of the advantages of being married is that there is always someone else off whom to bounce ideas. If one of you tends to make hasty, emotional decisions, it is good if the other is a methodical thinker so that there is a balance and less chance of the hasty one not weighing the downside of any proposed resolution.

Some people find it impossible to make a major decision. If one of you finds it difficult to arrive at a decision, the other may find it easier to bring things to a head. Summarizing the good and bad points sometimes helps the procrastinator or the fence-sitter to the point of decision.

A husband and wife should feel comfortable making joint decisions about their life, with neither being "in charge." This equal sharing of wisdom and responsibility should be relieving, even to traditional men, and empowering, even to traditional women. It should also prevent fights for power—and bitter recriminations later.

Shared decision making does not mean that both of you must agree all the time. Try following the method used by Peggy and Rufus to decide where they should live. If you and your spouse are still at an impasse, try the following advice.

FIVE STEPS TO MAKING MAJOR DECISIONS

1. Clarify the real issue.
2. Write down all the different viewpoints concerning the issue.
3. Weigh the upside and downside of the different viewpoints.
4. Evaluate the costs (financial, emotional, etc.) of each viewpoint.
5. Make a choice and agree as a couple to accept responsibility for that choice.

If one person always gets his or her way, something is wrong. It does not help your marriage in the long run to bully, wheedle or otherwise insist on getting your own way all of the time. Regardless of the merits of the arguments involved, sooner or later this is experienced as a win-lose situation. In time, the one who mostly loses cannot help but feel increasingly alienated from the marriage.

Guidelines for Positive Decision Making.

♦ If the decision will affect both of you and the family, always involve your mate. Set your pace to accommodate the slower one of you. Don't close off consideration because you are naturally fast-paced or because you find it too difficult to tolerate the anxiety of indecision. Give yourself and your mate time to come to conclusions together.

♦ Respect and use each other's special expertise, and remember, both of you have valuable opinions and information to contribute.

♦ Move beyond the purely emotional reasons to the rational factors involved, then consider both. Emotional and rational factors are both important in coming to a satisfactory choice.

♦ Work out differences in the spirit of exploration. Give your differing mate credit for wanting the best for all of you, and for having as much intelligence and foresight as you.

♦ Back up your case with facts. Avoid yelling, out-talking, tantrums, anger and other attempts to intimidate.

♦ Listen carefully and be open to changing your mind. You get no points for rigidity.

♦ Know yourself sufficiently to recognize if you have inordinate difficulty in coming to a decision. Do you not really want what you think you should want? Do you not want to lose out on the alternate choice? Do you enjoy the interaction with your mate involved with working over the issue? Do you not want to risk either choice? Try to explore what is holding you back from deciding, rather than pushing through to do so.

♦ After you two have made a decision, don't back out. Carry your share of the responsibility. And never let yourself say, "Well, I could have told you," or "I told you so!" after the fact.

Always remember, you must seek equability between the two of you. For the sake of your ultimate happiness, every decision should contribute to a Win-Win balance in your marriage.

CHAPTER FOUR

Sex

"Sex can enhance love but is not love itself."
—Eric V. Copage
Black Pearls, 1993

An important part of marriage is the physical joining of the couple in the intimate sharing of sex. Intercourse is a natural, bodily need and the healthy expression of the love and pleasure of marriage.

We are all exposed to influences that shape our sexual attitudes, for better or for worse. Some of these are myths and teachings that become brakes on our enjoyment of a perfectly natural act.

Our sexuality begins to be shaped in our cribs. The infant who is lovingly cradled as she nurses at her mother's breast is receiving her first sensual influence. Gratification of her oral needs become associated with warmth and trust in relation to another person's loving embrace. The baby becomes aware of the difference between her own and her mother's body.

If all goes well, when the baby is relaxed and warm we can notice in boys an erect penis. There is a similar internal arousal in girls.

During infancy, the baby begins to explore his body, and learns that touching his genitals brings pleasure. How this early masturbation is managed has a lot to do with a person's ability to enjoy sex later in life. At the same time, the child is learning bladder and bowel control, what gender he and she belongs to and the obligations and privileges of that sex. When developmental milestones of independence are encouraged with the same loving acceptance, the toddler safely greets her independence. Whether the infant and young child meets anxious, harsh, punishing or cold treatment during this key period of sexual identification, or warm affirmation, has lifelong effect.

Even if the young child grows in the most supportive and benign home, his or her own fantasy life can influence later attitudes. Castration fears, self-punishment and anxiety about their sexual curiosity and ruminations, the way their parents model their own bodily acceptance are all factors with which the child contends.

During adolescence with its bodily changes and urgencies, and self-consciousness about what young persons consider their acceptable and horrible physical features, the influence of their expected acceptance or rejection by the opposite sex as well as the world's treatment of them, shape again what will be their attitudes and behavior in the marriage bed. The more we feel good about the person we are, the more able we are to give and receive pleasure.

Sex during courtship happens whenever two people have the opportunity. The couple needs privacy, even if they are living with other people in close quarters. However, a married couple's lovemaking should be an unassailable part of the marriage. Furthermore, this is one area in the marriage where it doesn't pay to be shy. If either of you is less than satisfied with your sex life, do something about it now.

I'm an old-fashioned woman. I refused to have sex with Keith before our marriage so I had no way of knowing that he was into X-rated videotapes. Keith is willing to make love without watching a tape first, but he doesn't get much out of it. We have the best sex after he has watched part of the movie. It makes me very unhappy.

Ingrid should not *say* anything to Keith about this. Since she— Ingrid—is sexually inexperienced, her energy should go into accepting the way he is now and learning how to turn him on more than the movies do. There are plenty of helpful books and tapes, both video and audio, on the market for her to choose from. The key for Ingrid is to enjoy the learning experience, rather than make Keith feel as if she is doing him a favor. If she addresses this issue with real enthusiasm, the X-rated videos will disappear.

One mistake that couples make is to assume that because they are in love, their desire for sex will occur at the same time. Like everything else, sexual styles are very individualized. The key is not to build sexual frequency into an issue of monumental importance. Try to wait out a period of disagreement. After being married for a few years, your desires in this area usually start to run along the same lines. Whatever you do, don't talk the subject to death. God forbid you should make any kind of formal agreement. This would put sex on the list of your regular tasks and you don't want to do that.

It is worth noting that desire for sex can fluctuate during times of stress. Do not panic. This does not mean that you are no longer desirable to your mate. Feelings of unworthiness will cause you to elevate the lack of sex into a major problem and, again, that must be avoided.

If your mate is under no particular stress, and his or her desire seems to have waned, take a look at the level of respect and trust in your marriage. If there are problems here, changing your cologne, hairstyle or nightwear will not help revive your mate's interest in sex.

As in all others, we cannot help but reflect our past teachings in this area. Sometimes, these teachings are implicit assumptions from our observations and experiences; sometimes, they are the direct result of what we have heard from parents, friends, movies and the media.

Of course, we have always ignored the myths (such as that Blacks are wilder in bed than whites) touted by the dominant culture and not allowed them to affect our marriages. We know that those myths are just one more way of saying that Blacks are not quite civilized. We know that the dominant culture has to create many myths and burden us with many false labels in order to justify the continued systematic racism against people of African descent.

That is not to say that we have not picked up some harmful ideas that could haunt us in the bedroom. For example:

♦ Black women have often been told "Men are dogs." This means that women cannot trust men. Men are believed only to be after sexual conquests not a loving, caring relationship with a woman.
♦ Men have told each other that women want to consume them, castrate them, tie them up and imprison them.
♦ Women are told that it is up to the man to give her an orgasm. They are told that if the man did it right, she would have thrilling sex.
♦ Men are told that real men are athletes in bed. If a man cannot perform, it is because he has lost his virility, or is with the wrong woman.

♦ Both men and women are told that the most successful sex is characterized by simultaneous orgasm.

♦ Women are told that if they have not achieved orgasm they are "frigid" and never will achieve orgasm.

♦ Both men and women are told that if they have not brought their partner to orgasm they have failed, or perhaps that their mate no longer loves them.

♦ Both men and women are told that you can't have good sex without reaching orgasm.

♦ Women are told that it is not ladylike to want or enjoy sex. Their role is to serve men and make them happy.

♦ Both men and women have often been exposed to the idea that Black women are either frigid or loose.

♦ Both men and women are told that Black men have larger penises than white men.

♦ Women are told that if their husband cuts down on the frequency of sex or cannot perform it is because they are too fat, are no longer attractive enough to him, or that the husband no longer loves them.

♦ Both men and women are told that if their partner really loved them, he or she would know what they like without being told or given a hint.

♦ Women have learned that it is shameful to show or to explore their bodies. They are told not to derive pleasure from the manipulation of their own bodies. They are told to regard their bodies as flawed and unacceptable.

These are only a few of the interfering beliefs that might haunt a couple. The habit of being an evaluating spectator to our sexual performance and experience is a sure damper. Being a critical director of our mate's every movement is another. Not freeing ourselves from the cares of the day for those moments does not help, nor does using sex for dominance or punishment.

When you are angry with each other, the sexual part of the marriage theoretically should be a safe haven but it doesn't usually work that way. Problems should be resolved before they grow big enough to come into the bedroom.

Lack of sexual appetite is another problem frequently reported by both men and women. Sometimes, erotic films, stories and books shared together help solve this problem. Sometimes, a change of routine and habitual sexual practices help. Shared sexual fantasies can titillate. Two contemporary African American female writers who focus on Black women's sexuality are Julia Boyd and bell hooks. Their books are available in most libraries.

But suppose we diligently free ourselves of negative myths and beliefs, and do all we can to enhance our coming together, but continue to have real trouble? Suppose that no matter how aroused we feel, we cannot achieve an erection, or we ejaculate too soon or penetration is painful or we would rather go to the dentist than have sex? At this point, you need to acknowledge that something may be seriously wrong.

The good news is that the psychological and medical professions have made great advances in the diagnosis and treatment of sexual disorders since the ground-breaking work of Kinsey in the 1950s. We no longer assume that all sexual dysfunctions are social and psychological in origin. Some are precipitated by medications; hormonal changes in the body; physical changes in the body not necessarily due to aging; and reversible consequences of aging. Some problems the two of you may have agonized over are easily reversed by a few sessions with a behavior-oriented psychotherapist. Some people respond to a combination of behavioral and medical treatment, and some to painless medical care. The point is not to be discouraged by trouble. Get the right help.

Guidelines for a Positive Sexual Relationship Through the Years of Your Marriage

♦ Free yourself to enjoy your body and to give and receive pleasure from your spouse. Express delights with sounds of joy. Communicate with your body. Save the talk for some other time, except for love talk.

♦ Be experimental. Push yourself to try out new ways, new games, new play, new settings, new sexual adventures with your spouse. Leave shame out of it, but respect the limitations of your mate.

♦ Men, take your time. By nature, women are slower to arousal than are men. Women, get yourself ready both physically and mentally before you meet your husband. You can be on your way to climax on your own.

♦ Always remember that you are making love. Keep your love-making central. And keep things fun.

♦ As to frequency of intercourse, try to be responsive to each other's appetites. Find some way of clearly communicating your readiness to each other. Private signals can be fun. Yes, women can initiate, too.

♦ If you find yourselves with very different preferences, talk it over. Sex should not be a chore.

There is no evidence that good sex alone can keep an otherwise bad marriage going for very long. But there is much evidence that it enhances reasonably solid marriages. By definition, problems with sex affect both parties. If there is no blaming of self or partner, these problems actually can serve to consolidate your marriage. When you work on them together, your shared concern is a binding force. The resolution of the problem becomes a marriage strengthening celebration.

Finally, keep in mind that marital sex is most satisfying when there is a degree of calm within the relationship.

CHAPTER FIVE

At Least We Have
Our Health

"The head and the body must serve each other."
—Wolof proverb

When we are feeling good, the world looks brighter and we are filled with hope. Our attitude is positive and loving. It seems that all things are possible. Good health plays a strong role in the lives of happily married couples.

As a race, we have to start taking better care of our health. Consider the following:

In comparison to the larger European-American population, our life span is six years less for Black women and eleven years less for Black men. According to the 1994 U.S. Department of Commerce Economic and Statistics Administration, Bureau of the Census, the life expectancy for Black men is 65.5 years; for Black women, it is 73.9. If we contract cancer, only 50% of us survive it. One out of every three of us suffers from high blood pressure and one in ten has diabetes. We are also twelve times more likely to be obese.

Yes, it is possible to get help for these afflictions but it makes more sense to change your habits and try to avoid falling prey to them in the first place.

As a people, we tend to avoid seeking medical care until our pain or discomfort becomes intolerable because either we do not have access to decent medical care or we distrust the medical profession.

Historically, we have had good reason to view health care practitioners with some suspicion. In her excellent book, *Good Health*

For African Americans, Barbara Dixon says that "during slavery, doctors advertised in newspapers for sick or injured slaves on whom they could conduct surgical demonstrations and experiments. Autopsies were never performed on whites in the South; almost all dissections were performed on black corpses. Blacks rightly feared the hospitals, expecting that they would be allowed to die in order to supply cadavers for medical research."

After slavery ended, African Americans were only allowed to use medical facilities allocated for Blacks. Naturally, these centers were shamefully underfunded with poorly trained staff (Black doctors were not allowed to obtain any postgraduate medical education such as internship or residency) and rudimentary treatment.

In 1932, the United States Government started paying for the infamous Tuskegee study. In that federally sanctioned and funded experiment, four hundred African American men were told that they had "bad blood" and that the government would give them free treatment for this affliction. This was a lie. All of the men really had syphilis. All of them were given fake medicine (usually sugar or water pills) to "treat" their illness. All of them were allowed to suffer untreated for forty years so that the government could study the natural course of the disease.

Yes, we've had good reasons to avoid members of the medical profession, but this is all the more reason to practice preventative medicine by following a healthy diet, exercising and eliminating nicotine and excessive alcohol from our lives.

Taking better care of ourselves will lessen the frequency with which we have to visit a doctor and decrease the possibility of a serious illness where a prolonged hospital stay or treatment program is the only answer.

Nutrition

We need to examine our nutritional habits to ensure that we are not hampered by preferences with which we may not even agree. If we are older, and have been used to down home cooking, we may be adhering to those childhood tastes without updating our cooking to cut down on the fat, the salt and the heavy emphasis on meat. For example, smoked turkey wings make as good a seasoning for greens as ham hocks or fatback, and are a lot better for you.

There is more information on nutrition and fitness available now than at any other time in our country's history. If you can't afford to buy books, get a library card and borrow them for free.

EASY STEPS TO BETTER HEALTH

♦ Stop smoking.
♦ Avoid fried foods.
♦ Spend time with others who are trying to take care and control of their health.

Someone has to take on the role of family nutritionist. Years ago, it was the acknowledged responsibility and privilege of the wife and mother to make sure the family ate fresh, well-prepared food. Women took pride in their table, and were rewarded with the daily pleasure they saw in their families' appetites and the praise the women received. Now, with gender roles challenged in many ways, the wife and mother's domain as caretaker of the family's diet is no longer built into the wedding contract. Sometimes, neither husband nor wife know what's for dinner on a given evening because neither has assumed the responsibility to plan for it. Obviously, this does not make for healthy eating. It is up to the couple to negotiate meal planning and this is one area where it doesn't pay to slack off.

Mental Nourishment

In addition to eating right, we need a lifestyle that will support our physical and mental health. That lifestyle includes exercise; quiet time; active interests; loving support and laughing fun with family and friends; and work that is financially rewarding or in some way meaningful. For many of us, the spiritual nourishment of our religion is necessary for a fulfilling life. A full life, like a healthy diet, includes many elements in balance and moderation. Most of the above elements may be achieved as a couple. The more we join together, the more we secure our bonds of intimacy. Being healthy and feeling reasonably contented will keep us close as two vital and positive persons.

Exercise

Nick came home tired every night. He headed straight for the couch, shedding his suit jacket and tie on the way, and did not get up until it was time to go to bed. Alyce even brought his dinner to him. He ate while watching the news and whatever followed it, and then dozed off until it was time for bed. Saturdays and Sundays, he slept until noon and hardly dressed except when Alyce forced him to do so. He said that he worked too hard and was under too much stress to have the energy for anything but rest at home. Alyce, however, decided that she did not want to just work and sleep, or just work and watch Nick sleep. She joined an exercise club which she used several mornings a week. She felt so energized and trim as a result of this exercise that she began to attend her sorority's meetings and even volunteered for one of their committees. Nick began to notice these changes, and especially that she was not around much of the time. Alyce encouraged him to join her at the club, which he eventually decided to do one Saturday afternoon. He remembered lifting weights as part of his teenage push for muscles, and he found that he enjoyed competing again for more endurance. Without saying much he decided to kill two birds with one stone: get back in shape and spend time with Alyce. Together, they went to the gym a couple of times during the week and on Saturday mornings. Nick found that he had more energy, was having a better time at work, and that life had room for much more fun.

As Alyce and Nick demonstrate, one member of the couple need not follow the pace of the least active member. Persue your own activities. If you are enjoying and benefiting, you may well inspire your partner to join you. Setting an example usually works. Nagging and scolding rarely do.

Make Life Feel Rewarding

Hinton had accumulated thirty years as a handyman at a garment factory. He fetched and carried, and was at the bid and call of the operators and everyone else. He felt that he was being more and more patronized and affectionately disrespected. He regretted that he had not paid more attention to improving himself for better job opportunities. He was beginning to feel quite demoralized.

When one of this friends asked him to help out with a boys' recreation center that his church was trying to establish, Hinton agreed. The more involved with the boys he found himself becoming, the more he gained their trust. He found that they looked for him, sought his approval and admiration for their achievements, and his advice. He also found that he could be helpful to some of the mothers, who turned to him because of his influence on their sons. His pride in his work reinforced a pride in self. Hinton believed he began to carry himself differently enough to be treated with more respect at work. Certainly, life seemed more rewarding as he became a more contributing, more active participant. The better he felt about himself, the better mate and family member he became.

Quiet Time

Another factor in a healthy lifestyle is the regular opportunity for quiet, private time. Meditation is ideal. Meditation is simply sitting quietly while focusing on your breathing, or on an object in sight, a sound, or favorite word, while tuning out your worries, plans and the usual content of your thoughts. Meditation requires practice and results in many physical and mental benefits. Your creativity and energy is enhanced; your blood pressure is regulated; your metabolism is more efficient; your outlook on life becomes more positive. Try meditating twenty minutes a day. Both of you can meditate in the same room, so that you are together though nourishing your inner selves.

HEALTH TIP

Take a meditation course, or read a book that describes the methods of meditation. It is a practice that will enhance your life.

Do Something For a Reason Other Than Money

A hobby or an interest is another element of the foundation of a healthy life. Any hobby works. James collects stamps. Theodore is a Civil War buff. Rose bakes and decorates fancy cakes. Francine repairs small electrical appliances. Lillian and Herb follow their favorite jazz artist. Doing something for the sheer pleasure of it adds spice to our life. If it happens that both you and your mate share the same interest, that is an extra bonus to your coupledom. Do not make the mistake, however, of demanding that to be the case. If your interests differ, you have an opportunity to learn from each other.

Stress

There is no such thing as a stress-free life, no matter what your race or gender. However, African Americans have to deal with a disproportionate amount of stress on a regular basis. Barbara Dixon says, "Scientists have always intuitively felt that anger is linked to the unusually high rates of hypertension and other diseases in blacks. In the last few years, new studies have emerged to support this hypothesis. People, black or white, who suppress their anger have higher than average blood pressure. Since black people must cope daily with the insults of racism, large and small, they are likely to have more anger to suppress than whites. This swallowed anger is thought to be a major reason for stress-related diseases among blacks."

Too much stress can damage your physical, emotional and mental health.

Since it is not yet possible for us to prevent this type of stress, it is essential that African Americans (particularly the men) learn ways to deal with it to prolong their lives. Make a list of at least five activities that you find pleasurable and do one thing from the list each day.

TIPS FOR REDUCING STRESS

♦ Avoid people and places that always upset you.
♦ Find something to laugh at when life gets you down.
♦ Talk over your feelings and concerns with your wife, a preacher or mental health professional.

George and Earline would often find themselves lamenting the state of things for Black persons and other people of color in America. They would read the paper and discuss articles, particularly those that emphasized crimes supposedly committed by Blacks and Hispanics; that told tales of American welfare recipients while omitting the fact that the majority of people who receive welfare are white; that argued that affirmative action was unfair, etc. Each of these discussions left George and Earline more angry, more depressed and more frustrated.

When their older child entered kindergarten, things changed. Instead of sitting around complaining, they both sprung into action. They became active members of the Parents' Association. George was eventually elected president. Earline formed committees to deal with school problems such as asbestos in the building. Through her committees she demanded assignment of a reading specialist from the school district office and the enforcement of higher standards of cleanliness in the school cafeteria. Both George and Earline learned much about the politics of school management and how to function as community leaders. They found themselves making a difference. Eventually, their school activities weren't enough to satisfy them, and they became admired community activists in their district. They were often too busy and tired, but were happier and more fulfilled than ever before.

Yes, actively making a difference by changing the world for the better is deeply meaningful. It is one thing to feel oppressed. It is quite another to feel that you are a constructive, active warrior in the fight to change your situation. Whether you form a caucus at work for mutual support, or demonstrate against a toxic dump in your community, or adopt any large or small, popular or unpopular cause, your physical and your mental health will benefit from your positive activity. You will no longer be a passive victim. As a result, your relationships at home should be less tense, more positive and more committed.

We should consider it to be an obligation to our mate, our other family members, as well as to ourselves to protect our health in all areas. Obviously, a healthy lifestyle has no room for smoking at all or drinking to excess, and certainly not for even the recreational use of drugs. When you are feeling good about yourself, there is no need for such distractions. You can love others best when you can love yourself.

Taking care of yourself is an expression of that love.

CHAPTER SIX

The Higher Power

"Only God has kept the Negro sane."
—Fannie Lou Hamer
We Are Not Afraid, 1962

Every couple has different ideas about how much of a role spirituality will play in their union. Some go to church on Sunday but don't further participate. Others get involved with committees, clubs or the choir which meet during the week. Many couples don't go to church or get involved with organized religion, at all. What is important is that the marriage have a spiritual dimension, that you both believe in a power higher than yourselves and try to live righteously both as individuals and as a couple.

Marriages that have a spiritual dimension stand a better chance of surviving. When a husband and wife both are seeking a high quality of spiritual life, they try harder to avoid selfishness. When the inevitable disagreements occur, prayer helps the couple to regain peace and eliminate bitterness.

Religion was a central part of Black life in Africa. The Africans were mostly Muslims before they were forcibly removed from their homeland and converted to Christianity in America.

In order to control their captives, the slave owners usually emphasized those parts of the Bible that spoke of docility and obedience as requirements for entry into Heaven after the life on earth was over. During our terrible (and lengthy) period of captivity, it was the faith, the slave preacher and the songs that lifted our spirits when the burden became too much to bear.

Now, we are not limited to Christianity. There are Black people affiliated with every religious denomination that exists in America. However, most African Americans who practice organized religion fall into one of two groups: Christian or Muslim (Nation of Islam). Usually, when there is a discussion of "the Black church", we refer to the Black Christian church.

Both churches were born in protest.

Richard Allen was born in Delaware in 1760. He was a slave who became a preacher. After purchasing his freedom, Allen relocated to Philadelphia in 1786 and joined St. George's Methodist Church which had a predominately white congregation. Allen spent a lot of time preaching to other Blacks in the city. He urged them to join the church and save their souls. Allen was a very powerful speaker and he converted many people to his way of thinking. Soon, a large number of African Americans had joined St. George's church and the white parishioners decided that segregation was the answer to their increasing discomfort. One Sunday morning, Allen and a fellow influential Black clergyman named Absalom Jones were astonished when they arrived at the church and were ordered into the gallery where the other African Americans had already been led. Allen and Jones sat in the gallery that morning but they never returned to the church and convinced the rest of the African American population to abandon St. George's, as well. Richard Allen then established the Bethel African Methodist Episcopal Church which was the first major Black church in America.

Elijah Poole was born in Sandersville, Georgia in 1896. At the age of 27, he moved to Detroit and became a factory worker. Seven years later, Poole met a peddler named Wali Farad who had founded Detroit's Temple of Islam. According to Farad "the word Negro was invented by whites to separate blacks from their African and Asian brothers. Since Christianity is the religion the white man used to enslave blacks, only in Islam can the black man find justice." Poole, who had become dispirited after experiencing the same kind of racial discrimination in the North as he had back in Sandersville, became a part of Farad's fledgling movement and Farad renamed him Elijah Muhammad. When Farad disappeared in 1934, Elijah Muhammad became his successor. Under Muhammad's direction the Nation of Islam grew beyond the city of Detroit. Its message of economic self-sufficiency and Black pride appealed to thousands of African Americans. By 1960, the Nation of Islam consisted of eighty temples and 30,000 members. Malcolm X became one of its most famous members and because of his popularity and tireless campaigning on behalf of the Nation, the number of temples and its membership tripled over the next few years. Today, Islam is a major religion among African Americans.

Both institutions teach forgiveness, which is another reason why a couple may benefit from having a sense of a higher power in their lives. It is impossible to remain married for any length of time without committing some kind of offense against your spouse. It is also impossible to maintain a satisfactory level of civility in a marriage relationship without forgiving those offenses.

It has been said that the time to go to God (or Allah) is before you need Him. Many of us believe that statement in theory, but don't find the time to worship on a regular basis. However, when life deals us a crooked hand or when our spirits receive a major blow, we pray. Once the crisis is past, we forget about God (or Allah) until the next time.

No matter what your religious beliefs are, giving thanks to some higher power on a daily basis can help you put your challenges in the proper perspective and make you stronger as a couple.

PART TWO:

Family Ties

CHAPTER SEVEN

The In-Laws

"Family for blacks in South Africa means everybody: grand-parents, aunts, uncles, cousins, nephews, nieces, the lot. The concept of the nuclear family is foreign to us."
—Mark Mathabane
Kaffir Boy In America, 1989

We are using the phrase "in-laws" in this chapter for the sake of familiarity, but it is really a European concept used to describe the people who are biologically connected to your spouse. "In-laws" implies a relatively limited role for these relatives in your lives and, in fact, it would be hard to translate the phrase "in-law" into any African dialect. Extended family is a better way to describe the relationship between a married couple and their birth families in West African society, from where the majority of our ancestors came.

The heart of West African society was the total family unit. In other words, marriage did not mean that a man and a woman joined hands and set up a house where they did their own thing, oblivious to their families of biological origin. Quite the contrary. The married couple kept strong ties with their biological families and the "in-laws" were considered an integral part of the whole unit. They were not interlopers who simply had to be tolerated at certain times of the year. In those communities, a person's life depended on the well-being of the tribe as a whole. In fact, the families became linked and used their combined strength to increase their overall influence. After our ancestors were torn from their homelands by slave traders, they still found ways of giving each other encouragement under the most brutal system imaginable.

During segregation, the Black community came full circle. Families had to depend on everyone, even the most distant relatives, to survive in such a dangerous and psychologically harsh environment.

After the Civil Rights movement, African Americans were compelled to accept the Post-Industrial Revolution European concept of nuclear family, often with disastrous results.

Now, when so many of the families in our communities are on the verge of collapse under the strain of issues and political decisions beyond their control, we have to pull our families together again. We have come this far because in the worst of times, we have pulled together and held each other up. We need our families. It is time to turn this situation around and bring the aunts, uncles, cousins and grandparents back into our lives.

The In-Laws Have To Adjust, Too

When the marriage is new, extended family on both sides go through their own period of adjustment. It takes time for them to figure out just how much (if any) a part they will be allowed to play in your new lives. They know what the family network has been like up until now, but that doesn't mean the "stranger" is going to leave it just as is. They are nervous.

When Nancy and I were first married, we moved to a suburb about an hour away from my mother-in-law's house. The first week, she and Nancy's stepfather came over to help us paint and then they just disappeared. Although Nancy talked to her mother on the phone, we didn't actually see them again for six months. I started thinking that maybe they weren't too crazy about Nancy's choice of a husband. When we finally had them over for dinner, they explained that they were giving us a chance to settle in and waiting for an invitation. I appreciated their consideration. Things have been fine since then. We are all very close.

—William

Many black families stayed close after segregation ended. However, when a person who has been raised differently marries into a close-knit unit, friction is not unusual.

George and Shari are a perfect example. George is one of five children and has a host of aunts, uncles and cousins. They support each other and enjoy each other's company. Shari cannot abide George's allegiance to his family, even though they are kind, generous people who never interfere in their marriage.

GEORGE: *I come from a large, close-knit family. Shari dislikes them even though they have never given her reason to. It really makes me mad.*

SHARI: *It's not true that I don't like them. It's just that they are all obsessed with each other.*

COUNSELOR: *Shari, the word you used was obsessed. Can you give us some specific examples?*

SHARI: *First of all, we are talking about a lot of people. Aunts, uncles, cousins—they're all over the place. When George was promoted last year, the phone rang with congratulations for two days straight. When his cousin lost her husband to cancer, it was all George talked about for weeks. He worried about her until I finally made him stop because it was just so ridiculous. His cousin wasn't destitute. In fact, every time I saw her she looked just fine.*

COUNSELOR: *George?*

GEORGE: *I can't believe Shari thinks she stopped me from worrying about my cousin. All she did was make me stop talking about it in front of her. She is just jealous because her family only gets together for weddings and funerals. On those occasions, they make polite talk for a few hours and then rush to their cars like they can't wait to get away from each other. I've tried to make a difference but nothing seems to work.*

COUNSELOR: *Do you mean that you've tried to bring Shari's family closer together?*

GEORGE: *Yes. When we first got married I talked Shari into having several get-togethers at our house. I figured that over time, they would connect like mine and my kids would grow up like I did.*

SHARI: *I told him it wouldn't work. We don't want to be all over each other. Why can't loving George and doing right by him and our children be enough?*

GEORGE: *I think Shari is just related to some people. They are not a real family at all.*

COUNSELOR: *Hmm . . . are you saying that families who differ from yours are not real?*

GEORGE: *I didn't mean it like that.*

COUNSELOR: *Perhaps not, but you do need to give that remark a lot of thought. Okay?*

GEORGE: *Yeah.*

COUNSELOR: *Shari asked a question earlier which has not been addressed. She wanted to know why just being a good wife and mother isn't enough.*

GEORGE: *Give me a break. I'm a good husband and father. Why isn't that enough? Why do I have to give up my family, too?*

COUNSELOR: *How does George's family treat you Shari?*

SHARI: *They're nice but I don't need to be bear hugged every time I see somebody.*

GEORGE: *Do you see how petty her complaints about my family are? Shari's behavior is embarrassing. She's not exactly rude to them but . . . I guess the word is indifferent.*

SHARI: *He just says that because I'm not all over the place kissing kids, stuffing myself with greasy food, laughing at the same old jokes and trying to talk over that old timey music which is always way too loud.*

GEORGE: *Shari spent a lot of time around my relatives while we were dating. She knew the deal. Why didn't she bail out then? I'm not giving up my family for anybody.*

This couple has a serious, marriage-threatening problem, even though on the surface the conflict seems simple. The word "family" means different things to each of them.

George was raised to believe that "family" means mother, father, aunts, uncles, cousins, grandparents and everyone in between. When someone is doing well, everyone is happy and shows it. If tragedy strikes, they all feel the other's pain.

Shari simply has had a different experience. To her, "family" is George and their two children. She has married into a family whose habits she cannot understand and, as a result, feels frustrated and unappreciated. George's last statement was very hurtful to her. She is not "anybody." She is his wife.

This is where acceptance comes into play.

♦ Like far too many women, Shari fell in love with George and figured that she would change her man's habits once the ring was on her finger. This is why she didn't "bail out" while they were dating. Shari is learning that she cannot change George or anyone else. She must accept the way George interacts with his family or he will end up resenting her and acting out in other ways.

♦ George cannot make Shari's family relate to each other in a different manner. Nor does he have the right to try. He also cannot meld Shari's kin into being one with his own family.

♦ If Shari would relax when in the company of her in-laws instead of looking down snobbishly on their ways, she might find herself having a good time.

♦ George wants his children to have the same sense of bountiful love and security that he did. This is wonderful, but Shari does not place the same value on this that he does. As long as she doesn't try to prevent their children from having this nondamaging experience, he has to let it go. Every effort he makes to change Shari's way of thinking will only serve to create distance between them.

♦ Shari is guilty of "me" thinking and is also very insecure. At the very least, she needs to stop making disparaging comments about George's birth family, especially since they are kind people who have done her no wrong. Having embraced her as one of their own, they would also celebrate her highs and be there when life deals a blow. In our rapidly changing world, we can all use this kind of support.

♦ George should apologize to his wife for the word "anybody" and never refer to her that way again.

Putting Your Spouse First

In order to stay happily married, both husband and wife have to separate to some degree from the birth family. Here are some healthy examples of putting your spouse first.

Jennifer says that her sisters accused her of setting back the cause of women twenty years because she does all the cooking, cleaning and ironing, even though she has a full time job. "I like to do those things myself. What they don't know is that Aaron is so grateful, he showers me with love and affection and takes me everywhere I want to go. Plus, he insists that I spend my salary on whatever I like. He also pays the major bills. I haven't told my sisters all of this because it is simply none of their business. Aaron and I are very happy."

So far, Jennifer has managed to ignore the pressure from her sisters. Over time, the pressure could increase or just become tiresome. Jennifer needs to stop them before this happens. Otherwise, she may start having doubts about the lifestyle that she and her

spouse have created. Jennifer and Aaron have created an arrangement that suits them. Nothing else matters.

Lillian's story is very different. Her parents have good reason
to worry about her and she feels guilty for staying married and
causing them so much concern. Nevertheless, she has chosen to
put the needs of her spouse over the wishes of her biological family.

*My father and mother decided early in their marriage that they
would have just one child. They had both grown up in large families
during the depression and reasoned that if hard times came back,
it would be easier to make it if there were only three people to
feed. They were great parents and I grew up in a warm, nurturing
environment.*

*When it was time for college, I decided to major in Art History.
My father started to talk me out of it but Mother would have none
of it. She was totally supportive. By senior year, I had switched
to Business Administration. I think they were relieved but there
were no lectures, no speeches. They accepted my decision without
comment. Their support gave me the confidence I needed to get
through graduate school and land my first job, as product manager
for a cosmetics firm.*

*We continued our close relationship until I met Carl. They took
an instant dislike to him. I held firm and we married three years
after our first date. Carl and I have been married for five years.
During much of that time, he has been trying to find himself. Carl
did not have the family support that I've had. I've taken that into
account whenever he makes a mistake. First, he tried getting into
medical school but that didn't work out so he went to Wall Street.
Since he is basically a gentle man, that cut-throat atmosphere went
against his nature. He was unemployed for about a year before
he decided to go back to school for his M.B.A. I was thrilled.*

*And then came the blow that almost destroyed our marriage.
I learned that Carl had fathered a child when he was a junior in
high school. He should have told me long ago but was afraid, for
some reason, that I would leave him. Everyone knew about his
son, Raheem. That is, everyone except me and my parents. I wasn't
upset about Raheem's existence. It was the years of deception that
made me question his integrity and caused me to be very angry at
his family, as well, for not telling me.*

*After his confession, Carl decided to be a responsible father
and quit grad school. He took a job so that he could pay child
support. Raheem's mother put the boy in an expensive private
school. Carl now pays half the tuition as well as some of the other*

expenses which go with raising a child. I try not to be bitter but we rarely have extra money anymore and our lifestyle has changed. My parents and I don't get along anymore. They say that I should get out of this situation while I'm still young. I'm the first to admit that Carl has done me a great wrong but we're working through it.

My parents believe that Carl is using me and that he only told me about Raheem because the mother had tracked him down and threatened him with a suit in Family Court. Mother says, "Everyone can see Carl is no good. You're the only one who can't see it."

Lillian obviously feels that she and her husband can overcome their challenges. She has made a decision to work on her marriage and, although her parents are understandably worried, they sound like people who can be reasoned with. Lillian should have a private talk with them in which she makes it clear that although she understands and appreciates their concerns, they have to respect her position.

Lillian should also let them know how much she misses the warmth they used to share and her hopes that it can continue in an adult-to-adult fashion.

The case of Jennifer and Aaron and that of Lillian and Carl are prime examples of the importance of seeking and maintaining a proper degree of separation from the birth family.

A lot of times, the situation is not half so serious. A partner who feels jealous is capable of figuratively waving the marriage license around out of insecurity or an irrational need to control the other. A controller's first step is to isolate the spouse from his or her birth family. In these cases, there is no empathy, acceptance or "we" thinking at work. It is simply bad behavior that should not be tolerated.

Partners Behaving Badly

I hate my mother-in-law and my feelings will never change. When Paul and I started dating, I was seventeen and he was twenty-nine. My father found out and became enraged. He threatened to kill Paul if he ever caught us together. Paul's mother was scared for her son. She also did not approve of me because of the age difference. She accused me of trying to trap her son. I can understand that but what she did a few weeks later was unforgivable.

She called my house one night right after the news went off. It was close to midnight and she was roaring drunk. She demanded that I stop seeing Paul and called me a little yellow trouble-making whore. She continued to rant until I got tired of being insulted and hung up on her. The next day I told Paul about the phone call. He hugged me and told me not to worry about it. After I turned eighteen, my father backed off but Paul's mother didn't. She came to our wedding and was hardly civil to me.

A few months later she came to our house carrying a tureen of chicken n' dumplings. I snatched the meal 'cause I didn't feel like cooking, and slammed the door in her face. That was the night that Paul and I had our first fight.

—Frances

We are living in an age when handguns are far too available. So, a threat to end someone's existence is not taken lightly. This woman was frightened and probably tried to talk her son out of continuing the relationship with Frances. When that failed, her fear reached a level that she could not control.

It would be hard for anyone to forget such a disgusting phone call, which is one reason why the mother-in-law should have tried to make up long before the nuptials. But she didn't. Paul feels that his mother was trying to make peace and that Frances behaved badly when she snatched the food and slammed the door. He is right.

Paul also feels that the feud needs to end. He is right about that, too. He loves his mother and Frances loves her father. The four of them should go out to dinner on neutral territory and air their differences. Frances should be heard. Mother-in-law has to apologize for the phone call and her rudeness at her son's wedding. Father should apologize for threatening harm to Paul. After that, Paul and Frances should take control of the situation by firmly vocalizing their love for each other and their refusal to tolerate anyone in their lives who can't accept their commitment to each other.

Then, for the sake of the marriage and grandchildren to come, the hatchet should be buried.

I was born and, through my high-school years, raised in Cleveland, Ohio. I am one of three children. My father was a truck driver and Mom stayed home to take care of us because neither of my parents liked the idea of latchkey kids and all of our other relatives were in the South. Whenever we went to Mom and Dad with a problem, we were encouraged to come up with possible solutions on our own. If we got stumped, then they would help. However, they never just fixed a situation for us.

Gloria was from Miami. We met during freshman year at college in Ohio and clicked right away. The next three years went by quickly. We shared everything and joked about what our children would be like.

We got married at City Hall the day after graduation. Gloria wanted to go home and, since I'd never been out of my home state, I was anxious to see more of the country. My folks accepted my decision to move to Miami. We have only been married a year but I'm tired. Gloria won't do anything without talking to her mother first. If she has a problem, she runs to her mother, who fixes it. I only hear about the issue after the solution has been decided on.

Let me make one thing clear: This is not my mother-in-law's fault. Gloria gets on her nerves, too. She has told me more than once that in a way, she was relieved when Gloria did not get accepted into any of Florida's good colleges.

Gloria had always been too dependent on her. She'd hoped that four years away at school would change the situation.

Instead, Gloria called her long distance every day for four years. I never saw this side of Gloria while we were in school.

—Freddie

Freddie needs to team up with his mother-in-law and have a discussion with Gloria. Each of them should air their feelings and discuss the impact that Gloria's behavior is having on their lives. In a kind, supportive and nonthreatening manner, Gloria needs to be told from now on that mother's answer to run-of-the-mill problems will be a firm, "Talk that over with Freddie."

I had just come home from the gas station where I work as a cashier. My feet were tired and my clothes were sweaty and stuck to my body. Vernon came home and took pity on me. He told me to take a shower and relax while he looked after the kids. Vernon bathed and fed them. I was thrilled when he decided to run the kids over to his sister's house so we could go out to eat by ourselves.

When we got there, Debbie wasn't doing anything. Normally, she is out on a date, searching for Mr. Right.

Vernon and I were relieved to find her curled up in an armchair with some romance novel and spooning strawberry ice cream into her mouth.

The kids ran in and jumped all over her like they always do.

Normally, Debbie starts squealing and thanking us for surprising her with the kids but that night was different. She looked like she had been crying. She sent the kids into the kitchen, put her hands on her hips and demanded to know what was going on. Vernon explained the situation and she got highly upset.

We were confused. It wasn't the first time Vernon and I had dropped the kids off without asking. In fact, she always seemed to get insulted if we asked her to "sit" for us. She always used to say, "I'm always glad to see my babies."

Anyway, Debbie told us to take the kids back home. I asked her how she could hurt the kids' feelings like that. Then, I got mad and cursed her out. I let her know where I thought all of this was really coming from. One of her boyfriends probably dumped her and she was taking it out on my kids.

I pulled my kids out of her house and drove off, leaving Vernon in the middle of the floor babbling an apology to her. I was furious with him because we had done nothing to feel sorry about. I let him walk the twenty blocks back home and didn't speak to him for a week.

—Marie

Marie had every reason to be shocked and upset by her sister-in-law's behavior but she was wrong for using profanity. It has never solved anything. Most importantly, Marie should not have left Vernon without a ride home just because he didn't agree with her approach to the problem. Vernon's sister obviously had made plans to spend a quiet evening at home with only a pint of ice cream and a new book to keep her company. Debbie is entitled to do that without feeling guilty or having Marie jump to conclusions that have substantial base in reality. Just because Debbie was inside her home instead of out at a nightclub does not make her time any less precious. Next time, Marie and Vernon should ask in advance and use this incident as the reason if she has the nerve to start protesting that her nieces and nephews are welcome anytime.

I grew up in a foster home after my mother was killed in a car accident. I don't know who my father is or whether I have any other relatives so I was happy to marry Teddy. He came from a real family and I looked forward to being the daughter that his mother never had. Boy, was I disappointed! Teddy's mother is boring and stupid. She is always whining and wringing her hands over some trivial issue. We can never have a pleasant conversation.

All she does is complain about her life. After the first two years, I decided to have as little to do with her as possible. I leave the twins at her house when I have errands to run. Teddy resents this.

First, he accused me of "just using his mother for baby-sitting." I said, "Fine." So, I started leaving the kids with my girlfriend next door. After a few months, he got mad because his mother wasn't seeing her grandchildren anymore. I can't win.

—Chris

Chris has had to deal with tragic and very serious issues early in life. Therefore, someone's everyday complaints probably make her extremely impatient. Having a worrier for a mother-in-law just sets her teeth on edge.

Chris does not have to give up her dream of being a daughter. In fact, this is a good way for her to learn what a mother/daughter relationship is really about. A kind and loving daughter would realize that her mother's world is obviously far too narrow and take steps to expand it. They could make a joke out of it. "Hey Ma, you and I will take the kids to Disney World together if you promise to stop whining for two straight weeks."

Finally, Teddy could take the kids to see their grandmother without waiting for Chris to do it first.

My husband and I have been married for twenty-five years. We live in Brooklyn and have two teenaged boys. Last year, my mother suffered two strokes. After her recovery, she could no longer work and I brought her up from Memphis to live with us. We have a spare bedroom and she tries to stay in there when Jim is home but he still complains.

The kids adore her and, since I've always been a housewife, she is good company for me during the day.

Jim resents her presence in our home and treats her badly. He curses her out when he gets angry and it makes her shake out of sheer nervousness. My mother is eighty-three years old and has never given Jim any reason to dislike her.

I've argued with him about his behavior but his position remains the same. He wants me to put my mother in some old folks' home and I refuse to do that. I've overheard the children talking about the way he treats Grandmama and they sound very angry.

I would just take her and leave but I don't have any job skills or work experience. Nevertheless, I'm beginning to wonder how our marriage can survive under these conditions.

—Antoinette

No one should spend the last years of her life in such a situation. The image of a frail, elderly woman quaking in fear at the sound of her son-in-law's footsteps is nauseating. A senior citizen center can't be worse.

However, professional help is in order here, whether Antoinette's mother stays or goes. Jim needs to understand that his sons are learning from him:

♦ how to disrespect women and children by using filthy language in his home;
♦ how to be stern, inflexible and downright mean, even if it makes the wife and children unhappy;
♦ how to treat an elderly parent.
   When he becomes a sick old man living in one of their homes Jim should realize his children might remember his behavior.

My husband and I are in our late fifties. All three of our children are out of the house. I thought that we could start traveling and having fun again, but Reginald has been harboring a grudge all these years and refuses to take me anywhere.

We got married when we were just out of our teens and I was jealous of anyone who hung around him. Even his relatives. Over the years, his large family drifted away. Reginald now has bitterly informed me that there were picnics, card games, weddings and other celebrations to which we were not invited. He is not lying when he says that I would have made his life miserable if he had insisted we attend any of these events. And, I would have never let him go alone.

Now, he says that we're not going anywhere. He says that we will just grow old around the house alone, without friends or family (he recently barred mine from the house), just like I always wanted.

He is wrong about that. If he doesn't change his mind, our marriage will be over even though I still love him.

—Carrie

Reginald is very angry and has been plotting this move for many years. However, he can't put the blame for this situation totally on Carrie's shoulders.

It is true that his spouse was supposed to come first, but Reginald forgot that this sentiment was supposed to be reciprocated. It was not. Right from the start, Carrie was thinking "me" and not "we."

Reginald should have recognized this and done something about the unfairness of his situation years ago.

Reginald should not have allowed himself to become completely alienated from his biological family because of Carrie's irrational insecurity and selfishness. It took two people to create the current state of affairs and both are equally responsible for it.

That said, it is not healthy for two people to be locked in a house with only anger and bitterness for company. In fact, it sounds downright dangerous.

Marriage counseling is the only alternative here. Otherwise, the kids will end up getting involved and taking sides or the situation could end up as a tragic case of domestic violence.

A therapist can help Reginald work through his anger and help Carrie find the reason for her extreme fear of abandonment. In between sessions, they should travel. For the first year, Reginald can pick the destinations.

Some people are just impossible and their natures don't change when they become in-laws. It is nice when members of the extended family are peaceable, fun-loving human beings who don't interfere in a couple's life, but that isn't always the case.

In-Laws Behaving Badly

Every time Leslie's mother comes over, I end up with a headache halfway through the visit. All she talks about is her other children and how well they're doing. We live in a fifth-floor walkup. Her eldest son has a six-bedroom home in Baldwin Hills. We can barely afford a weekend at a bed-and-breakfast. Leslie's baby sister and her husband visit Europe twice a year. On and on it goes until the door shuts behind her.

—Hugh

When siblings earn more, live in fancier homes and take nicer vacations, the new couple can feel deficient or even embittered if they measure their own lives against these standards. However, a couple with a fulfilling life (close friends and diverse activities) can have a healthy interest in the family and manage to stay close to them while still feeling good about their own life together.

Leslie's mother may be under the mistaken impression that her insensitivity will cause Hugh and Leslie to work harder for the type of lifestyle that she and her other children seem to value. Or, she may just be suffering from a bad case of meanness. It doesn't really make a difference.

Hugh and Leslie have to approach her with love before the next visit, explain how badly she makes them feel and gently tell her to cease and desist.

My brother-in-law has been after us to go with him to Las Vegas for the last six months. It isn't that we don't want to go. We just can't afford it and, besides, we want to be together right now. We've only been married for a year. Over the past twelve months, there have been two weddings and a reunion in my family. I tried to explain this to my brother-in-law the other night but he hung up on me. I'm a peaceful woman who believes in turning the other cheek but it really made me angry.

—Cathy

People forget what it was like during the early years of their marriage. A newly married couple must get used to being with each other. On top of adjusting to the relationship there are work, household duties, hobbies that should not be abandoned and leisure time with friends. In-laws would do well to look back and remember and avoid pressuring either the new husband or wife to visit more often until their lives settle down a little. Everyone also needs to remember that each spouse has a biological family.

Cathy is dealing with a bully and bullies just get worse with time. She has to tell her husband about the hang up and insist on receiving an apology from her brother-in-law before he is allowed to call her house again. Turning the other cheek won't work here. She will just get slapped on the other side of her face.

My wife is afraid of her mother, who is a strong woman with a big mouth and a way of making anyone who doesn't see things her way feel real stupid. Everyone in their family agrees that it is best to stay on Naomi's good side. As a result, she runs our house.

We have the jobs she thinks we should have and we are raising our son in a way which makes her happy. When Sheila and I are alone, we make lots of decisions. Neither one of us admits that all of our plans are subject to Naomi's approval.

My wife wants to have another child next year but I just don't know.

—Ralph

Ralph and Sheila should postpone the decision to have another child until they become adults themselves.

Secondly, assuming that neither Ralph nor Sheila can get a

company transfer to Buenos Aires, here is a recipe for achieving adulthood and regaining self-respect.

♦ In a calm and unthreatening manner, Ralph should approach his wife and unburden himself. He needs to ask Sheila just to listen until he has articulated all of his concerns, fears and frustrations.
♦ Ralph should also ask his wife to stand firm the next time the two of them make any kind of plans for themselves or their son.
♦ When the next opportunity arises, Ralph and Sheila should present their mutual decision to Naomi as a couple. They should hold hands and look directly at her while speaking.
♦ Most importantly, they must go through with their plans, no matter what Naomi says.
♦ Repeat as necessary.

Kim's mother was such an active woman before her husband died. We used to complain that we didn't see enough of her. Since Pop's heart attack, she has made us her whole life. She visits every weekend and expects Kim and the kids to be around for her the whole day. This has been going on for the past six months and it is driving the whole family crazy. I can't say anything to her without seeming cruel and Kim refuses to "hurt Mama's feelings."

—Bob

This is really sad. Kim's mother is probably so lonely and grief-stricken that she doesn't even realize her constant visits have become a nuisance. This isn't bad behavior, because there is an absence of malice on her part. She wasn't always this way. It is to Bob and Kim's credit that they haven't hurt her feelings. Mama needs:

♦ Grief counseling.
♦ To resume her hobbies. Perhaps her friends could be persuaded to drop by and catch her up on what she has missed.
♦ A brand new activity in which to get involved.

Toward the Future

In *The Encyclopedia of Black America,* editors W. Augustus Low and Virgil A. Clift remind us that most of the mainstream writers on the Black family have "operated under the assumption that black families should be changed, in essence, to become more like ideal white families."

We don't need to change. What we do need is a discrimination-free society in which to exist and not another government study or think-tank analysis.

Low & Clift go on to say that "one of the advantages of most black families has been their tremendous adaptive flexibility, that stoical ability to survive. Family ties have always played an important role in the African American community. Historically, we have had to share food, clothing, heartrending loss, money, housing and information about activities taking place in the dominant culture that threatened our very survival as people."

If you live far away from your family or if you belong to a large group of people who are spread out across the country, think about holding an annual family reunion.

Family reunions can be touching events where we honor our kinship. That is, if it is properly organized.

If you are in charge of planning a family reunion, here are some tips for making it successful.

♦ Organize small groups in charge of food; entertainment; games; transportation; space; family history commemoration; finance.

♦ If the reunion will last over several days, consider holding some innovative workshops in parenting, African American history, career planning or community activism, and contact experts who would be willing to give a brief lecture for a small fee.

♦ To avoid last minute scrambling or omissions that cause hurt feelings, pull together a master list of names and addresses. Remember to give everyone at least six months' advance notice.

In general, try to get along with your in-laws. Think of your new family as individual people with their own hopes, dreams and personalities.

Relate to each person in the family as an individual. If you have a problem with a particular person, don't talk disparagingly about "the family." Talk the problem out with that one individual. Stick to the issue you are angry about and don't insult others who have nothing to do with the problem. Statements like, "All you Wilsons get on my nerves" are simply not acceptable.

CHAPTER EIGHT

Parenting

"I looked at that kid for a long time, I felt something impossible for me to explain in words. Then when they took Natalie away, it hit me. I got scared all over again and began to feel giddy. Then it came to me. I was a father."
　　　—Nat "King" Cole
　　　　Unforgettable: The Mystique of Nat "King" Cole, 1950

A baby is not the answer to any problem that is plaguing a marriage. If you're not feeling loved by your spouse or are afraid that the marriage is falling apart, look elsewhere in this book for possible solutions. If there is already stress in the marriage, the pressures of bringing up a new baby may just break the fragile strands that are holding it together.

If your marriage seems solid, and both of you want a baby, it is important to talk about your husband's fear as well as your own. Men worry, too. Husbands share the same issues with their wives, but from their own perspective. For example, husbands worry about their ability to be a good father. They worry about whether the child will look up to them and whether they can earn enough to support a child; they worry about their wives forgetting them to give all the attention to the new baby. Women's worries include fear of "failing" to get pregnant; the pain of childbirth; making the grade as a mother; being tied down to a baby; working outside the home while mothering, versus not working and so being eliminated from the career track. Both parents need to be concerned about the economic burdens of parenthood, and about losing their lover status with their spouse. All of these concerns are legitimate and frequent, whether or not acknowledged. They should be talked out with one another.

Even if all of these issues have been settled, this still may not be the best time to have a baby. Ask yourself the following questions:

♦ Are you or your spouse planning a return to school in the near future?
♦ Are you doing well financially?
♦ Do both of you have time to devote to the child?
♦ Will at least 80% of the expenses be covered by health insurance?
♦ How much time will you receive from your company for maternity leave?
♦ Who will care for the infant when the caregiver returns to work?

If You Have Trouble Getting Pregnant

Infertility is defined as the inability to get pregnant after trying for at least a year, or not being able to carry a pregnancy to term. Only a physician can determine why you cannot get pregnant or cannot support a full-time pregnancy. An infertility specialist can help you understand

♦ what causes infertility;
♦ which course of treatment is best for you;
♦ how to deal with the emotional and psychological impact of infertility.

Pregnancy and Childbirth

Like everything else, pregnancy and childbirth can be intimacy enhancing or alienating, depending on a couple's approach to the issue.

The decision to have a child should be a mutual one that has been given a lot of thought. It is an enormous responsibility to take on years of full-time care for another person.

The way we react to the idea of becoming a parent is directly related to how we perceive our own childhood and the nature of our emotional ties to our parents. Compound these feelings with society's teachings about the way one should feel about parenting, and with fears about whether you can make the grade as a good (perfect?) parent, and things get very complicated. In fact, as these feelings get stirred up, we may become anxious, confused and ambivalent. Don't worry if you have some negative feelings about what is supposed to be "a blessed privilege." If you are experiencing too much fear and anxiety, then you need to deal with some of these issues before deciding to become pregnant.

Sometimes, it is not your own concerns but your mate's reactions that bother you. You may want the reassurance provided by a wholly ecstatic reaction from your spouse. Any doubt you detect reinforces your own. We may even see your spouse's doubt as a rejection of you. If you do, it is a sign that you might stumble into the pitfall of over-identification with the child you might have. You may already see the child as a little "you" rather than a separate human being.

You need to seek true understanding of yourself and your mate.

Laura and Dave had been married for ten years. They had a comfortable relationship centered around their respective careers. They were the typical two-career professionals who were always busy, always moving ahead. They did commit themselves to time together—at least one day on the weekend and one evening during the week. They enjoyed each other's company. Both came from relatively close-knit families, although there was not time for much visiting.

The two extended families and some close friends got together for a party for Laura's 35th birthday. Among the gifts was a silver teething rod that had been in her family for a number of years. The note said, "It's your turn to use this. It's later than you think. What are you waiting for? Happy Birthday." Laura did not ignore this gift, even though she and Dave had not seriously considered having a baby. Somehow there always seemed to be more time ahead. But now, at 35 Laura could no longer deny that they had to come to a decision about parenthood. They spent the next several weeks speaking of nothing else. Unfortunately, they echoed each other's ambivalence. When Laura spoke of the joys of having a child, Dave outlined the problems, and when Laura talked of the disadvantages, Dave proved how each could be overcome. Finally, they decided that they needed objective help in deciding.

Someone suggested a marriage counselor.

They spent the first part of the first session convincing the therapist that they were happily married, proud and pleased with their lifestyle, and wished to talk only about whether they should have children. They emphasized that they never made decisions based on what others expected or did. Neither was sure that they were cut out to be parents, although the idea was somehow intriguing. They liked the idea that their children would be smart, good-looking, cultured and successful reflections of themselves.

As Laura and Dave proceeded in therapy, they uncovered several previously unrecognized concerns that were contributing to their inability to come to a decision.

For example, Laura worried about maintaining their marriage. She believed that just as her parents valued her for her good looks and academic success, so did Dave. She assumed that her tall, slim body, smart clothes and corporate success were the assets that attracted Dave and maintained his interest.

How would he regard her with a fat belly? What if she were never able to get back down to her current figure that she worked so hard to maintain? Somehow, Laura had developed the fear, which she knew to be illogical, that having a baby was equivalent to opening the flood gate to repeated pregnancies, no longer taking care of herself and no longer being a part of the struggle in the outside world. Digging further, she found that the fear covered a partial wish. Part of her wanted to slow down. In addition, Laura longed to be loved for herself, not for her accomplishments, but she had given up that possibility a long time ago.

Laura questioned her potential for successfully taking care of a baby or children. She thought back to how lonely she was as an only child, and vowed that she would have two children or none. But she could not imagine herself with two or three children. It's one thing to be efficient in an office with subordinates and secretaries, and at home with one other person, but with three or four children? The vision grew worse as she talked about it. Furthermore, she knew that her parents would love becoming grandparents. Laura did not want to give them that satisfaction. Her own childhood had not been happy. Her parents were too restrictive and intrusive, too subtly punishing, but she could never retaliate or protest because they were loving on the surface. And, besides she did not know how she would fare in the competition with her mother. There seemed to be lots of roots to the negative side of her ambivalence.

Dave's concerns were fewer, but not necessarily less important. First of all, he wanted to protect what he had. He loved Laura and he loved both being in love with her and her love for him. He wanted to remain the center of her life. He had seen how the wives of his friends turned from their husbands to preoccupation with their babies. And he had seen those marriages erode. He also *wondered what would be expected of him. Would Laura continue to work? Could he alone be able to keep up their lifestyle? Would he be expected to do more housework? Or spend the time he needed to prepare for the workday tending to the baby? Could he be a good father? Dave had had a wonderful father. He felt that as far as his father was concerned, he had come first. Dave felt he still could talk to his father about anything and find both comfort and wisdom. He doubted that he could be half as good, or even good enough as a dad.*

Both Laura and Dave believed that down the road they were likely to regret a decision to have no children. They worked diligently and persistently through their therapy. As they shared their fears, they grew closer and became more sensitive to each other's needs. It was this hearing and sharing that provided reassurance to each of them of their mate's love and acceptance. It also provided the opportunity to teach each other how they could best go about mutual problem solving.

Laura was coached on how to gain a better understanding of her parents as individuals with individual histories. She was helped to retrieve their life stories by spending time interviewing them about their own parents and grandparents, their early life experiences, disappointments, triumphs and dreams. Laura's parents were delighted to respond. They wanted to retrieve and pass on those memories, and they were so happy that their daughter was interested. Laura began to see them not as flawed parents, but as normal humans with particular life struggles. As they emerged as whole persons, she could better understand and accept them and their behavior. She found herself less resentful. And as she learned to deal with her parents not as child to adult, but as adult to adult, she found that she felt more in control, and more honest. She also found that both her mother and father responded positively to this more mature relationship. They actually became friends. The intended dividend of this work resulted in the evaporation of some of her negative concerns about a baby.

This work took about six months of weekly meetings. Laura and Dave were told to take the next six months to go back to their normal schedule, but to make no decision about children during that time. This was intended to provide the space for the first six month's work to be absorbed, and not to result in undue influence or a backlash decision. Laura and Dave were given an appointment for six months later, when, presumably, they would be in a position to arrive together at a decision. When they did return, they seemed more content and even happier. They reviewed their original apprehensions, laughing at some, figuring out how they would help each other with others.

Together, they agreed that not only did they want to have children, but eagerly looked forward to doing so.

Unfortunately, Laura and Dave returned to therapy two years later because of their distress about the failure to conceive. Each month, as her menstrual flow appeared, Laura grew more and more depressed. This was her first encounter with defeat. Dave was also disappointed, but was more worried about Laura. The counselor was pleased to note the effects of the earlier work. They knew how to listen to themselves and to each other. They knew how to communicate caring. There was no sign that they were succumbing to the worst pitfall of all for couples who are having trouble conceiving: blaming. Blaming oneself or blaming one's mate leads to no good. Not conceiving is a mutual problem, and an act of God. Once Laura could move beyond her despair, they decided to go into action. They sought help from a highly regarded fertility clinic. It was understood that Laura would require extra support from Dave, and that it would be important for Dave to participate with Laura in every step of the process. He went to all of the examinations, he gave her the daily injections that were required, heard the news about the status of things along with Laura, cried with her when the first implantation did not succeed, and finally, rejoiced when the second try worked.

Finally Dave and Laura gave birth to beautiful twins.

And through it all, they became even more intimate and happily mated.

African Americans have always regarded raising children as an extremely worthy function, even though it has never been easy to raise a Black child

Rather than concentrating on what has gone wrong in our past, we, as a race, should praise ourselves for the remarkable job we have done, sometimes with little or no resources.

During slavery, African American children were denied real parents who could make decisions as to their well-being. Youngsters ran semi-naked around the plantation until they reached working age, which normally commenced after the sixth birthday, when the little ones were assigned to carry water out to the field workers. Four years later, the children were given regular places. They were forced to work in the fields or in the Big House, where they handled the lesser needs of the master's offspring under threat of severe beatings. There were very few exceptions to this pattern.

Once legal slavery ended, thousands of African American children still had to work in the fields with the parents, who were now called sharecroppers.

Even now, raising a Black child is not the same as raising a white child.

The Black child grows up in a country where the majority of decisions that will impact him are made by whites, most of whom are primarily concerned with issues which impact their dominant culture, not the needs of African Americans.

All parents must help their children acquire the skills that will help them perform successfully as individuals, in their own families and as citizens of the larger world. The Black parent has an even bigger job. White couples do not have to:

♦ socialize their children to function successfully in a Black-controlled world;
♦ teach their children how to thrive in spite of other people's perceptions or expectations.

The mainstream approach to child rearing is fine, but our children need a little more to protect them from some of the psychic harm of second-class citizenship.

To start, if your local school does not offer courses in African American history, you and your spouse can put aside two hours a week and teach your children yourselves.

Another custom that is beginning to catch on is called the Rites of Passage. These programs are springing up around the country. Charles and Sarah enrolled their daughter, Jackie, in one such program. They said, "When Jackie turned twelve, we started to worry about drugs and pregnancy. Even though Jackie has always received a lot of love and has been a good student in school, we figured our concern couldn't hurt. We enrolled her in the program and she and loved it. There were classes on valuing the body, spirituality, history and cooking. There were a lot of events we could attend to see what the kids were learning. Jackie made a lot of new friends. One of the other girls is now her roommate at college."

If there is no Rites of Passage program in your community, perhaps you, a relative, or someone else could be persuaded to start one. The essential components are:

♦ A lecturer with a thorough knowledge of African as well as African American history;

♦ related films;
♦ related field trips;
♦ workshops that teach specific skills which can be used in everyday life;
♦ events which involve parents and extended family;
♦ ceremonial activities;
♦ a final ceremony which family, friends and neighbors can attend.

One of the reasons why the lives of our children have changed is that we have moved away (sometimes physically, sometimes psychologically) from the extended family. If both parents are working and Grandma lives far away, children don't have anyone to turn to when they are at risk. In households headed by single female parents, small children are sometimes cared for into the early evening by day care centers. This means the children rarely come into contact with the elders during the week. If the family elders are only visible during the holidays, children can't get to know them and take their advice as seriously as past generations did.

We need to turn this situation around.

To ease some of their pain and to keep a sense of self, our children, regardless of the financial resources of their families, need to be exposed to situations where the focus is on African American customs and issues. They need a space where they are allowed to relax and be themselves, a place where they are valued and shielded from comparison with the dominant culture.

When the Baby Comes

After the baby comes, the husband and the wife's life is very different from their lives in the childless couple stage. With the baby comes the sleepless nights, the frequent feedings, the requirement for constant care of a demanding infant who is getting his first taste of life in the outside world. With the baby also comes exhausted parents, and a mother who is still physically sore, and emotionally fragile. This is the stage of family life—with its demands for change in order to find ways to meet everyone's needs—that sends more couples to therapy than any other stage except when the first child reaches adolescence. Expect to be under stress. Get the kind of help you need, if not from a therapist, from a wise family member, friend or neighbor, or from a hired housekeeper.

The first problem to be solved is the sharing of the required parenting. Since the mother gave physical birth to the baby, and thousands of years of tradition and necessity have required the mother to be the baby's caretaker, it is assumed that she is naturally comfortable and knowledgeable about taking care of an infant. Her mere man of a husband is assumed to know nothing about doing so. This is a dangerous situation to fall into. Both parents need to learn how to handle the baby, and to feel comfortable in doing so. And both need to assume responsibility, and in fact, equally share the awkwardness and the joy of caring for the baby. Lamaze classes and baby care classes, which both parents attend together prior to the birth, help a great deal in this regard.

If the baby is breast-fed—the healthiest alternative—obviously the mother must take care of the infant's meals. The father, however, can get the baby for the mother and return her to her crib or bassinet when feeding is over. Decide who gets up when, who bathes the baby, who puts her to sleep, gets her ready for the day, changes her diaper, takes her out for strolls. These duties should be divided as evenly as possible. It is best for couple intimacy, and for the infant's psychological and physical well-being, for the infant to experience, from the beginning, two different handlings and bondings with two different parents. Initial bonding takes place through the giving and receiving of physical care.

Mother, do not make the mistake of thinking that you are the only one who can take proper care of the baby. You will end up doing it all, which will be too difficult for you, too alienating of the father from his child and too undermining of your marriage. And if you hover over your husband to supervise and criticize how he handles the baby, you will bring about the same results.

Some men are better at managing baby care than are their wives. Many men, however, have been taught that they cannot do so, and worse, as a real man, should not do so. Luckily, we are living at a time when those notions are changing. Men have permission now to be "tender," and many real men are letting themselves go. It has been found that African American men are more likely to help with household chores and with childcare. The more this is the case, the more stable the marriage, the more secure the children and the happier the household.

When the New Father is Unhappy

When a new father wants to bolt, or withdraws from the excitement around the new mother and baby, or even feels repelled from his wife and child, it is frequently because of his old insecurities. Is he up to managing all of this? Is this woman he married now just a mother, or can she still be a lover? Does he now become just "a parent" or is he still attractive to women? Is he going to be abandoned by his wife?

It is not too difficult to become afraid at first. And fear makes you want to run. If you find yourself in this situation, calm down. Be patient with yourself. Sometimes, all you need is some time to adjust. Try to become acquainted with the baby.

If you don't begin to feel better after a couple of days, get help as quickly as possible. A trusted minister or priest or a professional mental health counselor is necessary. Be sure to let your wife know what you are feeling. You will need her help to get over this hurdle.

The Stay-at-Home Parent

We would all like our children to have one parent at home all day. If you can afford it, fine. However quitting a job requires careful thought and planning because a lack of money brings a different type of problem into the marriage.

Practicality and financial considerations aside, you need to think hard about whether both or either of you will be able to sustain this arrangement.

Lisa and I had been married for six years when I decided to stay at home. We had a three-year-old son at the time. Lisa and I had worked very hard to get our careers established and some money in the bank. I'm an accountant and she teaches science at our local junior high school. Since Lisa had to be at the school by 8:00, it fell to me to get our son fed, dressed and delivered to the baby-sitter. Every morning, he would cry as I headed out the door and it broke my heart. I started wondering if I could practice my profession from home so that my son wouldn't have to be away from home all day.

Even though I felt bad for my son, not working at all was not an option. That would have emasculated me. I know other guys do it but I also know myself very well. I had to be the breadwinner.

So, before I broached the subject to Lisa, I had to figure out how to generate enough business working out of our home, so I started doing some research.

During one visit to the library, I read through two years worth of back issues from Black Enterprise *and* Success *magazines. I got very excited. It was time to talk to Lisa.*

At first, she wasn't convinced that I could provide a substantial income for my family by providing accounting services exclusively for other people who work from home. She was concerned that we would begin having serious financial problems by the time our son started school. I told her that I didn't want my son to end up with a weary father and an exhausted mother arguing over who was the least tired and prepared to check his homework.

Lisa finally gave in and I was off and running.

That was seven years ago. Business has been steady and all three of us are happy with our lifestyle.

—Alan

Neha always thought that she would welcome the opportunity to stay at home. She had been working since she was fourteen-years-old. Sometimes, she'd had two jobs. She was tired. When Neha got pregnant, she and Colin figured that they might be able to make it on his salary alone.

Neha was excited when Marva was born. It was like playing with a wonderful, living doll. As the years went by, they had to decide whether Marva would go to nursery school three times a week. They read that this experience helps the child to make favorable progress when she reaches kindergarten. Unfortunately, Neha and Colin could not afford the recommended programs. As an alternative, Neha organized a play group where she and several friends and neighbors took turns supervising a group of their children. At the same time, Neha found herself getting restless. She missed the routine of getting up at the same time every morning with thoughts of all the things she had to accomplish that day. She missed not having to keep up her wardrobe and circulating in public. She found she even missed the relationships at work and feeling productive. She missed receiving a paycheck and feeling entitled to spend money because she had earned it. She missed being able to answer with pride the question of what she "did."

Yet, Neha felt privileged that she and her husband alone were raising Marva, that they did not have to drag her out of the house on cold snowy mornings and come home too tired to fully enjoy their daughter.

Neha and Colin decided that when Marva was old enough to attend a full day in public school, Neha would return to work.

Once that decision had been made, Neha began to enjoy being a full-time mother to Marva. She took a course in the evening to keep up her job skills, while Colin spent time with Marva. She also put aside time to read more newspapers and newsmagazines so that she could keep up with the outside world.

Staying at home is a major change for a woman who has always worked. Some women take pride in their role as mother and home-maker and enjoy leaving the rat race behind. Other women feel incomplete, like shirkers. They become very insecure because they feel more dependent on their husbands.

The parent who stays at home is not always in an enviable position. At minimum, he or she has two jobs: parent and house-keeper. If that spouse also works from home, then we're talking about three jobs. The partner who works outside the home has one job and needs to respect the efforts of the stay-at-home partner.

Two cars collided on a quiet suburban street, shortly after 10:00 A.M. on a weekday morning. People who lived on the block were alarmed and ran out of their homes to investigate. Once they found that the driver and passenger were both okay, the people took a good look at each other. They were all men—stay-at-home dads. The wives had good-paying, professional jobs and most of the men had work that they could perform from home, while they cared for the children.

Most African American couples do not live like this, but when fathers do stay home, there are special problems. Both men and women have been indoctrinated with the idea of the man as bread-winner. Couples who decide that they will not be chained to tradition, still often find themselves resenting the role reversal. Women feel deprived of a full nurturing role. Men feel that they are losing their manhood. It is not easy to admit to this, so they don't and hostility builds.

Be honest and frank. Right is on both sides. Then, do not be afraid to change if the course you have chosen is not working out.

Building a Foundation

The best school and teachers in the world cannot take the place of parents and extended family when it comes to giving children encouragement, love and security. African Americans must parent their children so that they:

♦ learn to thrive regardless of other people's perceptions;
♦ are able to move comfortably in both the black world and the white world;
♦ know about their family roots to anchor their identity as part of an ongoing family tradition;
♦ know about the cultures of Africa and the contributions of African Americans to all facets of American life;
♦ appreciate the fighters against slavery, for civil rights;
♦ appreciate those who are fighting today for fairness in education, economic justice and political influence;
♦ appreciate their own special beauty of skin color, hair texture, facial features without comparing those to European standards;
♦ know how to respond if they are stopped and questioned by police or shopkeepers, even if they are completely innocent of any wrongdoing.

A child with caring, loving and responsible family role models has the best chance of making something of his or her life. Although children who aren't lucky enough to have these types of models can do well, it is twice as hard for them. Remember, children hear what you say but they do what they see you do.

Great Expectations

I met Ayanna when we were both seniors at Howard University. She is from Louisiana and had spent her teen years going to school during the day and hustling money from gullible tourists at night. She and her crippled mother lived on that money. Ayanna was never bitter about her life. In fact, some of the funniest stories I've ever heard are Ayanna's tales of New Orleans after dark.

I grew up in Baltimore. My teen years weren't as colorful as Ayanna's, but they were hard, too, since I never had any money.

Ayanna's mother died the summer after graduation. My family and I were not close, so Ayanna and I took a bus to New York and got married at City Hall. After our "wedding," we stood outside on the street staring at each other. We each had one suitcase and nowhere to go.

We met up with a buddy of mine who had graduated the year

before. He was living in a studio apartment in Brooklyn and was kind enough to give us temporary refuge.

Ayanna got pregnant right away and my friend moved out.

By the time Richard was born, I was working as a production assistant for a radio station and Ayanna was an assistant account executive for an advertising agency. Things were still tough because those jobs didn't pay much.

Anyway . . . that was a long time ago. We have our own home now, two cars and advanced degrees. We are proud of ourselves but Richard is another story. I just don't know what we're going to do with that boy.

Ayanna and I have always tried to instill in Richard the values of high goals and hard work but our words seem to be falling on deaf ears. We have given him every advantage but nothing seems to mean anything.

Every six months, Ayanna makes up a new itinerary for Richard. We sign him up for a combination of athletics, creative arts and at least one extra-curricular intellectual pursuit. We have no intention of losing Richard to the drug dealers, thugs or the criminal justice system.

Last month, Richard's Saturday schedule looked like this:

9:00 A.M.	*Breakfast*
9:30–Noon	*Yard work*
Noon–1:00	*Lunch*
1:30–2:30	*Tap*
3:00–4:00	*Soccer practice*
4:15–5:00	*Computer class*
5:30–6:30	*Dinner*
7:00–9:00	*Family games, discussion*
9:30	*Bed*

The first time Richard cut classes, I talked to him and he promised never to do it again. I had to keep Ayanna calm; she was very upset about it and became angry when I dismissed the incident as a boyhood prank.

Ayanna was right.

The next time, Richard played hookey for the whole day. This time, I hit him. We couldn't ground him because at the time he was taking karate and learning to bowl. All those lessons had been paid for. Instead, I made him start a scrapbook of articles on successful Black men. We discussed each executive profile and I carefully explained what each man had to do to reach the highest levels in his field. Richard seemed interested and I thought the project brought us closer together.

I was wrong.

A few weeks later, he got caught stealing a bag of potato chips and his last report card was atrocious. We cannot understand how Richard has turned out so lazy and irresponsible.

—Steve

Executive profiles don't mean much to a twelve-year-old boy. He was interested in the project because of the amount of time he was spending with his father. That is why when the project ended, so did the closeness and Richard was alone to be chauffeured about from activity to activity once again. Family counseling is needed here, since Ayanna is likely to object to pulling the boy away from her carefully scheduled way of life. In fact, because of her background, threatening to upset the careful structure she had erected would be a threat to the marriage. Since Steve and Ayanna started out with nothing and are living prosperous lives, they obviously know about setting their goals high and working steadily toward accomplishment. They expect their only child to be a high achiever as well, and he just might be if they just stop scaring him. He hears their words and sees a mountain of tasks set before him. Afraid that he cannot possibly scale that mountain, he turns around, goes back to the ground and stays there.

Yes, Richard's behavior is inappropriate. Yes, something must be done about it. However, it is important to look at the problems that lie behind his antics and correct those problems. Then, the symptoms will go away by themselves.

Naturally, Steve and Ayanna can't understand why Richard is behaving so badly, but their imagination is running too far ahead. There is no reason to grab the "endangered black male child" ball and run with it. Richard is a normal kid who is scared of the impossible demands that are being heaped onto his twelve-year-old shoulders. "Where has he learned to be so lazy and irresponsible?" The boy barely has time to think because his parents are so afraid of his getting into trouble. Instead of being involved in two activities in which he really wants to participate and in which he might do well, the child wakes up with every minute of the day accounted for—doing things he never asked or wanted to do. Why should he be grateful or feel happy about his exhausting plight?

WHEN THE KIDS GET ON YOUR NERVES

♦ Take a nice long walk.
♦ Do some deep breathing exercises.
♦ Send them to their room and read the next two chapters in the book you're reading.
♦ Put on your favorite dance record and do a solo.

There is No Such Thing as a Perfect Parent

For many, the essence of married family life is the intimate merging of the creative energies and loving responsibility that is a man and a woman joining forces to nurture each other and the coming generation. The children you have produced are the fulfillment of your bonds with each other. There is no investment you can make that will give you greater lifetime dividends. While you cannot stay married because of the children, the children have a great stake in your marriage.

By overcoming hurdles before they are mountains, including the hurdles of parenthood, you strengthen the children and strengthen the marriage.

Keep your focus on your coupledom. Be sure to have dates with each other, protect your private time together and remain romantic. Do not look for identical attitudes toward child raising. The children know how to accommodate themselves to your differences and thrive with them.

Enjoy your children together, meet the challenges together of protecting and raising them and when that task is done, be proud together. There is no job harder than being a good parent. Don't beat yourself up if you make a mistake. Just give the child a huge smile and keep going.

Fifteen More Steps to Successful Black Parenting

1. Make sure your children get to know themselves—their strengths, weaknesses, fears and dreams.
2. Get the children to try things they are fearful of failing. If they do fail, celebrate the fact that they made the effort in the first place.
3. Let your children explore.

4. Never let them hear you use the "N" word.
5. Never let them hear you denigrate Black men or women as a whole.
6. Love and cherish your spouse and make sure the children know it.
7. Set limits. Encourage your children to participate in deciding what those limits should be and how they should be enforced.
8. Have conversations with your children. Listen to them. You learn more that way.
9. Make sure they know and respect the history of African Americans.
10. Teach responsibility for self, family and community.
11. Stress the importance of a good, formal education.
12. Discuss negative media images with your children and help them write letters to responsible parties.
13. Give them lots of hugs and kisses.
14. Remember that children do what you do and not what you say.

CHAPTER NINE

When Mom Puts the Child First

"Excessive or prolonged stress, particularly in the form of frustration, fear or anxiety, is distress, and it leads to disease."
—Gail C. Christopher
Black Pearls, 1993

The child grows inside the mother's body for nine months. So, the pregnancy starts an attachment between mother and child the father can only marvel at. Yet it is never healthy for a marriage to be centered around a child.

It is not healthy for the husband, who in extreme cases, is essentially being told that the word "we" no longer means the couple. It means the mother and child. Whether he fights this unilateral decision or not, he will suffer and hurt deep inside.

It is not healthy for the wife, because deep inside she knows the situation is unfair and that it needs to change but she is too anxiously rigid or too afraid of relinquishing her new-found power to do anything about it. If she loves her husband and has a conscience, she looks at him and his humiliating situation and feels guilty.

Most of all, it is terribly unhealthy for the child who decides early on that

♦ women are the boss;
♦ men must be stupid or women wouldn't have to rule them;
♦ Daddy has to obey Mommy just like I do;
♦ something must be wrong with me because Mommy watches me so much.

When Dad allows himself to be ignored by Mom while the child is in infancy, there is little hope of turning the situation around when the child gets older. Without professional marriage counseling, the husband looks up one day and realizes that he has become the second child. He finds himself with a TO DO list designed by Mom to which he must adhere or face serious consequences. Like a child he starts

♦ behaving badly when she is not around as a form of rebellion;
♦ running away from home, either physically or by mentally withdrawing into his own world, sometimes taking a substance (usually excess food or liquor) for company.

The mom who gives most of her attention and emotional life to the children is not creating a healthy example of marriage for them to use as models.

One man told us that his "wife lost interest in sex after our son was born. At first, I thought it was a temporary thing but he is four-years-old now and she has not changed. When she does give in, it is hurried. I feel like I'm just another item on her list of things to be done." There is no way to stay happily married without true intimacy, and true intimacy cannot survive under this type of circumstance. As of this writing, the couple is seeing a marriage counselor twice a week.

It is particularly important for Black children to see African American men and women treating each other well and working together to accomplish the goals they have set.

We dated for seven years, then lived together for two years before we got married and bought a fabulous house in suburban Houston. We were happy during Anne's pregnancy but ever since Jade was born, nothing and no one else has mattered to Anne. When I get home from work, we eat dinner together as a family. After that, she takes Jade upstairs to her room and the two of them stay there for the rest of the evening. I watch TV downstairs in the den until it is time for me to go to bed. I've tried talking to Anne about the situation many times. Jade is now five-years-old and I still get the same answer: "You're a grown man, that's my baby."

—David

Anne only agreed to see a marriage counselor after David threatened to leave her if she didn't. Because she didn't want to go to work and get a sitter for Jade, Anne wanted to keep her marriage together. In the first session, it was apparent that she was just going through the motions.

DAVID: *It's not that I don't love Jade, but for the past five years our lives have revolved around her.*

ANNE: *You know, I've read about this type of situation where men were jealous of a baby but I never thought David would act like this.*

DAVID: *Jade is not a baby and I'm not jealous of her—I'm just sick of the way you act.*

COUNSELOR: *Both of you are talking in generalities. Let's get some specific incidents on the table. Anne, you first.*

ANNE *(sighing): This is all such a waste of time.*

COUNSELOR: *Okay. David, you first.*

DAVID: *I don't like the fact that the children in my family are never invited to Jade's birthday parties. I don't like the fact that we haven't been out to a movie, dinner, party or any other social event alone together in five years. I don't like the fact that Anne hovers over Jade so much that my daughter can barely breathe. Shall I go on?*

ANNE: *No. I've heard enough. We've been through all this before, David.*

COUNSELOR: *David has heard your answers to his complaints but I haven't. Would you mind telling me your side of the story?*

ANNE: *Not at all. I'm not leaving Jade with baby-sitters. So, unless it is a family gathering or another occasion that she can attend with us, we stay home. We'll have time for dances and movies when Jade is old enough to stay home alone.*

COUNSELOR: *I believe that David is saying he does not want to live like that.*

ANNE: *I'm not leaving Jade.*

COUNSELOR: *Why not?*

ANNE: *Because she needs me.*

DAVID: *Jade does not need you after she goes to bed. Why can't she sleep over at one of my sister's houses while we go out.*

ANNE: *Forget it.*

COUNSELOR: *Why?*

ANNE: *Look, I'm really sorry that David has dragged us all in here but I'm not going to change my mind.*

COUNSELOR: *Anne, do you agree that two people have to compromise in order to have a happy marriage?*

ANNE: *Yes, and I let David do whatever he wants about other matters but Jade is a different story.*

COUNSELOR: *Let's backtrack for a moment. Why aren't the children in David's family invited to celebrate Jade's birthday with her?*

ANNE: *The children's parties in David's family are so tacky. Everyone crams themselves into one apartment. The adults eat fried chicken, drink beer and talk while the kids run wild. Then someone feeds the kids hot dogs or hamburgers and they play pin-the-tail-on-the-donkey, everyone eats cake and the party is over. No one does that anymore. It's old and tired.*

COUNSELOR: *Do you have any sort of celebration for Jade's birthday?*

ANNE: *Yes. I rented* The Discovery Zone *one year, two of her friends slept over last year and we all made a birthday breakfast. This year I'm having a "make your own sundae" party at our local ice cream parlor.*

COUNSELOR: *Fabulous. Is there a reason why David's young relatives have been left out?*

No Answer.

DAVID: *Tell her, Anne.*

ANNE *(defiantly): They just wouldn't fit in, that's all.*

COUNSELOR: *Why not?*

DAVID: *Because they're Black. That's why.*

COUNSELOR: *You're Black. Anne is Black. Jade is Black. What is the problem?*

DAVID: *We live in a predominately white neighborhood. I worked my ass off to get us to an upscale neighborhood so that when Anne and I had children, they would grow up in a safe, clean environment. Not so I could forget who I am or where I came from. If I'd known Anne was going to act like this, we would have stayed in the old neighborhood.*

COUNSELOR: *Anne?*

ANNE: *Jade had a little Black child over once. I don't know what David is talking about.*

DAVID: *Do you see what I'm up against? This marriage is over.*

Anne was dealing with class and racial issues such as self-hate. The therapist saw that although marriage counseling was definitely needed down the line, Anne needed to see a therapist on her own for a while. David agreed to stay in the marriage if Anne would act on the therapist's referral.

When this couple finally came back to marriage counseling two years later, things had changed. Although Anne still didn't think David's family was good enough to allow her daughter to spend a night in their homes, she was trying hard to overcome her snobbery. In the meantime, a wealthy teenaged white girl had become the couple's official baby-sitter. Anne and David were going out alone at least twice a month and were a lot happier.

The coming of the children can create emotional problems centering around the relationship between husband and wife. One problem is that some women change their whole life in order to make the new child its focus, and they dismiss the husband's needs along the way. Anne became so insecure about her perceived inadequacies that she felt she had to prove herself through her child. Anne feels inferior because of her race, so she is determined to merge Jade into the white world. Anne was also self-conscious about her own background she wanted to separate Jade from Neville's family, whom she regarded as even worse than her own. She felt unsure that she was doing the right thing so she refused to listen to Neville or to anyone who might convince her that she was wrong. Having the baby brought out her possessiveness. She found it hard to allow Neville to be an active parent. Her need to be totally loved and important to someone caused her to lavish all her attention on her child to insure that Jade would love her back in the way she so desperately needed. This love affair with a child leaves little room for attending to a husband, who is then expected to care for himself.

Other ferociously attentive mothers turn to their children because they feel lonely and unloved by husbands who don't seem to be interested in them. Husband and wife have stopped talking to each other in any meaningful way. They spend little or no time together. They have not nourished the intimacy of their marriage. Attention to the baby becomes the wife's weapon of retaliation and compensation.

Neville's refusal to tolerate Anne's behavior and insist on counseling saved their marriage. Other men are too proud to admit they feel lost and sad, so they just let the situation drift on. Some become absorbed in their work or in another woman who is more attentive to them.

Colin never threatened to leave his wife, even though he had been miserable since the birth of his eight-year-old son. Since his father had walked out on the family when he was young, Colin vowed to stay with Delissa until his boy was grown.

Delissa knew how Colin felt about marriage. Since she had no fear of losing him, she completely ignored his feelings about most things. Colin found himself with no free time on the weekends for friends or family. Delissa made sure he had errands to run or something to do until late evening on both Saturday and Sunday. His friends drifted away and his family teased him that he was "henpecked."

Colin didn't care. He stayed with his son until the boy won a scholarship to an exclusive prep school. The child was now fourteen and entering the ninth grade. Since it was a four-year school with college to follow right afterwards, Colin felt free to leave the marriage.

Delissa was stunned.

Desperate to save her marriage, she enlisted their son's help in getting Colin to agree to marriage counseling. It was a hard sell because he was very bitter but they eventually came in.

After a few months of sharing his pain, Colin realized that he didn't really want to leave Delissa. He just wanted to hurt her.

Delissa was willing to do the work required to keep her marriage together but she did make one important statement early on. "You never resisted anything I said or told me that you were unhappy with the way things were," she told Colin.

Most of the time, the woman who puts the child first starts to feel all powerful. It is a short step from there to treating her husband like the household's second child.

The husband then starts feeling resentful and either finds a way to get even or becomes withdrawn, filled with anxiety and stress.

In either case, the couple becomes emotionally distant to the point where the word "marriage" is a misnomer. They turn into two people who are just coexisting under the same roof with a piece of legal paper filed away.

Many women pretend that they're not shutting the husband out and they devise elaborate schemes to cover their true intentions.

Dominique started off by shutting me out but I knew what that would lead to and put my foot down on day one. So, she let me bathe and feed my son but I was so busy trying to read the four pages of typewritten instructions she gave me that it didn't work out. He would cry, loud and hard. One day, I was reading and feeding him. He started crying so hard, he was making choking sounds. I panicked and called out for Dominique. When she ran into the room and took him from my arms, I noticed a triumphant little smile on her lips. I hated her at that moment.

—Jacob

It does not take four pages of text to explain holding a baby and placing a bottle between his lips. This was a control issue for Dominique.

Jacob's resentment festered, he stopped trying to bond with his son, and, eventually, he used Dominique's controlling personality as an excuse for acting out in the company of other women. It almost destroyed what little was left of their marriage. Rather than let things get to this negative point, Jacob could have found a parenting class and gained the confidence he needed to feed and bond with his child, in spite of Dominique's attempt at sabotage. Then, he confidently could have discarded her "instructions" which were only designed to make him nervous, in the first place. The conflict within the marriage would not have gone unresolved for so long and with such nearly disastrous results.

More importantly, Dominique needed to do some soul searching. There is no "we" thinking at work if you continue in a practice that is unfair and that makes your spouse feel miserable and rejected.

Some mothers don't realize what they're doing. Jai was one of them. "Our baby was a wonderful surprise and she was a low birth-weight baby, so it took a while for her to get home. I was so afraid that she would die that I couldn't let her out of my sight. Ike had to stop me one day. He held me in his arms and said, 'Honey, you fuss over the baby all the time. We haven't had a conversation about anything else in almost three months.' I felt awful but we ended up laughing about it and going off to the movies. We've enjoyed our daughter together ever since."

All marriages must be nurtured and a husband should not be treated like a second-class citizen in his own home.

CHAPTER TEN

Coming Together on Discipline

"My mother was always very fair . . . She let me do what I
had to do . . . even when we couldn't see eye to eye on things,
we could at least discuss them."
—Queen Latifah
Ebony magazine, December 1993

In the past, African Americans have been accused of having rigid
child rearing methods. The collective memory of dangers surrounding incompletely socialized children and youth, especially
boys, has led to the traditional strictness of Black parents.

We all know the old way. It was very simple. Children did
what they were told or got a whipping. To resent our parents and
grandparents for this would be unfair. Black parents have had to
set up many restrictions and harsh penalties for breaking them.
This was necessary in order to protect their children.

During slavery and segregation, Black children had to obey
orders from any white citizen, instantly and without question. They
also had to know how to submit to the humiliating Jim Crow laws
without showing any sign of impatience or anger. Anything less
could cost them their lives or jeopardize the town's entire Black
community. Therefore, whipping was a survival technique passed
down from generation to generation.

Even today, a misstep by a Black boy or man can result in hard
times for the entire Black community, but our position in this
society has improved enough that we can afford to explore other
methods (aside from hitting) of disciplining our kids.

What Is Discipline?

When the disciplining of children is mentioned, most people think of the punishment of infractions. Discipline is more than that. It is what the elders used to refer to as home training.

The expectations you have for your children from their time of their birth; the way you accept them, encourage and discourage them; the way you show them concern and respect; give them tasks within their ability and model the behavior you expect—all comprise the foundation of discipline. If you invest in establishing the behaviors you admire during their early years, your children will incorporate these standards and you will reap the dividends when they reach the perilous shoals of adolescence.

EXERCISE: WHAT IS DISCIPLINE?

Do a pop quiz. Write 10 things that come to mind when you think of discipline for children. Ask your wife or husband to do the same. Then, both of you compare the lists. Some lists are punishment oriented. Some refer more heavily to the rules of living. What were your associations? How similar or different are you in your basic outlook? How similar do you have to be in order to have harmony in your family?

A basic issue to remember is that children want to please their parents. They also model their own behavior after that of their parents. Children are on your side.

As children develop, their need for parental guidance and control changes. The infant's task is to figure out the difference between his own body and that of the mothering one. The eighteen-month-old carries his mother with him everywhere and needs her help each step of the way. He looks for admiration and praise for whatever he produces. The two-year-old seeks to separate her will from that of her parents.

The six-year-old will wear the clothing chosen for her. Once off to school, the child will work out ways of being in the world of strange adults like teachers, and of other children. How popular, how smart, how strong, how pretty, how tall—these are the child's preoccupations. Along the way, he or she must push against the boundaries to explore what kinds of behaviors are acceptable and safe. The eight-year-old insists on privacy and a closed door. The sixteen-year-old insists on picking out her own clothing.

When adolescence arrives, it demands that the youth not only continue the search for acceptance or the effort to excel in the outside world, but to experiment with what it means to be an adult. In this context mild rebellion, the adolescent version of the two-year-old's "nos," tests out separation from parental protection.

Although all of these developmental stages may present occasions for parental guidance in the form of punishment, it is more helpful to regard those occasions as opportunities to guide and teach. The young child needs to explore the world as it unfolds before him. He touches, he drops, he falls, he spills and mixes things. The adults teach him what is safe and what is not, what can be handled and what is better left alone. While some of that teaching may need to be emphatic for the sake of the child's safety and the convenience of the others in the household, none needs to be harsh. Preventive vigilance, a sharp "no" or bodily removing a toddler from danger, will teach and keep him safe, while you protect his curiosity. Later, the child needs some explanation about why some behaviors are unacceptable to you, along with consistency on your part.

Punishment, if necessary, needs to be fair, proportionate to the infraction, and connected to it. It also needs to be rare.

If the preceding years went well, during adolescence, you, as a parent, get your payoff. If both of you have proved reasonable, can be talked to and confided in, can listen, can be counted on to express your feelings and opinions, and are consistent, your teenager will have less need to go to dangerous extremes to rebel. These are the years that bring the most conflict in families. The teenager pushes for a different kind of relationship with parents, perhaps one that affords her more respect as a thinking person, and more age-appropriate independence. This can upset the entire family balance.

Most referrals for family therapy occur when the oldest child has entered adolescence. This is the time of strain for families and marriages. Husbands and wives need to be careful not to take each other for granted. The main excitement in the marriage is the teenager's life. Don't let this happen. Now is the time for you to stimulate your marriage. Share a lot, talk a lot (if even about the weather), laugh a lot. Go out together. Have dates. Stimulate your sex life. Make it your business to have fun. Perhaps one of you finds it easier to deal with the teenager. If so, that one might take the lead in managing rules and their infractions, backed up by the other. It is all right to disagree, but better to have a united front. Look for agreement, and talk everything over as you go.

Young children seem to accept spankings, not beatings, from their parents. Older children are more likely to see such actions as aggressive. Even though children may stop the wrong or dangerous behavior when spanked, it has not been found that this form of punishment is more effective than other kinds. Consider time outs; withdrawing privileges; and firm, brief lectures.

There is no getting around the issue—how to discipline the children is a matter with which every couple has to deal. It is also an issue which highlights differences in background and the fundamental attitudes of your two separate biological families. We all know that children will upset us at times. Men and women also agree that children need rules and limits. It is only when a couple tries to agree on how to react when the rules are not respected or the limits are overstepped that there is conflict.

Carter and Sylvia sought counseling early in their son's life because they were fighting about this problem. "I used to say that if I ever had a child, I would never hit but my feelings have changed. My son is now tall enough to reach the knobs on the stove and Sylvia's lectures did not make him stop turning them on. So, I hit him. It was better than waiting for him to burn himself or to set the house afire. Anyway, Sylvia had a fit over the spanking. It is ridiculous. My mama used to hit us when we deserved it and she was not a child abuser. She was the best mother in the world." Sylvia shook her head as Carter was speaking. "I don't want hitting in the house. We could have simply taken the knobs off when the stove was not in use." Carter scoffed at this. "He has to learn not to play with any stove. You can't talk things out and reason with a four-year-old and we can't ask our relatives and friends to remove their own kitchen knobs before we come over."

Carter had a point.

Constant bickering about how to handle the children can push a couple apart. This rift between Carter and Sylvia had to be closed, quickly.

Since the problem in their marriage was confined to this one subject, the counselor referred them to a series of parenting seminars.

After six months, Sylvia understood that simply lecturing a child will not bring the desired results. She started taking away her son's playthings one at a time whenever he broke the rules. It didn't take long to bring his behavior under control.

In the end, Carter knew that he was right when he said that Sylvia's "talks" were useless. He also understood that punishment does not have to involve hitting.

They were happy with their new choice.

Scott travels a great deal on business. He feels guilty about it but he works for a public relations firm that has offices all over the world. He spends most of his time on planes. Since he doesn't see Betty and their only son as much as he'd like, he tries to make up for it by indulging little Jodie's every whim. When he is home, the eight-year-old breaks every rule and routine by which he and Betty normally live. Betty has asked her husband for his support, but he refuses to speak firmly to the boy and make him behave. Scott says, "I can't be the one to chastise Jody when he does something wrong. I have far too little time for him as is. I don't want those precious hours to be used for anything except fun."

Scott and Betty were smart enough to realize that unless they came together on this issue, Jody's antics were going to escalate. They compromised. Scott didn't have the heart to correct his son but he agreed to help Betty by gently ceasing to play with his son until the boy addressed his mother's concerns.

The next time Scott was home, he interrupted their board games three times so that he could complete tasks that Jody was supposed to have done for his mother. Three weeks later, Scott came home to find that Jody had taken it upon himself to make sure this time there would be no interruptions. Jody had created his own TO DO list earlier in the week. Every single line was marked DONE, and had been done by Jody.

It is all right if Daddy is more strict than Mom, or vice versa. Children accept and even work within these differences. But when the differences are great, or when you and/or your spouse do not accept your differences, this produces marital strain. It gets even more complicated when you are living in a dangerous neighborhood, where serious restrictions must be placed on your child for safety's sake. It is worse when you have to work hard and are still poor or are just about or not even making ends meet, so that you are always worried and tense and have little patience. Add to this mixture your own temperament and how your child's temperament fits with yours—whether he is a seeker of your approval or a challenger.

As with all things, it is a good idea to talk together about your concerns. Try to be specific. Don't say things like, "You are unreasonable." Instead, be specific. Say something like, "When you told Anabel that she had to come from shopping after an hour and you would not listen to her, I thought you were unreasonable." This provides the opportunity for you to think about the fears or other concerns that underlie your decisions and expectations about your child's behavior, and also better to understand your mate's position. Aim towards mutual agreement about principle. For example, going downtown or to the mall for shopping is all right, within the time limits set by you and agreed to by the teenager. To go to the mall to hang out will not be allowed.

What do you do when there are impasses? A couple can bicker constantly or fight, either privately or in front of the children. One member may give in voluntarily or with great resentment, or he or she may try to undermine the other by colluding with the child.

Andrea and Quentin found themselves in increasing disagreement about their reactions to their children. When the children were young, the differences did not seem very great. Andrea said "no" and "don't touch" frequently to the toddlers and Quentin was more laid-back and indulgent, but then, Andrea was dealing with them most of the time. As the children grew older, the differences between Andrea and Quentin grew more marked. Quentin found himself always defending them against Andrea's punishments and tongue-lashings. In turn, she would turn her rage on her husband. When their daughter reached adolescence, Andrea made an issue of any minor lapse. A sloppy room or grease left on a washed glass could cause her to rant and rave for hours. She seemed to be suspicious and distrustful of the girl and imposed what Quentin thought were excessively harsh punishments for relatively minor infractions. Husband and wife developed mutual contempt for each other's attitudes. Their disagreements over the kids grew ever more sharp, and there was more and more rage attached to those reactions. They fought through the children.

In counseling, it was established that they both agreed their children were basically responsible, respectful and doing well, both socially and scholastically. So why the anxiety about their daily behavior? Beyond Andrea's admitting that she was the more anxious one, the rest was a mystery. Only gradually did it emerge that while they both appreciated some aspects of each other's style— Quentin's easygoing ways and Andrea's pushing energy—they both were repelled, as well. Characteristically, the more Andrea sought to control and correct, the more Quentin protected. The parents' drama was acted out in regard through the children— safer targets than each other.

Andrea was a temperamentally high-strung person who was raised to waste no time, tolerate no laziness and be ever on the move upward. She feared and hated any traces of laziness she detected in herself. Her mind went to images of strung-out bag ladies or drug-addicted out-of-wedlock mothers on welfare. She transferred her fears of disaster for those who do not toe the line from herself to her children.

On the other hand, Quentin rebelled early in life from his mother's nervous pressures. With a mixture of affection and exasperation, his mother still describes him as a "stubborn brat." He both recoiled from but found familiar comfort with female nervous energy. He thought there was nothing really wrong with Andrea that a little calming would not cure. The more the parents focused on their own issues through therapy, the less pressure was directed to the children. Both parents noticed that the children seemed to thrive better than ever, with less rather than more scrutiny.

Andrea and Quentin's situation illustrates an issue of discipline that is easy to overlook. Our angers and frustrations with our job, or with significant persons in our life who let us down or bother us, or with the other parent, are often misdirected to concerns about the children. This is a "kick the cat" phenomenon. The children's health, safety, behavior, schoolwork, social life—we can use all or any of these to explain our unease and make the kids objects of our built up rage. Couples can help each other, as well as the children, if they consider such issues when they find they are having trouble agreeing on the discipline of their children. The more you deal directly with the source of your frustration, the more it will help you to be a little more objective about the children's behavior. The more objective you are, the more wise and effective you will be in reacting to them.

You can see that discipline does not always mean punishing. Now, let's see why discipline does not have to involve hitting.

Why Hitting and Punishment are Different

Melvin, aged four, had a habit of throwing toys at adults when he couldn't get his way. Once, a plastic truck hit his father in the eye. Nelson took all of his toys away for three days as punishment.

Arela spanked him. "I had no intention of waiting for an injury to myself," she said. "Besides, I had already spoken to Melvin about throwing things. I don't care whether Nelson liked it or not. I'm not having it."

—*Arela*

First of all, any sentence that starts, "I don't care," when referring to a partner's opinion or feelings, is a dangerous sentence. You are always supposed to care.

Nelson had already made Melvin pay a consequence for breaking the rules. When Arela meted out her own punishment, Nelson saw it as a repudiation of his own solution. If Arela had spanked Melvin out of fear of future injury to herself, her action wasn't fair. The child was punished for something he *might* do at some future date. Most dangerous of all is that Melvin now understands he can make his parents stop speaking. That is a lot of power to give a four-year-old.

But what about more drastic differences, like spanking or not spanking? If one of you believes that there is nothing wrong about administering corporal punishment, and the other abhors any kind of physical force, especially on children, you need to talk out your differences. Often, even if one person understands the other's point of view, the couple continues to disagree.

If you hit a child, he'll stop doing what you find is annoying you, because it will cause him more physical pain if he continues. However, he has not learned anything about the behavior itself. The next time, he will simply be careful not to repeat the act in your presence.

If you punish a child properly, he has time to think about his actions and realize that his act was selfish, disrespectful or in some way dangerous. If he is helped to truly understand the act and its consequences, he will behave even when you are not around to hit him.

Since it is impossible to follow a child at school, on the street, with friends or later, when he starts working, it makes sense to teach him to control himself simply because it is the right thing to do.

If you choose corporeal punishment, you should know that hitting only works until the child reaches adolescence. Once he is no longer a child, what you have is a young man who has never been taught to look within himself and think about what his behavior means. For this young man, self-control only means avoiding the pain of getting caught. This is one of the reasons teenagers commit crimes.

Remember, what method of discipline you use depends on the type of results you want.

How To Punish a Child Properly

More than anything else, kids need consistency. If something is the wrong thing to do today, it should be the wrong thing to do tomorrow. Children should not be punished just because you're in a bad mood. Make sure that your actions and your words match.

If you tell a child that if he continues to misbehave, all toys will be put away for three days, do just that if he doesn't stop—no matter how much it hurts the both of you. Make sure the child understands that the choice not to have toys for three days was his own. He was warned and, therefore, had a decision to make. Now, he must accept the consequences of that choice.

Do not get emotional. Just follow through on your warning. This is excellent preparation for real life.

FUNDAMENTALS OF DISCIPLINE

There are two basics to remember. The first is that discipline is not a matter of punishment only. The second is that you and your children are on the same side.

POSITIVE DISCIPLINE TAKES PLACE WHEN:

♦ You show the expectations you have for them from the time of their birth.
♦ When you show them that you love and accept them even when you accept some behavior.
♦ When you encourage some of the things that they do, and discourage them.
♦ When you show them concern and respect for them and for others.
♦ When you give them tasks within their ability level, help them if necessary and praise their accomplishment.
♦ When you always model the behavior you expect from them.

These are the daily behaviors that comprise the foundation of discipline. If you invest in establishing the behavior you admire during your children's early years, they will incorporate these standards and you will recognize the dividends when they reach the perilous years of adolescence.

Sometimes, we forget the second basic issue in child discipline: children need and want to please their parents. They cannot help but model their own behavior after that of their parents. Children are on your side.

Present a United Front

Even though we believe that punishment works better over the long haul than hitting, this is a decision that has to be left up to the individual parents. However, no matter what type of discipline you settle on, it won't work if the child senses that one parent does not agree with the plan. Even a toddler can sense a conflict between parents' points of view. Children are very intuitive and they will learn to play one of you against the other. Make a plan and never let the children see you sweat about it.

Handling a Delinquent Child

According to *Black Americans: A Statistical Source Book,* 60,026 Black adolescents under the age of eighteen were arrested for violent crimes in 1993 and 158,850 were arrested for property crimes (which includes robbery, arson, etc.). In comparison, during that same year, 57,123 Caucasian adolescents under the age of eighteen were arrested for violent crimes and 412,348 were arrested for property crimes. Although it is true that our children are targeted far too often by law enforcement and unfairly arrested, in this chapter we are focusing on those who commit crimes and are justifiably detained.

Trouble with a wayward adolescent can strain even the most stable marriage. Only incompatibility or adultery cause more of a threat to the union. This is one reason why it is important to raise children who are able to discipline themselves when you are not around to do so. It is very hard for any parent to accept when a child goes wrong. Far too often, we beat up on ourselves in the mistaken belief that our parenting skills had to be wrong somewhere along the line. It is important to remember that children are exposed to other children, mass media and adults with bad intentions. You are not the only influence in their lives.

I was actually married when I met Olivia, even though my first wife and I had stopped loving each other a long time before. We needed some time apart so I left Fayetteville and headed for New York to visit relatives. That was the summer I met Olivia. Six weeks after we met, I went back home and filed for divorce.

I married Olivia a year later, when she was five months pregnant with our own child, Bert, Jr.

Junior started cutting school in the seventh grade. If it had been up to me, he would have been grounded for the next school year but Olivia said that I was too harsh. She said that he was just going through a phase. By the following year, I had started smelling reefer when I got home in the evening. The air was also too per-fumey. Like he had sprayed something to cover up the scent.

Olivia and I started to keep a closer eye on him.

When he got himself arrested at fifteen for drug possession, I blamed Olivia for having been too soft on him. We argued for weeks. Some of the things we said to each other are too horrible to repeat. Finally, we were exhausted and simply walked around the house like zombies, sleeping with our backs turned at night. I started thinking that this marriage was going down the drain, just like my first one. I didn't want that to happen but I didn't know what to do.

One evening, I was watching a special on TV about a boot camp for boys who were headed for trouble. I copied down the information and confronted Olivia. At first, she cried and protested but in the end, she agreed that if we could get Bert, Jr. accepted, it would be an act of love.

Junior bopped in around midnight with the usual smirk on his face and I told him the new deal. He turned to Olivia. Her eyes told him that this time, she was standing beside me.

It took a few months but Junior finally went away to "boot camp." We went into marriage counseling right after he left to talk about some of the issues that had been raised during this time. It went well and we started rebuilding our lives.

We did not let Junior break up our marriage.

As hard as it may be to accept it, trust your gut feeling if it seems as though something is amiss with your child. Forget shame or the idea that your dreams are crumbling. Those responses only lead to nonaction. It is important that you face the situation head on. Living in denial will not help your child. If your kid gets into trouble more than once and he is under eighteen-years-old, you will find yourself caught up in the juvenile court system. This means an endless round of interviews, reports and social workers who have the power to separate your child from the rest of the family by declaring you "unfit" or saying that your parenting is inadequate, neglectful or in some way cruel. If you refuse to cooperate with the social service agency that is prying into your personal affairs (sometimes quite rudely), this is considered an admission of guilt.

There will be no trial.

Moreover, if your home is declared "unsuitable" (and therefore, presumably, responsible for your child's youthful offender status) on the whim of a case worker who is angry at your resentment of her presence, all the other underage children in your home will be removed, as well. In light of the highly publicized cases of children being murdered by their parents, not many judges are going to risk their careers by ruling in favor of the parents against the advice of the social worker, even if his instinct tells him that the social worker is being petty or vindictive.

Social workers and the Bureau of Child Welfare wield awesome power. Their word is the last one, so it is important that you go along with their demands until the situation is resolved and they are out of your life.

If you sense that your child is headed for trouble, handle it immediately by getting professional counseling for him and family counseling for everyone. If you can't afford counseling, contact your local church and ask the pastor for assistance in getting your child into an appropriate program. This will help you and your child get to the root of the problem and expose the real issues so they can be overcome. It will also help you if the child does not straighten up and a state employee asks what you have done to help him.

If you do not take action, the pressure and legal issues involved with a delinquent child may tear your family apart.

Remember, the parenting years do not last forever. If you are lucky and work hard, your marriage will.

CHAPTER ELEVEN

Stepfamilies

"Little by little the bird makes its nest."
—Haitian proverb

With so many single-parent families and marriages that end in divorce, it is not uncommon for newlyweds to have children from previous relationships who play a role in the new union. If you (or your spouse) find yourself in this situation, remember that the child's life has changed dramatically from the moment you got (re)married. He now officially has a new stepparent, new grandparents and other people who are now related to him by marriage.

When the one you love joins you in marriage, and one or both of you have children, you face a particular challenge: making one family unit out of two. Don't worry. African Americans historically have handled new additions to the family with open arms, loyalty and generosity. We have always been more likely than other groups to welcome children and the elderly into the home, even when our resources are already strained to the limits. That strength of perseverance exists within you. All you have to do is relax, have faith and tap into it.

Basically, there are two different opinions about managing the family unit. One is to meld the two groups into one. That is, to parent all the children without regard to the biological connections. The other approach is to maintain the integrity of each original family grouping, but to cooperatively interact for shared responsibilities in managing the children and the household.

Regardless of your joint decision about the basic organization of your new family, you must keep primary your marriage commitment to each other. The foundation for everyone sharing the same home should be your love, loyalty and support of each other. The two of you must know that you will always find understanding and help from each other, whether or not you agree and regardless of whose biological children are involved if either of you have problems concerning them.

No matter what, you and your mate must present to the world a solid, united core. It is the foundation of your new family. This does not mean that you withdraw love or attention from the children you brought into the marriage. Separately, and together with the other family members, they should be helped to feel assured that your love has been expanded, not redirected.

The Fantasy

Many people envision one large blended family, where everyone gets along with love and loyalty, and any biological or historical differences become so softened that they disappear. Well, that does happen, on television. Real life is a little too complicated for such a situation to come about very readily.

In most cases, the biological children do not tolerate sharing their mother or father equally with other children. They count the number of peas dished out on each other's plates. Even the smiles they receive are compared. And sometimes, the two sets of children are just too different to like each other or to get along. In addition, children do not accept from a stepparent what they will put up with from their biological parent. A yell or a reprimand, punishment or restriction may be seen as proof of the stepparent's evil intent, or a demonstration that this rival for their natural parent's affection and loyalty is their enemy. In fact, children may actively fight against becoming too close to or feeling love for the stepparent because they believe that to do so would be an act of disloyalty to both biological parents. And, as we mentioned before, it is easier to take out resentments on a stepparent.

Forget any fantasies you had before the wedding and handle each situation as it arises. It is not easy to combine two families, each with its own values, traditions and expectations. Since it often takes years to work through all the resentments and conflicts, couples should not berate themselves for failing to make the process seamless or painless.

The Age of the Children

A second consideration is the age of the children. The younger the child the more likely he or she will be happy to have a new daddy, and even will accept a new mommy. It seems that fathers are somewhat more readily replaced, if only because it is a little easier for the child to regulate closeness to a working father, than to someone who is in a mothering relationship.

Much depends on when and how the original parent was lost. In the case of desertion or death, young children will gradually accept an interested, caring adult as a parent. It is important to follow patiently the pace of the individual child. Mostly, children first need to feel reassured that their remaining natural parent will not also leave, and that they will still be loved and cared for by that parent despite the new people entering their lives.

The older the child, the more wary or resistant he or she will be about the interloper. Teenagers, who tend to give all adults a hard time for good developmental reasons, can be downright hostile or even combative. The older the child, the more careful the new parent must be in imposing new limits on the youngster's behavior. With teenagers, it is best to leave the discipline to the biological parent. Just be an approachable, understanding and wise adult who can listen to a young person and *if asked,* can come up with helpful advice. Remember, *if asked!*

The Family Dinner

The family dinner table has been found to be the one most reliable influence in making for a cohesive family unit. It is worth the sacrifice in busy or otherwise disorganized lives to eat together to stay together. And please, make dinner pleasant. Do not correct, scold or bring up punishable acts at dinner.

Treat it as an oasis of peace.

It is a good time to share the events of each other's day, or even problems encountered, without invoking a lecture or a reprimand. It may be better for everyone when dinner is a collaborative affair. Rotating teams of parents and children could share the tasks associated with preparing and cleaning up after a meal.

If the Stepchildren Seem Out to Get You

It may be very difficult for you to do this, but try very hard not to take an angry stepchild's antics too personally. It will help if you focus on the child, rather than on your own hurt or angry feelings. Above all, do not join the war. A child's ability to delay gratification because of future consequences has not yet been firmly established, nor has their ability to inhibit or redirect a momentum, or put reason over passion. Children deal in extremes.

When you take the time to try to understand the warring child, you maximize your opportunity eventually to achieve family harmony. For example, ask yourself: What have this child's experiences with other adults been like? Children who have experienced early loss of important parental figures are scarred. As a result, many avoid attachment to adults.

Did the child stay with a relative on whom he or she was imposed? If the child was left with grandparents in the islands or down South, then forced to leave that home and parent in order to join the resettled parent, who is now a stranger, imagine how scared he is inside.

Observe the warring child's style. Some children fly off the handle then cool down relatively quickly. Some simmer for a long time. Whatever the case, don't react too quickly. Parents often escalate a dispute to a full-fledged battle that takes on a life of its own.

Words Do Not Have the Power of Actions

Hard as it is to believe, children, even through adolescence, model themselves after the important adults in their life. No one is more important to them than their parents, including their stepparents. If you observe carefully, after a period of time, you might even begin to notice this. If the child has never been treated with respect, he or she may not treat others with respect, especially at times of stress. If there is a lot of yelling, screaming and berating in the household, chances are that quiet acceptance will not characterize the child's reactions. Your behavior will always be more important than what you say or the behavioral standards you tell the kids they should have. Words, no matter how often repeated, do not have the power of actions.

The Weekend Stepchild

Spending only weekends with the remarried parent is a very different situation from living full-time with a stepparent.

The weekend child is essentially a visitor. There tends to be less at stake in this situation. It is to be hoped that she will become a comfortable visitor, who fits harmoniously into the household's rhythms. The child knows that she will soon be home so she won't fight as hard against things she does not like. The downside is that the child is often confused, especially if the households function very differently. In addition, the child is provided with a golden opportunity to play one parent off the other and one household off the other, thus dodging responsibilities by escaping to "where I'm really understood." Especially tempting to many children is having all three or four parents fighting over or about her. Let the natural parent know that you are ready to support her routines and standards for the children. If their bedtime at home is 8:00 P.M., when at your house, they should not stay up until 10:00 P.M. If they are expected to keep their room clean at home, then their space in your house should be kept orderly. Let the natural parent deal with the children's protests and with whatever discipline seems necessary. Under these circumstances, the stepparent's role is to be a loving, interested adult friend, rather than to exercise the full responsibility and privilege of parenthood.

It is hard enough to get close to our own kids. Establishing a relationship with a child who is the product of a partner's ex-marriage or relationship can be extremely difficult. The core of the problem is that the average child always hopes that his parents will get back together. Unless one of the child's natural parents is deceased, he carries this hope within him, whether he gives voice to it or not.

As the stepparent you represent a threat to that fantasy.

It is not unusual for a child to carry around this deep-seated desire straight into adulthood, even when all of the evidence shows that this wish will never—and should never—come true.

There is absolutely nothing you can do to make a child stop secretly wishing that his parents will rediscover each other. It will be easier for you to empathize with your stepchild if you are the child of parents who never married, or if you grew up with divorced parents.

Whatever your background, the first rule of stepparenting is never to talk about this secret fantasy unless the child brings it up himself.

My stepson is ten years old and he hates me. Jerome and I have been married for four years. Joey dislikes me more each year and is beginning to answer everything I say to him with hostility or sarcasm. I'm ready to tell Jerome not to have him over anymore but I know that would start World War III.

Jerome has talked to Joey about his attitude but all he says is that, "I have a mother and Micki has hurt her a lot. She never wanted you to break up."

—Micki

This child obviously has been told or overheard a lot of angst-filled stories from his mother. He feels her pain and he can't be nice to the enemy. As long as his mother is filled with sadness and anger over the end of her relationship, this child cannot form a loving relationship with Micki. He is going through a lot of turmoil because his mother is so self-centered.

Jerome needs to handle this. First, he should speak to Joey's mother and try to make her understand that she is hurting their child a lot more than she is hurting her ex-husband and his wife. The mother needs to understand that because she has allowed her emotions to take control, her child is turning into a bitter little boy who can only grow up to be a bitter man. Jerome should ask her to think about this fact and whether it is what she really wants for their son. Next, Jerome should have a talk with Joey and insist that he talk to Micki with respect.

The most important thing in any stepfamily is that the two of you, husband and wife, must remain committed to each other and to your marriage. If it doesn't work out with the kids, breaking up the marriage shouldn't even be an option. This definiteness of purpose will communicate to relatives, stepchildren and friends alike that the two of you intend to be together no matter how many challenges are thrown at you.

Things had been simmering between Sadiqua and Gene's daughter, Madeline, since the courtship began four years ago. Sadiqua had always taken the mature, adult approach but nothing seemed to work. Finally, after Sadiqua corrected this girl who was finger-painting the living room wall, Madeline turned to her and said, "Don't tell me what to do; you're not my mother."

Sadiqua made Gene take the little girl home.

The couple came in for counseling a few weeks later when communication between them had completely broken down. Gene was enraged because Sadiqua wouldn't allow his only child to come back into their home.

After a few weeks of learning how to be a stepparent, Sadiqua relented. Since Madeline had been allowed to create drama before, naturally, she responded to Sadiqua's admonishment with the same response. This time, Sadiqua's correct response was:

No, I am not your mother. I am an adult and you will respect that. I'm sure that if you had done (this) in your mother's house, she wouldn't like it, either. In fact, you would probably be in a lot more trouble than you are right now. From now on, you watch your mouth or you will be punished.

The Other Parent

Sometimes, the other biological parent is an interfering, over-controlling or over-protective type who feels compelled to manage the child/stepparent interaction. Some use the child to retaliate against the former spouse, or to manipulate the lost spouse into greater involvement with the old household, almost in denial of the breakup. Some are determined to punish the new family for being.

Under these circumstances, it is all the more necessary for the new couple to be on each other's side and drawing ever closer. Your mate has very limited influence over the behavior of his former wife or lover. It is less than useless to feel unprotected by him and to demand that he change her negative behavior. To begin to blame each other, or to reject each other's frustration, is to let your marriage become controlled by outside persons.

It is best to develop a cooperative relationship with the parent you are joining or replacing in your marriage. Emphasize that you both have a common interest in supporting the best interests of the same children. You will have to demonstrate that you are not competing for the love and loyalty that naturally goes toward the natural parents. Make it clear that you are not out to show your husband or your wife that you are a better spouse or even a better mother or father than the ex.

If You Don't Like Your Stepchildren

Stepparents have their own difficulties in accepting the new children. Do not feel guilty if you find yourself resenting the demands of caring for someone else's children, even the children of the person you love. It is easy to build up negative attitudes toward children who seem not to respect you, or who have habits and behaviors that you dislike. It is natural to feel a little jealous of those who are loved by your mate, especially if at times the mate seems to take the child's side over yours.

It is certainly easy to take the side of your own children in a conflict with your stepchildren. It may be worse for you if your stepchildren do better in sports or at school than your own children. There are, indeed, many difficulties with which stepparents must contend. But these are *your* problems—yours to understand, take responsibility for and solve. Avoid the temptation to dump the problems on your mate, or worse, to blame him or her for their existence. Bringing things to the point of crisis with an "It's me or them" statement is almost guaranteed to lead to disaster.

What to do? If you need to discharge your anger or frustration, this is one occasion when you need to choose a person other than your mate with whom you are free to talk. Ask that person not to respond by giving you advice, but just to listen, and to keep all confidential. That means that you have to trust this chosen confidante. Avoid friends and family members who are a part of your family's daily social life. They will remember and, perhaps, resent your mate, the children or the ex, long after you have forgiven all and have worked out the situation. Better to choose a work mate, your wise grandmother who lives in another state, or even a relative stranger.

If this does not help and you can't cool off, get to a professional counselor right away.

Grace sought counseling because she was having problems get-ting close to Dwayne's eight-year-old daughter. Dwayne had visita-tion rights which included two overnight stays each month. Brooke was a sweet little girl who talked and laughed freely with her father. When Grace tried to have a conversation with her, she responded in a polite, reserved way. If Grace planned an outside activity for the three of them, Brooke never turned it down—she just walked through the event with an obvious lack of enthusiasm. "It was clear that she didn't want to get close to me yet there was nothing that I could complain to Dwayne about. The child did everything that I asked of her," Grace said.

This was a relatively easy problem for Grace and the counselor to work through.

Grace was advised to make plans for herself and Brooke that did not include Dwayne.

The first event was a Halloween party to which Grace invited six other neighborhood children. Dwayne left the house shortly after his daughter arrived.

The party was a huge success. Grace and Brooke spent the next hour preparing refreshments, choosing spooky music and hanging paper jack-o'-lanterns. They had just changed into costumes when the other kids arrived. Dwayne came back home just as the other mothers arrived. Grace kissed Brooke good-night and went to bed.

Over the next few months, Grace and Brooke developed a relationship with this small group of mothers and children. Dwayne cooperated by not getting involved with any of the fathers and staying away from the house during these special visits.

At the end of nine months, Grace and Brooke had: friendships with people unknown to either of Brooke's parents; a thick photo album to show Dwayne which Brooke and her new friends had put together and shared memories of good and bad times.

It is essential for new stepparents to forge their own relationship apart from their partner. There is no other way to start on the road to closeness. Not only that, but it takes some pressure off the biological parent to not have all interactions flowing through him.

Darren and Charmaine each came to the marriage with a teen-aged son who would be living in the household with them. Since they were so much in love, it was a big disappointment to them when one problem after another began to surface.

Darren's first wife had died when Michael was in kindergarten, leaving Darren to raise the boy alone. Michael was a kind, well-mannered young man of 16 when his father married Charmaine. He had always longed for a mother and sibling, so he was delighted when Charmaine and Salvatore moved in.

Charmaine's ex-lover had refused to marry her when she became pregnant with Salvatore. She went to live with her mother and the two women did an excellent job of raising Salvatore, who had just passed his seventeenth birthday when Charmaine got married.

Darren and Charmaine could only afford the two-bedroom

apartment that Darren was already living in, so they gave the biggest room to the boys.

Although Michael and Salvatore knew and liked each other, neither of them knew how to share close living quarters with another person. Michael kept his music playing constantly. After Salvatore complained, the parents bought headphones for both boys.

The second conflict started because Salvatore liked everything neat and tidy. Michael often had to step over piles of his own clothes to get in bed. Darren eventually trained Michael to show respect for his roommate by putting his belongings away after each use.

Darren and Charmaine tried to put out every fire but the incidents still grew in number and intensity. They were also struggling with their own issues, such as gaining true intimacy and not having enough money.

Things came to a head over their son's social lives.

Charmaine didn't allow Salvatore to stay out past 10:00, even on weekends.

Michael didn't have a curfew. All Darren asked was that the boy leave a number where he could be reached and Michael was very good about that.

Naturally, Salvatore wanted to have the same privilege. Charmaine wouldn't stand for it. The tension in the household got so bad that everyone was miserable.

Charmaine decided to invest her Christmas bonus in a series of counseling sessions for the entire family.

In the end, some ground rules were laid down for the boys so that they could peacefully coexist in their shared room. Bins were supplied in which each boy deposited the day's various possessions. This helped Michael, in particular, to keep his belongings off the floor. They agreed that each must respect the other's belongings and boundaries. Punishment for breaking the rules of behavior they worked out were established. Both rules and punishments were posted in their room.

Both boys were given a midnight curfew on the weekends. Neither one of them was allowed to hang out on school nights. They all agreed that the boys were to apply the procedures they had practiced in counseling to settle their own disputes. They were not born for their parents to act as referees.

It frequently happens that problems, even severe ones, leave things better off than if they had never occurred. In the case of this family, Darren and Charmaine gained a better understanding of each other's sensitivities, and were more lovingly assured of each other's caring support as a result of their collaboration in dealing with the series of problems caused by their sons. They worked well together; each felt understood by the other and found they could depend on each other when things got tough. Including their sons in their problem solving helped gain them mutual respect and more responsibility all around. The additional dividend was peace for the family and more private time for Charmaine and Darren.

A brand-new stepfamily encounters numerous challenges. Each member has had a loss and there is

♦ no common family story;
♦ no common set of beliefs;
♦ no common ways of accomplishing things.

Therefore, creating a stepfamily that works takes time and a lot of effort on the part of both adults and youngsters.

A new stepfamily has to learn to make decisions as a family. The children must also feel that no child is more important than the other.

Professional help is recommended if a child is consistently hostile toward one particular person in the new family or a spouse becomes hostile toward a child or too stressed-out to deal with the situation in a positive way.

Stepfamilies should not expect miracles. They must give themselves the time to establish their new relationships and develop their own traditions.

The key is honest communication.

Jealousy

Justine was an intelligent little girl who was perfectly happy as the only child of her mother, a single parent named Helen. The two of them shared everything, including a bed, even though Justine was ten years old. Helen rarely dated, and she gave most of her leisure time to Justine. They lived in San Francisco and spent their time cooking, watching videos and collecting stamps. They went on vacation three times a year and celebrated Kwaanza by inviting friends and family from all over the Bay area.

Then Helen met Bryant at a conference on Black parenting.

Bryant had a daughter who was the same age as Justine. Her

*name was Marisol (after her mother who had died during child-
birth) and she was a stunning beauty who modeled for print ads
for major catalogues.*

Justine envied Marisol's beauty.

*Marisol lived with her maternal grandmother until Helen and
Bryant got married. The couple bought a three-bedroom condo-
minium so that each girl could have her own room. Everyone
except Justine was happy.*

*Helen watched in alarm as her young daughter began to lose
weight, fly off the handle at the slightest provocation and become
an introvert.*

*After giving the matter a lot of thought, Helen realized that
Justine was simply jealous because everyone they knew raved about
Marisol's beauty. Before she could figure out what to do, Justine
approached her and her request was simple. "Mommy, can you
please send Bryant and Marisol back to where they came from?"*

Helen explained that she loved Bryant and it would make her
very unhappy if he were to go away. She also told Justine that it
would be just as wrong for her to separate Bryant and Marisol as
it would be for someone to separate her from Justine.

Helen and Bryant asked their visitors not to fawn over Marisol.
It wasn't good for either child because Marisol was becoming
extremely conceited.

They also bought Justine a piano since she had always seemed
musically inclined. They hired an excellent teacher and Justine
soon received her own share of adulation when she played for
their friends and relatives.

A further consideration within stepfamilies is the issue of discipline. Most biological parents want the stepparent to contribute
a loving atmosphere and some financial help but do not like the
idea of the stepparent getting involved in punishment, particularly
if that punishment is physical.

This is something that should be worked out between the two
of you before the child arrives whether to stay or visit. Nothing
is worse than allowing a youngster to think that he can start the
two of you arguing. Decide beforehand and present a united front.

*Oliver only gets his son on weekends because of the custody
agreement between him and his first wife. Since Oliver divorced
Martin's mother to marry me, he is extremely vulnerable to the
feelings of guilt that the boy raises in him. He spends all of his*

extra money on Martin and the presents have become meaningless since the little boy has more toys than any child can ever play with.

He makes sure that it is his extra money being spent so I can't say anything.

Even though Martin no longer wants the treats, it has become a game with him watching his father sweat to come up with the latest demand.

I don't like it.

—Eunice

This is a case where it is best for the wife to do nothing. Oliver is taking care of his financial responsibilities around the house and uses his own pocket money to ease his conscience.

Eunice has the husband she wanted and Oliver has to learn that there are some things that money just can't buy.

Until Oliver learns that lesson on his own, there is nothing Eunice can do or say that will not alienate him. Criticizing his son's spoiled demands certainly won't help the situation.

Elaine learned this the hard way. She and Gary shared a rambling farmhouse with their natural daughter, aged five, and Gary's two teenaged daughters. "Gary is good to all the kids but he doesn't like it when I start criticizing the older girls," she says. "I think I should be able to voice my opinion about the girls' behavior without feeling as though I'm walking on coals."

One way for Elaine to handle this is to wait until Gary is having a problem with his daughters and then mildly give her honest opinion about the situation. He cannot accuse Elaine of picking on his kids when he has initiated the discussion. If this method doesn't work, marriage counseling is the next step because Elaine has to have a voice in her own home.

Some General Guidelines

1. Treat your mate's children as if they were your own.
2. Understand that this man by marrying you has made a statement to the world that he has decided to trust you with her life. His child did not make that choice. She has basically been told that she just has to accept Daddy's choice.

3. Since the child did not choose you as a friend, you will have to earn his trust.
4. If the child's mother is alive and unmarried, she will harbor hopes of a reconciliation for a long time (even if life in the household was miserable because of their unhappiness with each other). Even if she really likes you. Accept this as a psychological reality and don't take it personally.

Claude and Janice had only been married for five months when his sister's children were seized by the Bureau of Child Welfare. Claude knew that his sister had been using crack and he berated himself for not keeping a better eye on the situation at her house.

When the social workers called because he was the closest living relative, Janice could see in his eyes that he wanted to take the three small kids but was too afraid to ask her. She empathized with his dilemma. If it were one of her sister's kids she would definitely fight anyone who tried to put them in foster care. So she gently told Claude to let them come.

What she didn't know was that Claude would get carried away. He was so stricken by the children's plight that he became oblivious to Janice and her needs. Although Janice still treated the children well, she resented her husband and started going out alone to bars at night after everyone else had gone to bed.

When Janice started leaving the house at night, it was a cry of pain that Claude was smart enough to hear after a few weeks. One morning she woke up to the sound of muffled giggles. Curious, she followed the sounds into the kitchen. Claude and the children had made her favorite breakfast and decorated a chair with crepe paper and balloons in her favorite colors. Mystified, Janice asked what the occasion was and the answer was: "It's just because we all love you."

Claude waited until after breakfast to apologize for his insensitivity and told her that he had talked to the Bureau of Child Welfare about some family members approved as baby-sitters so they could start going out together again.

When Claude's sister came out of a rehabilitation program a year later, she found her children happy and healthy, with a couple who were very much in love.

PART THREE:

Home Life &
Leisure Time

CHAPTER TWELVE

The Need to Be King

"Sometimes I want the will to make myself master of Rome, at other times the opportunity.

—Hannibal

There is an unending list of things for couples to fight about. Whether we choose lots of issues on that list, or stick with just a few, the underlying issue that most of these topics represent is usually power. All men are conditioned through the socialization process to believe that they are naturally endowed with all the necessary qualities of leadership and that women should play a subordinate role at home and in human affairs. Black men are affected by these same stereotyped roles of men and women. To some degree, they internalize the same values of male supremacy that men of other races do. However, the Black man has been historically denied the opportunity to act on these values outside of his own home.

It was the young brother who was most desired by the slave traders and as a result, there were more enslaved men than women on many plantations. We will never know for sure, but it is safe to assume that although he was treated as less than human from dawn till dusk, the Black man was allowed to be "the leader" once he returned to the cabin at night.

Right after President Abraham Lincoln signed the Emancipation Proclamation, African American males started claiming "their rightful position" as head of the house. In fact, local custom in the South during the early days of Reconstruction gave him the right actually to contract his wife and children out for plantation labor, without his wife's consent. The wives did not routinely resist this custom, simply because there weren't many other jobs available to a Black woman. Some Black women tried staying home to watch the children, like many white women did. This plan usually failed, because sharecropping did not pay enough for the Black family to exist on the labors of just one person.

Once she had to go back to work, the Black wife wanted an equal say in matters pertaining to the family away from the fields. The Black man did not want this. He said that he needed his wife to just treasure and shield him from the brutality that he encountered every day in his dealing with the dominant culture— not to share in his limited decision-making power. A significant number of women went along with this situation on the surface and used subtle and creative methods to influence family and household matters.

During modern segregation (from 1900 to the early 1960s), some Black men experienced a measure of power. Black men owned retail stores, moving companies and other essential enterprises needed to maintain a community's viability. Black newspapers reported on life and Black doctors tended the community's sick. There were also Black-owned theaters, inns and hotels that thrived because the people in the community had no where else to turn for these services, without being exposed to the humiliating Jim Crow laws. However powerful in their own communities, Black men were forced to swallow their pride and behave in a subservient, almost childlike manner whenever they came into contact with members of the dominant culture.

In 1968's *Soledad Brother,* George Jackson states that, "No man or group of men have been denuded of their self-respect, none in history have been more terrorized, suppressed, repressed and denied male expression than the U.S. black." The sisters have always known this and in the early 1970s, many female members of the Black Power Movement tried to compensate for it by deferring to all of the Black man's wishes on the homefront.

Over the past two decades, Black women have been moving away from this position for the sake of their own self-esteem and the good of their marriages. The Black woman has learned that hiding in the shadows so that her man can shine does not gain the man's respect (no one respects a doormat) and does nothing to advance the race as a whole. In her thought-provoking essay, *Double Jeopardy—To Be Black and Female,* Frances Beale observes that, "It is fallacious reasoning that in order for the Black man to be strong, the Black woman has to be weak."

Today, the Black man walks the streets every day with people moving aside as though he is a dangerous animal. Many people (including some of his own race) are using their talents to make money in the odious "Black male bashing" industry, and if he does not have a college education, it is becoming more and more difficult for a Black man to land a well-paying job. The world outside his home can be a menacing one and he risks his manhood in a hundred different ways every time he steps outside his front door. Many Black men who don't have positions of authority in the workplace or some other activity where they get a chance to show leadership (such as community activist or church deacon), try to compensate for their feelings of powerlessness by trying to rule their households. Although a lot of Black men have positions of power and authority, he still does not get the same respect that men of other races take for granted. Couples of all races go through power struggles, but African American couples have to be extra careful not to let the struggle for respect play itself out in their marriages.

Aquila and Homer sought help for a teetering marriage. He had told her that he would leave if she did not "straighten up." He complained of her moping around, having little to offer, not making their life at all interesting or pleasant. Certainly, she ignored his needs. Aquila complained of being overworked, feeling tired and sad, if not depressed, and somehow being on a treadmill with no end in sight. Homer had brought her in for therapy, but then consented to join his wife for a few sessions, in order to "help out the treatment." The initial consultation gave the therapist ample evidence that it was not only Aquila's problem that was at issue, but the couple's interaction.

Homer was a tall, slim man with a booming voice. Aquila was a much shorter, quite round lady who looked as burdened as she described feeling. They were both in their late forties. As in the first session, Homer did most of the talking, including interrupting and talking over what Aquila tried to say. He corrected her on matters of detail, and disagreed with almost all of her few opinions. It became increasingly more difficult to elicit her verbal participation in early sessions; ready tears were easy to call forth.

Homer was a fairly successful businessman. Aquila had worked in a clerical capacity throughout their thirty-year marriage. She had supported them while he went to school for a B.A. and an M.B.A. They had four children who were not on their own.

As the story unfolded, Aquila told of her trying her best to be the dutiful, "perfect" wife, mother and homemaker. She handled

*her jobs—whether employment outside the home or home duties—
with a demanding intensity. In fact, she prided herself on "having
it all." Her good-looking, educated and successful husband, her
good-looking, smart children and her showplace home were all
sources of confirmation. None of that confirmation, however, came
from her inner sources.*

*Aquila had always believed that she was a very lucky lady. But
as the children graduated from good schools and left home, as she
lost energy to work herself into a frenzy to entertain Homer's
business associates and friends, and as she began to feel that Homer
was treating her more like a servant than a cherished woman to
whom he was grateful, she developed two feelings, but she was
only consciously aware of one. Aquila knew that she often felt
lonely and sad. The unconscious feeling was increasing rage,
directed mostly against Homer, who used to be her hero. She
expressed this anger by such actions as "forgetting" to have his
laundry available before he ran out of clean shirts and underwear
and by hitting him once while they were both asleep. She grew
even angrier when her ostentatiously miserable withdrawal did not
elicit from him any sign of worried concern.*

*Homer was completely astonished that he could be perceived
as someone who could elicit anger. He had supported his family.
He was a Black man who had stuck by his children. He did not
drink, run around, or beat anyone. He was a real man. Aquila
had no reason to complain, let alone hold anger against him. In
therapy, they agreed that whenever Aquila resented any of his
words or actions, she would bring them to his attention. They
decided on a signal to do this. She would cross her index fingers.
The rules were that if he did not know what she was referring to,
he would ask. The first week was a revelation to him—the little
put-downs; the doling out of money, dollar by dollar, for household
expenses; the bragging about each thing he did and the ignoring
of what she did. They both realized that Aquila had not given
herself the right to object, or the permission to reduce her compul-
sion to please. She was feeling utterly powerless in the relationship.
Unfortunately, Homer had begun to see her the same way, as
powerless and worth little.*

With the help of the therapeutic situation, Aquila learned to
speak up and Homer learned to listen to her. They renegotiated
household duties, the management of the budget, and the planning
of their social life. Homer also agreed to try to pick up after himself.

Instead of her handing over her paycheck to Homer and receiving the day's expenses from him each morning, with explanations as to why she might need a little more on a given day, she kept her paycheck and used a new joint checking account for household expenses. Monthly, they sat down to go over their spending and the bills.

As to their social life, Homer agreed to help out when they entertained. Instead of ordering Aquila to create a dinner party and then attending as a guest, he was to help prepare the house, serve and clean up afterward. This latter was a significant improvement and went a long way toward removing Aquila's resentment and feelings of having been relegated to the servant category.

In this process, Aquila became and was seen as being an important person who warranted and demanded the respect of an equal partner in their long-term marriage.

The Need to Shield Him

Annemarie was 26 years old and her husband, Huey, the same age. They had been married six years when Annemarie started suffering from migraine headaches. Huey was frustrated by the attacks because Annemarie became immobilized and he was forced to handle the day-to-day problems of living, all by himself.

Both his and Annemarie's mother believed that it was the Black woman's duty to shield their men from every possible problem at home because of the racism and danger Black men face on a daily basis.

Until the headaches started, Annemarie made sure that Huey's life was as carefree as she could make it. If Huey didn't like a job, Annemarie told him to quit and then she worked overtime to pay all the bills until he landed another. Huey had been through eight jobs during their six short years of marriage.

If Huey was tired, Annemarie ran his bath, gave him a massage and did the cleaning after he went to bed. Huey always seemed to get tired after they'd had visitors and the house was a mess.

Huey had never learned to cook and Annemarie had never wanted to "pressure him" into learning. He had learned to appreciate French cooking while dating an exchange student in college. Annemarie collected French cookbooks and followed the recipes faithfully. She had to start every night from scratch because Huey disliked leftovers.

Huey had been raised to be active in African American affairs, so he volunteered at a community center for teenagers 15 hours a week. He spent a lot of time raising money for their activities and writing letters to Black professionals, asking them to donate time for inspirational talks. Annemarie felt it was important for Huey to keep his mind clear for this important work and she handled all their financial and legal affairs, to shield him from possible anxiety.

One night, Huey was driving home from a community meeting and was pulled over by the police, who proceeded to frisk and then handcuff him while he lay facedown on the sidewalk. He was released a short time later but the damage was done. Huey was tense, angry and withdrawn for a long time.

Annemarie felt sorry for him. She was reminded once again of the painful realities of Huey's life as a Black man. She started trying even harder to shield him from any aggravation and never told him about any of her own problems or disappointments.

Huey stopped acting loving toward his wife and Annemarie's headaches began.

Annemarie was treated by many medical doctors. One of them recommended psychological counseling, and since she had tried everything else with no relief, Annemarie agreed. She came to see that Huey was a grown man who had to face life's ups and downs without her behaving like a human shock absorber. He was no longer behaving in a loving manner because he no longer recognized her humanity. Huey no longer thought of his wife as a real person with needs, secrets and desires of her own.

Since both Huey and Annemarie had been brought up to believe that Black men and women should behave in the way each of them had been behaving, it was very hard for them to change. Huey's mother had treated Huey like a prince and he honestly did not understand Annemarie's problem.

With her therapist's help, Annemarie was finally able to give her husband a choice: Get help or lose me. He chose to go to counseling.

As Dr. Gwendolyn Goldsby-Grant points out in *The Best Kind of Loving,* her bestselling book for Black women, martyrs are not necessarily beloved. On the contrary, their partners feel guilty and resentful. And like children who look to their parents and other adults to protect them from their own excesses, arrogant husbands who go to negative extremes with their wives, deep down want and need to be confronted with limits.

Everyone is born with a need for power, and continue to have that need throughout their lives. Luckily, everyone is also born with a potential for power, which also continues throughout life. Feelings of power are created by our self-confidence; how successful we have been throughout life in exercising age-appropriate power; how others tend to respond to us, and various societal forces. It has been demonstrated over and over that a feeling of powerlessness is a menace to mental health, as well as to progress. It is also a symptom of emotional defeat and a cause for much trouble in marriage. When both members of the couple feel empowered in the relationship, the marriage does best. That means that each feels his or her contribution is appreciated and valued, and has equal shot at influencing what happens in the family. But there are forces that work against this sense of equity, especially for African American families. African Americans have been legally, economically and socially unempowered in comparison to members of the dominant culture.

For a successful marriage, the power positions may not be equal. One person may have a little more leverage because of income, dominance of personality, skill in manipulating others, or other factors. But there is an acceptable range. Beyond those limits, when one person acts as a boss with too little regard for the other, there will be trouble.

When you feel uncomfortable, that is probably a signal that a boundary has been reached. Fights over power can be very helpful, especially if it is understood what the facts are basically about. The disputes help to regulate the power division so that it becomes more satisfactory to both partners. And, of course, discussing directly the particular and the underlying issues is the best help.

This struggle between the sexes is intensified when the man involved has trouble remaining gainfully employed. As Susan Taylor observed in her November 1997 *Essence* editorial, "With few connections to land or power, and despite the economic success of a few brothers, too many Black men circle hungrily, wearily, on society's periphery, trying to find someplace to be somebody."

The Need to Work

Between 1979 and 1989, the average earnings of Black men in the United States declined while average earnings for white men increased during that same ten-year period. In fact, a study conducted by both the Russell Sage Foundation and Ford Foundation recently reported that among the 2,000 men surveyed, having dark skin decreased the possibility of getting work by 52%. So, the worth of an African American man should not be judged by the size of his bank balance or his position in the world of business.

Since American culture measures manhood by the size of the bank account, lack of work affects the Black sense of self and impacts on his relationships with his wife, friends, neighbors and relatives. They all start treating him differently. "Humpf, I knew he wasn't about nothin' anyway."

In other words, if you don't have work, you are considered a total zero. To be respected as a Black man is hard. To be respected as an unemployed Black man is next to impossible. Societal barriers that make it harder for Black men to get ahead in the workforce, make it extremely difficult for their marriages to work.

When a white man does not have any marketable skills and therefore, is without a job, he is called unemployed. When a Black man does not have any marketable skills and therefore, is without a job, he is *under*employed. In other words, it is assumed he is so far on the bottom, he will never get a job and his son won't get one, either.

Since more and more of the work for unskilled labor is now contracted out overseas, many Black American men of the future will not be able to work for one single day of their lives.

It makes sense that the Black man is apprehensive about showing up to say, "I'm looking for work." By telling him he is *under*employed, society assumes he gets the hidden message which is, "We don't expect ever to find you in our reception area filling out an application."

I took the first job I found but I have to find a way to land a better-paying job with good benefits and a future. My wife has been shouldering most of the financial burden for almost two years. It is killing me.
I no longer feel like a man.

—Herman

The fact that Herman took what job he could get until he could do better, says a lot about his character and love for his wife. While his desire to find a better-paying job is great, he needs to break his dream down into manageable steps.

The sense of accomplishment he feels after he completes each step will provide an increase in the confidence he will need to get ahead in today's competitive job market.

STEPS TO FINDING A BETTER JOB

♦ Use the library or the Internet to research the different types of jobs available in your geographical area.
♦ Decide which types of jobs sound the most interesting.
♦ List the prerequisite for each type of job.
♦ Decide how to achieve the required prerequisites.
♦ List the challenges that might have to be faced at home while trying to earn the necessary qualifications.
♦ List ways to lessen or eliminate those challenges.
♦ Make a list of places that hire people who do the type of work in which you are interested.
♦ Put together an effective resumé.
♦ Practice interviewing techniques.

Getting a job using this method is not easy, but it will lead to a more satisfying position than the method of taking any job, whether it truly interests you or not.

An additional benefit of this method is that any wife will have to admire a man who is working this hard for himself and his family.

But a Lot of Black Men Have Jobs

Yes, it is true that many Black men have jobs. But a lot of them don't, in spite of all their efforts to obtain one. It has always been easier for the African American female to find employment. Today, when a Black man without a college degree or word processing skills does find a job, it frequently pays below the amount of money he needs to support the household by himself. Often he also is expected to do a lot of bowing and scraping on the job in order to keep it.

Many of them cannot do that.

Shawna says that her husband complains constantly about the race issue and how it affects him on a daily basis at work. She is tired of hearing it and feels that Jerry has a tendency to dramatize the incidents he tells her about. His constant complaining gets on her nerves. Shawna has tried everything to cheer him up.

Shawna first has to realize that Jerry's complaints are legitimate. He has good reason to feel despairing or cynical. In order to ward off a full scale depression, she can do some things to help him.

First of all, she should stop trying to make Jerry feel better about the incidents. Consoling him on a constant basis will become draining for Shawna. After all, she has a job, too. Also, some types of consoling can be misinterpreted as pity.

Asking Jerry to stop complaining will make him feel that his wife is sweeping his problems under the rug or that she considers her issues more pressing. What Shawna should do is listen, and show her husband that she believes in every detail of the events he describes.

Shawna should also validate Jerry's concerns by showing distress at what he tells her and by assuring him that he has every right to complain.

In fact, to get Jerry's thoughts moving in another direction, Shawna might even magnify the events by talking about them in a more negative tone than he does. After a while, Jerry will start to think about ways around his dilemmas in order to minimize his wife's aggravation. The upside to this method is that Shawna will help her husband to think more positively about his options without angering him.

LOVING SUPPORT

When he finally does bare his soul and tells you what is going on in his head and heart, treat the knowledge like a rare jewel. Never taunt him with what you know, no matter how angry you get. Otherwise, you can't blame him for not confiding in you in the future.

My Wife is Too Domineering

Joan and I came very close to divorce court about four years ago. When we were going together, she was sweet and laughed a lot. After we got married, Joan turned into a drill sergeant.

She bought this huge black ledger with rows and columns and wrote in it all the time. I glanced at the book one day and there were lists and notes regarding every detail of our lives. I didn't say anything until she started demanding that I do things, instead of asking me.

I asked her to stop but she became more controlling than ever.

Things came to a head when she faced me over the breakfast table one morning. Joan informed me that she'd written to our landlord, the utility companies and the bank, informing them that she was now in sole charge of all our affairs. She told me that it was because I worked so hard "and didn't need more aggravation." I was no fool. Joan was a control freak. That was the morning I gave her an ultimatum: we either get some help or I'm gone.

—Dushawn

Joan was one of six children, raised by a single parent. Most of the women in her extended family are also single parents and she did not know how to interact with a man when it came to running a household. Joan was used to the woman having all the power and control.

Although she wanted to stop bossing her husband around, her fear was too great. She was afraid that if she wasn't on top of everything, something important would slip through the cracks and the family would fall apart.

Marriage counseling did not help Joan overcome this fear, so she embarked on a course of individual therapy. Although Joan did not choose to share the suppressed pain therapy helped her face, she did acknowledge that letting go of the need to control her husband is what saved her marriage.

Although Joan really did have a serious problem, as a group, African American women have always been labeled as "domineering" or "overbearing." The majority of these accusations are simply offshoots of an unfounded damaging and extremely hurtful stereotype.

I am Your Husband . . . Not Your Son

Hyacinth is eight years younger than I am. Normally, I didn't date women so much younger, but there was something about her that caught my eye. Once I got involved with her, I realized that she cared about me more than any woman I'd ever met. Although Hyacinth fell in love with me first, she never tried to pressure me into making a commitment. I finally asked her to marry me because I was afraid of losing her.

Hyacinth is such a sweet woman, I don't want to hurt her feelings by speaking sharply, but her constant hovering over me is starting to get on my nerves. She picks out my clothes and lays them out for me to wear to work the next day. When I decided to change jobs, she went through the want ads and circled everything she thought I was qualified for, before I even had a chance

*to decide what kind of work to look for. If I sneeze, she rushes
out to the drug store for cold remedies. I've tried to hint that it is
all too much but she doesn't get it. I've decided to try marriage
counseling and hope she agrees to go.*

—Neville

Of course, Hyacinth agreed to go. Neville wanted her to and
that was reason enough. She learned in counseling that telling
Neville what to do made him feel that she had no faith in his
ability to figure things out on his own. He felt insulted.

A marriage is a union between two adults who ultimately are
responsible for their own behavior. When a wife goes from supporting her husband to babying him, it puts him in a childlike position
which he resents. Unless the situation is turned around, it can ruin
a marriage.

Marriages usually don't start out this way. When a newly married couple sets up housekeeping, the wife sees her husband as an
equal who is capable of developing his potential. As time passes,
the wife may see her husband handling things in a way she does
not consider productive. If she steps in with unsolicited advice, the
husband believes that his wife finds him incompetent.

Change wasn't easy for Hyacinth, but Neville was patient with
her attempts to try. Little by little, she learned to wait and see if
Neville needed her advice with something he was trying to accomplish before offering her opinion. Over time, she discovered that
following this new plan, her own life became easier and less
stressful.

Black Men Making a Difference

In the early 1970s, The Black Panther Party for Self-Defense
were staunch champions of the self-help concept. They practiced
what they preached by forming much needed and very successful
free breakfast programs and free health clinics in Black communities across the country. They also sponsored hundreds of free food
giveaways. The Party called all of these services "survival programs." Today, many Black men are running community-based
programs which are just as necessary to our survival as a people.
For example, an organization called 100 Black Men of Chicago
says that its mission is "to improve the quality of life of our citizens
and enhance educational opportunities for African-Americans and
Minorities ... with a particular emphasis on young African-

American males." Some of the activities undertaken by the chapter since its founding are voter registrations drives; community restoration projects; African-American history contests; and career days. The group has been very successful.

All of our communities could use a program like 100 Black Men of Chicago. Encourage your husband and the other men in your community to channel their need for recognition, leadership and respect into creating and maintaining similar programs, rather than attempting to "rule the roost." Community service and stewardship will help to secure the future of African Americans, while attempts to dominate the home will only cause unhappiness and serious marital problems.

CHAPTER THIRTEEN

Domestic Drudgery

"Equals make the best friends."
—Aesop

The kitchen has long been established as the domain of the woman.

During slavery, Black female workers were genderless in terms of workload and certainty of equal punishment via the overseer's lash. The only place that she was recognized as a woman, and a woman with a certain amount of authority was in the slaveholders' kitchen.

After legalized slavery and its offspring, sharecropping, the African American female found that work as a maid was the only job that was always open. During the Depression she earned almost nothing even though most of the employer's housework fell on her shoulders and everything had to be cleaned manually because only the wealthiest families could afford the new technology like a vacuum cleaner or washing machine. Without these appliances, floors had to be swept clean and the families' clothes scrubbed by hand, leaning over a bathtub for hours at a time.

During the 1950s, the main job opportunities for uneducated Black women were as household servants, women whose workday was not finished until after the dinner meal was cooked, served and the kitchen cleaned.

What many of today's Black men don't realize is that they have a traditional place in the kitchen, as well. Through the Second World War, the galley was his place in the navy. In addition, before the Civil Rights Movement, male college graduates and Ph.D.'s found themselves happy to have jobs as cooks on the railroads.

When their livelihood depended on accepting kitchen duty, Black men were not too gender stereotyped to refuse duties in the kitchen.

Today, studies have found that Black men are more willing to share household duties than some white males. Those that refuse should know that sharing housework does not diminish a man's masculinity; rather it affirms a man's sense of fairness, love and security.

Sutton expects me to take care of all the cleaning, shopping and laundry because I am a woman, although he is "willing to help out from time to time." We talked about this before we got married and Sutton said all the right things.

After the first year, we started getting into this gender thing and I ended up doing all the chores. Well, I just stopped cold. The refrigerator became empty, the garbage piled up and the dirt was visible on the carpet. He got the message and for a while, he started doing his share of the work.

Now, I'm back to square one

—Lekesha

He stops helping. She stops cleaning. He starts helping. She goes back to cleaning. Couples have been known to do this cha-cha for years.

One way to wake a man up is to figure the cost of once-a-week household help into the next monthly budget and present it to him calmly. If he doesn't howl in protest and straighten up, then hire someone who could use twenty or thirty extra dollars on a weekly basis.

Either way, the problem is solved.

Jean and David have three teenaged children, so their house is a busy one. Even the basic household chores require a lot of planning. Jean says, "Our kids have always helped out around the house. Once every couple of months, we all sit down and talk about any problems that need to be worked out. Maybe someone has too many chores and something important is coming up. We talk about it, come up with a solution and then get it done."

Small children can do small tasks around the house. This will prepare them for performing bigger chores later on, thus taking the load off you and your husband. Work around the home also teaches them about team play and finishing a task they begin. These small successes help build early self-confidence.

Sharing the labor also sets a good example for children. The lessons of working together to achieve a common goal can carry on into the child's work life and his or her own adult relationships.

Our birth family has a lot to do with who we are and what we bring to the marriage. To stay happily married we have to get in touch with behavior we learned in childhood. Some of that behavior is good and should be kept and respected. Other behavior patterns are not productive and we need to learn new ways to replace the old.

What we're really talking about here is fair play. If you're a man and grew up in a household where males did not do domestic chores, stop and think for a moment. Both of you benefit from grocery shopping, having a clean house, making sure the bills get paid on time and maintaining an attractive yard, etc. Therefore, both of you should do the work that creates those benefits. Marriage is a friendship first, and a true friend would not sit by and watch the other work herself into exhaustion after a full day of working outside the home.

Men who have been brought up to think of domestic chores as woman's work need to discard this outmoded mindset in favor of teamwork. They just need to get the job done.

I had been running away from matrimony for over a decade. No matter how much I loved a woman, the minute she started hearing wedding bells, I was long gone. And then, I met Victoria. She had been married once and didn't want to go there again so I could relax with her. We enjoyed many of the same activities, like skiing and white water rafting. She was twenty-six and I was thirty-seven, but even the age difference didn't get in the way.

So, after dating Victoria for two years, I ignored my inner voice and asked her to marry me. She said no and it took me months to talk her into it. Victoria had had a big wedding her first time around so we just went to City Hall. We moved into my apartment because it was a one bedroom and she only had a studio.

By the end of the first year, I was ready to throw her out. Victoria was the nastiest woman I'd ever been around. She would step out of her clothes and leave them in a heap on the floor. I watched her pat perfume into her braids many times because she was too lazy to wash them. Dirty dishes were always piled up in the sink. And, unless I changed the sheets, they stayed on our bed for weeks. I decided to talk with her about it. She rolled her eyes until I finished and then said, "I knew I shoulda stayed single."

It felt like steam started coming out of my ears. I left my house and didn't come back until the next day. The place was immaculate. I took her out for dinner and apologized for leaving. She shrugged it off and everything was good for a while. A few weeks later, the place was a wreck again.

I started making plans to get out. Victoria must have sensed it because she found the name of a marriage counselor and asked me to go with her. I only went so that I could tell a judge that we'd tried everything.

—Eddie

Eddie rightfully resented his wife's messiness, which had started to blind him to the reasons why he fell in love with her in the first place.

But an interesting thing happened in counseling. Victoria had to deal with the fact that she had never behaved this way with her first husband, nor afterwards, when she lived on her own.

Victoria discovered that deep down inside, she was afraid of marriage. Her father had disappeared, leaving her mother to raise four children alone with very little money. Victoria's first husband had left her for another woman.

Subconsciously, Victoria was pushing Eddie away since she never really believed he would stay in the first place.

Once she started believing in Eddie's commitment, Victoria became her old self again.

HOW TO DIVIDE UP THE WORK

1. Make a list of all the chores you can think of.
2. Next to each chore, write down the first name of the person who does it now.
3. Next to the name write DM for "does mind" or DSM for "doesn't mind" doing it. Some people can deal with 3 bundles of laundry but get a headache at the thought of mopping a medium-sized kitchen floor. There is no right or wrong. It's a personality thing.
4. Look at the list. Is one person doing more than his or her fair share?
5. Are there chores either of you would like to exchange with the other?
6. Talk it out and then make a new list that is more equitable and less agonizing for both of you.

Some men and women dislike the idea of a paper which itemizes what they are supposed to do. If that person sees a chore that needs doing, he or she just does it. Yolanda, who is a publicist who is married to a busy stockbroker, says, "He cuts the grass, does repairs, food shopping and takes out the garbage. I cook, clean and write the checks to pay bills. We play anything else that comes up by ear."

For Yolanda and her husband, this method works and should be respected.

CHAPTER FOURTEEN

The Need for Social Outlets

"I do work very hard, and when I finish a project, I can party all night."

—Debbie Allen
Black Pearls, 1993

All people need a respite from work and other duties. During the 1950s in the South, church activities (suppers, revival meetings, etc.), family celebrations and people "stopping by" were the primary sources of recreation for Black people. Men also fished together while the women held their "silver teas" and raised money for church functions.

Clubs, sororities, fraternities and lodges have also been a refuge for the Black middle class. Most of these institutions flourished during segregation. They brought a measure of civility and grace to African American life and a respite from the angry outside world. Life is not nearly as harsh now, but we still need to take a break from our duties and socialize just for the fun of it.

Weekends and vacations are supposed to rejuvenate us. Some people do all their weekly laundry and housecleaning chores after they come home from work each weekday evening just so that they are free to enjoy themselves from Friday evening through Sunday evening. It is important that you and your spouse make room for fun events so that life isn't just a never-ending round of work, bills and family concerns.

Try to relax on these fun occasions and not let petty concerns get in the way of your having a good time together.

Let's look at the way two couples miss the whole point of socializing when they go out together.

Melvin's behavior at parties is just plain embarrassing. Sometimes I think, "If he does that stupid little dance he and his brother made up just one more time, I'll crawl under a table and never come out." I always wonder what everyone else in the room is thinking when he does that dance.

—Valerie

Valerie would be surprised to learn that other partygoers aren't necessarily having negative thoughts about her husband at all. In fact, they probably think he's quite a guy, maybe even the life of the party. Valerie needs to lighten up and enjoy the night. If a little dance is the worst thing Melvin ever does, she can consider herself lucky.

Every time my wife and I go to a place where food is being served, she always embarrasses me. Last month, I took Wanda to the Poconos for the weekend. They had a seafood buffet and I groaned inside when I saw it. True to form, Wanda made about six trips up there and filled her plate to overflowing each time.

I wanted the floor to open up so I could jump inside.

—Storm

Again, Storm was probably the only one interested in how many shrimp Wanda ate. They went away to have a good time and the all-you-can-eat buffet was included in a price that was probably pretty steep.

In any case, a spouse's flaws or eccentricities are not necessarily a reflection of you.

Friends

Women have a bad habit of dropping their friends when they find a man. This is a mistake. When you get married, the girls will understand that you can't see them as much as you used to, but there is no reason to drop them altogether. In fact, you stand a better chance of staying married if you keep your friends in your life. Otherwise, you risk trying to turn your husband into some sort of female confidante, a role he cannot and should not have to fill.

No matter how much in love you and your husband are or how strong your marriage is, the two of you cannot be everything to each other. You both need friends to socialize with on occasion, either separately or together.

Jurnee and I would feel suffocated if we didn't have a social life outside of each other. Once a month I go out with the boys and sometimes she and her girlfriends meet to go to the movies, concerts or just to have dinner. In between, our different friends drop by our house and everybody has a real good time.

—Ivan

Our house is always filled with laughter. Relatives, friends, our kids' playmates. Everybody is welcome and that means that Jerel and I always have plenty to talk about.

—Robin

My wife thinks I'm starting to become jealous because I don't like her going out with the girls anymore.
It isn't jealousy at all.
The problem is that when Keisha comes home after 6 or 7 hours away, I have to spend almost that same amount of time listening to her tell me about every single thing she did.

—Quentin

Partners who do go out with their friends alone should share some of their experiences when they get home. Just the highlight of the day, mind you—preferably something funny or a new discovery of a place you might visit together as a couple. Intimacy does not mean that you have to share every tiny detail of your afternoon out with the girls. Over time, you will both learn what stories are worth telling and which ones will make your partner's eyes glaze over.

I know a lot of women who don't want other females coming around. They feel that it is too much of a temptation for their husbands. I'm not like that. I feel that if Tim is going to be unfaithful, my not having friends isn't going to prevent it. I can't imagine a life without my girlfriends. We affirm and uplift each other in a way that is different than what happens between a man and a woman.

—Crystal

True friends enrich our lives and healthy friendships won't take anything away from your marriage. Good friends make you happier as an individual and that alone can make you an easier person with whom to live.

Lavinia is a 30-year-old librarian. Her husband, Vaughn, is a corporate executive. They are both kind, considerate and well-liked by their neighbors. Unfortunately, just about everyone in their upscale suburban community just outside Los Angeles has stopped inviting Vaughn and Lavinia to couples-oriented functions because Vaughn can never attend. Vaughn works overtime during the week and spends weekends studying for a law degree, even though he already has an M.B.A. When he isn't working or studying, he is exercising at a trendy gym. Vaughn defends himself: "Yes, I would like to go to some of the barbecues, card games and cocktail parties that Lavinia and I get invited to, but the business world is getting meaner by the day. I just can't afford to waste time like that."

Unusual? Not really. With all the downsizing and corporate games being played out in today's business world, many people, particularly African Americans, are terrified of getting caught up in a company's streamlining efforts. Through therapy, Vaughn was helped to realize that taking a breather now and then is not wasting time. Actually, going to a party or event probably replaced time Vaughn was bound to spend either in a hospital trauma unit, suffering from a stress-related heart attack, or in divorce court.

Unwinding with other couples who have similar interests is a mini-vacation from the daily rat race. The way it was going, Vaughn was working himself into a state of bad health and driving Lavinia to find a completely solo social life. Neither of these situations were good for the couple. For the sake of his health and marriage, Vaughn began to put aside at least one evening a month to socialize with his wife.

Reesie is a wonderful wife and mother. No man could ask for more, and that is why my situation is so frustrating. Right before our engagement party, she and I agreed that we would have two children and that she would stay home to raise them. Neither one of us wanted our kids brought up by relatives and baby-sitters. This worked for us until recently. Kevin is now thirteen and Lena is ten. They no longer come home for lunch and they participate in after-school programs, which means they don't get home until

5:00. Once breakfast is over and the three of us are gone, Reesie has nothing to do for the next nine hours. She dropped all of her friends years ago because she didn't want any other women coming to our house, so now she has nothing else to do but call me on the phone all day long.

Reesie calls to ask me what I want for dinner, to laugh at jokes that Lena made the night before, to tell me she loves me. I really am blessed to have Reesie and hate to sound like an ingrate but my boss is getting fed up.

—Victor

Reesie isn't unusual. Many women drop their friends because they fear that the friends might make a play for their husbands. As a result, these women wake up one day to find themselves lonely for companionship. Reesie needs either to go to work where she will have adults with whom to swap life stories, or find some sisterfriends who are home all day like she is. If she doesn't feel that work is an option, there are many other ways for her to meet women: doing volunteer work; taking adult education classes; or forming a literary club or an exercise group. Whatever her interests, Reesie needs to develop them and get a life in addition to the life she shares with her husband and children.

John belongs to a bowling team and he won't let the team's scheduled games get in the way of anything. His aunt asked him to drive his cousin home from college—John had a game. His cousin needed help moving household goods—John had a game. I needed him to watch our daughter one night when I had to go to school and the baby-sitter couldn't make it. John had a game. He gets very upset when I press him to do anything when the team is getting together.

—Meredith

John explained that the bowling team was his only social life apart from his wife and his job. The time he and his friends spent together was sacred to him. John apologized to Meredith for not skipping the game when the baby-sitter was unavailable. He assured her that if there was ever a serious emergency again, he would skip the game. Otherwise, he expected her to stop complaining about this one thing he did for himself. Meredith was smart enough to listen.

Ernest and I have been married for fifteen years and we've always done all of our socializing as a couple. We go out a lot and we also entertain at our home. Neither one of us knows people whom we consider more than casual acquaintances; these are the people we invite to our gatherings. Every April, we give an elegant cocktail party and the kids are sent to relatives. Everyone looks forward to it. We all dress up and have a lot of fun. Ernest and I don't have separate friends. I don't like to socialize without my husband and he feels the same way.

—Renee

We still say that a marriage is not supposed to meet your every need and that a couple should not make each other the only source of fun. However, this marriage has been working successfully for fifteen years. Ernest and Renee are happy with it and that is all that matters.

Using Friendships to Avoid Intimacy

Margot was a beach person. She loved to go to the Caribbean for vacations. On one such vacation, she was the object of more than usual attention from one of the hotel employees, a man named Don. He went out of his way to be helpful while he was on duty, offered to show her the island when he was off duty and pretty soon, they were dating. Margot was showered with so much attention and ardor that her head spun. When Margot returned from her vacation, Don called her every week and wrote her letters. Needless to say, Margot returned to that hotel whenever she could, eventually visiting almost every month.

The next year, she agreed to sponsor Don's migration to the States. They decided to live together, and, partially urged by Don's need for a green card, they married. It was very quick, very romantic and very exciting. After a few years, however, it became increasingly difficult for Margot and Don to remember those heady times. They had become almost completely alienated. Don was living his lifestyle, Margot, hers. They hardly ever interacted, although they continued to live together—with separate bedrooms.

Don spent most of his time with compatriots from his island. They had a club, they played soccer, they held dances, they earned money in the underground economy. (Nothing unlawful, but all "off the books".) He slept late, left during the day while Margot was at work, and either stayed out all night or returned in the wee hours of the morning when Margot was asleep. Margot had a high-pressure job which caused her a lot of stress. She worked long hours at her office, brought work home, was never caught-up, and eventually stopped cooling off with Caribbean vacations. In the beginning, she accompanied Don when he spent time with or visited his compatriots, but did not feel welcome—nor did Don encourage Margot to join him on these occasions. Above all, Margot was both bored and put off by the behavior and activities of Don and his friends.

Likewise, Don had no interest in Margot's activities and interests, which were intellectual and seemed to him to be too "white" and esoteric. They decided to make a try at keeping the marriage, although both thought that the only thing holding it together was the residence requirement for the green card. Neither had much hope of avoiding divorce.

It was obvious that Don was immersing himself in his many friendships to avoid dealing with the serious problems in his marriage. Treatment of this couple focused on recapturing the romantic excitement of their initial attraction, their sexual compatibility, their dreams of a future together. They were then introduced to several questions that they should have considered before they got married, namely:

♦ How does one merge two different cultures?
♦ What happens when someone leaves his country? Does he build a different way of life, mixing the new with the old, or does he try to duplicate what he left?
♦ How do marriage partners benefit from their differences instead of being pulled apart by them?

Margot was asked to take a two-week vacation from work, but to remain at home, rather than escaping to the Caribbean. Don was asked to remain away from his West Indian friends and relatives for that period of time. They were to devote that time to each other. The idea was to experiment, to investigate, to surprise each other, and to discover together areas of mutual delight. The two weeks were to free the couple from distractions while they dealt with each other, as happened when they first met. In addition, with the guidance of the therapist, the couple considered work options for Don. He found he could work with the same hotel chain that had employed him on the island. This was regular work which he enjoyed and at which he succeeded. Thus engaged, Don had less need to escape into an exclusively back-home, familiar and safe social world. As a working man he regained his sense of pride, no longer felt like a freeloader in what now he could regard as his own home, and even looked forward to spending waking hours in it with Margot. Margot appreciated coming home to a companion. They became a couple.

Like Don and Margot, many couples spend far too much time with friends or become workaholics in order to avoid confronting the serious problems in their marriages. If it seems that you or your husband have fallen victim to this way of life, invest in a marriage counselor to help you unearth the real reasons why you are spending so much time apart.

PART FOUR:

Mental Health

CHAPTER FIFTEEN

A Foot in Each World

"What amazes me is the naïveté of my white friends who believe that affirmative action and quotas have removed barriers for blacks."
—Lobbyist
Work Sister Work, 1993

When I get to work in the morning, I have power. I make decisions that affect thousands of people and cost millions of dollars to implement. I have a staff of twenty as well as three assistants, plus corporate credit cards and a company car. Yet, on the street, in stores and in other parts of my personal life, I have to be careful. I am a Black man and to forget that could cost me my life.
—*Johnnie*

When a human being has to disassemble and reassemble his thought patterns on a daily basis, it can lead to depression or a serious neurosis. If you feel that your perspective matches Johnnie's, it is important to realize that it is easy to transfer the resulting unarticulated anger onto your spouse. Seek the help of a trained professional who can assist you in channeling these strong feelings into more productive avenues.

Douglas is a senior manager at one of the Big Six accounting firms. He feels that the topic of race comes up far too often in his business life and he refuses to "play ball" when it means trying to appear raceless.
He watches in grim amusement as some of his African American

colleagues walk around with tightly pursed lips to make them appear thinner and he refuses to affect a prep school accent for the simple reason that he never went to prep school.

Douglas understands that playing the game would improve his chances of making partner. He realizes that his insistence on working hard but refusing to play the game means that he will never be offered a partnership in the firm.

Douglas knows that his wife, Sandra, backs him up in his decision, but when he sees the partner's wives traveling in company cars, he hates himself for what he is doing to his wife. Although Sandra seems satisfied with her lot and does not complain, sometimes Douglas feels a wee bit selfish.

Douglas makes a lot of money but his work life is lonely. Although Douglas has never rocked the boat or embarrassed his African American colleagues, the other Black managers know what he thinks of their behavior. They dislike him for it and take pains to avoid him. The white guys hang out together or with Black guys who pattern themselves after the rest of the group through word, thought and deed. So, for most of his waking hours, Douglas is isolated. Sandra is the only one who understands.

One day, Douglas was washing his hands in the men's room when a piece of paper someone had dropped on the floor caught his eye. It was a flyer aimed at white male executives. Douglas read:

S.A.M.E.

The Society for the Advancement of Male Executives is dedicated to eliminating the disadvantages many male executives and professionals face each day because of reverse discrimination. S.A.M.E. also wants to provide information and assistance to its members in order for them to advance in their careers, so that they can reach their full potential.

Douglas laughed out loud. He laughed for a long time and then he became enraged. By the time he got home, his body was dripping with sweat and both hands were shaking with anger. Sandra became alarmed and, with her help, he got out of the clothes that were clinging to his body. Embarrassed by the whole episode, Douglas started taking it out on his wife. Over the next few days he became verbally abusive and Sandra cried a few times before throwing a suitcase on the bed and threatening to leave. That made him straighten up. He had never behaved so badly before. Douglas apologized and Sandra accepted his apology. After a discussion, it was clear to both of them that Douglas had to find a new job or a new way of looking at the one he had.

After a three-month leave of absence, Douglas returned to work. While he was away, he joined the National Association of Black Accountants, 100 Black Men *and signed up for two* Black Enterprise *networking conferences. He attended at least two meetings of each organization. He felt rejuvenated, filled with optimism and less alone.*

Every situation is not as serious as the plight in which Douglas found himself. However, when we leave our mates in the morning and go out into the world to earn a living, it is very seldom that we don't encounter or hear about some race-related incident that makes us angry.

Niambi is an administrative assistant for a Fortune 500 company located in Dallas, Texas. Although the junior staffers usually don't barge in uninvited during conversations between managers, Niambi says "a white secretary or junior staffer thinks nothing of intruding into the conversation of Black executives. What upsets me is that they don't get chastised for it. If I tried that, I'd probably end up unemployed. My husband has observed similar situations at his office and we get angry about these things when we talk during dinner. He and I agree that their whiteness gives those employees carte blanche to do anything they please."

Cassandra weighs every slight that befalls her and classifies it as either intentional or unintentional. Most of the time, she decides to overlook the incident but while she is trying to decide in which category the slight falls, things are tense at home.

Aya was an advertising agency account executive who was hired through her company's affirmative action program. Although she had graduated from Smith College with a 4.0 average, excellent recommendations and a string of impressive internships under her belt, the bitter murmurings about the program which recruited her had begun to take their toll. One day, she confided in her husband who found her a copy of Marian Wright Edelman's The Measure of Our Success. *In it, Ms. Edelman noted that, "White Anglo-*

Saxon males never have felt inferior as a result of their centuries of 'affirmative action' and quotas in jobs from which Jews, racial minorities and women were excluded and too often still are." Ayer breathed a sigh of relief and her coworkers never realized why their words ceased to upset her and simply rolled off her back.

After a national news show did a story about children who were starving in Africa, a young white woman aired her opinion in the company cafeteria. "I feel sorry for those poor kids affected by the famine but what is the point of America feeding them for a few weeks when they will only return to starvation when our planes leave?" Niambi choked back angry words and left work that day with a pulsating migraine headache.

The kind of tension such situations cause carries over into our homes, whether we talk about our feelings or not. Sometimes, we can just look at our spouse and there is no need to say anything in explanation. We both know what is wrong. Our grandparents handled this part of their lives by turning the day's events into a kind of bittersweet humor. Some of this despair-turned-into-art still exists in the collections of tall tales, folk tales, toasting and other writings that can be found in the Black history section of most bookstores. Read these tales and marvel at the way our people have managed to create such richly textured material out of so much anxiety. Since working couples have so little time for each other to begin with, we should try not to let disturbing racial incidents we've encountered during the day ruin our precious evenings.

Two Solutions

Alonzo and Verona are an affluent couple who live in a suburb of Los Angeles. He is 35. She is 30. Both are California natives. Both were brainy enough to win scholarships to exclusive prep schools and Ivy League colleges. Both have high-paying jobs and wealthy friends. Since they are childless by choice, their money is spent on clothing, African American art and a five-bedroom house, complete with swimming pool and tennis court.

Alonzo, who considers himself quite a chef, also has recently installed a state-of-the-art kitchen.

Both work in the entertainment industry. Both are tired of being shut out of the networks that would enable them to rise to the top in their respective professions. Verona's supervisor routinely withholds information from her. Alonzo's boss barely acknowledges his existence, unless it is to criticize his work.

Verona wanted to chuck the whole West Coast scene and move to Atlanta, reasoning that they were both young enough to build new careers.

Alonzo was tired, too, but felt that leaving Los Angeles wouldn't help. Atlanta would simply be more of the same—that he and Verona would still be forced to walk the tightrope between Black and white worlds.

Alonzo and Verona spent a lot of time arguing their different viewpoints and discovered that as a result of this conflict they were becoming distanced from each other. Neither had the energy to stop the slow slide. They both started spending their evenings separately, with friends. Neither asked where the other was going or when he or she would return. Separate lives helped them escape the pain racism in their workplaces was causing. Finally, when they were both tired of running, they came in for counseling. Alonzo and Verona wanted peace of mind.

Eventually, Verona decided to leave her job. She joined the Black Filmmakers Foundation and started her own independent production company.

Alonzo took the memo route. He started putting all of his ideas, requests and replies to his supervisor's critiques in writing. After a few months, he noticed a change in his boss's attitude. Although he still hasn't been promoted, the two men have a much better working relationship and Alonzo no longer dreads going to work.

The suffering of this couple and others like them is caused by the knowledge that they are left out of the company loop and denied advancement opportunities simply because they are from a different cultural background.

In an effort to retreat from the discomfort of this knowledge and get information from more accessible sources, many Black professionals form their own support and informational groups and stop attempting to find acceptance among their white colleagues. Some whites in corporate life react with dismay when they hear that Black professionals find the office an unfriendly place to be and that at times we have to safeguard our sanity by distancing ourselves. Some ask each other what more could the Black professional want? They point to the fact that their company has more Blacks on staff now than it ever did and that its diversity program is supposed to be the best on Wall Street.

After a while, many members of the dominant culture throw their hands up in disgust and say, "The Blacks accuse us of prejudice and then they simply refuse to join us, even when we ask them to do so. When are they going to meet us at least halfway?"

Many whites honestly believe that saying "color no longer matters" will make the statement true. Once someone believes that race is no longer an issue, an African American who expresses different sentiments is mentally dismissed as a militant, a professional victim, or an irrational whiner.

Many Black professionals report that they've heard members of the dominant culture say, "We're just reacting to our own fear. If Blacks didn't commit so many horrendous crimes, there would be no racial issues."

WE KNOW THAT RACISM IS ALIVE AND WELL.

A Few Examples

♦ When a Fortune 500 firm has dozens of highly qualified African American executives on staff and only allows one to become a partner every other decade, it has nothing to do with the number of Black suspects currently on trial in the criminal justice system. It is a racial issue.

♦ When an African American novelist is told to make the dialogue between two people of color "more Black" or lose a valuable publishing contract, it has nothing to do with whether or not some notorious drug dealer has been apprehended. It is a racial issue.

♦ The fact that there are no Black (non-stereotyped) romantic comedies, nighttime dramas, soap operas, coming-of-age stories and movies-of-the-week which don't have race as the plotline, has nothing to do with the number of burglaries allegedly committed by African Americans in a given time period. It is a racial issue.

Naturally, when someone who is walking the tightrope hears such comments or notices among the dominant culture a bewilderment regarding racial issues, he or she can fall into a deeper despair. When you are living an experience, and at the same time being told that the experience does not really exist, it is all too easy to start questioning your sanity. Like everything else, what affects you affects your spouse. Don't fall into the trap.

Join support or informational groups where you can vent and share your feelings. Try not to bring the stress home—at least, not all the time.

CHAPTER SIXTEEN

How to Fight

"If fighting the battle is not for the sake of getting rid of an intimacy obstacle, but just a pet peeve, let it pass."
—Dr. Ronn Elmore
How to Love a Black Man, 1996

Ideally, marriage is a positive, loving, mutually caring and respectful lifelong alliance between two strong, fully self-developed adults. The idea of intimate marriage is not to melt each of you down to one indistinguishably fused whole. Nor is it to have the bigger, stronger one of you swallow the less assertive, so that there is only one opinion for both of you. These kind of arrangements are just as toxic to a strong marriage as one in which both of you are constantly enraged, fighting with no holds barred, over everything.

Even though you have come together partly because you share a common outlook on life and share similar values and goals, the fact is, you were raised in different families by different parents, were shaped by many different experiences, have learned different lessons and have developed different individualities. It is to be expected, therefore, that your opinions, choices and habits will differ from your spouse's from time to time. The differences between spouses enrich each spouse and the couple. It is also to be expected that each person will have the courage of his or her convictions and therefore, the most compatible of mates will clash from time to time. Then what?

Every loving couple has to learn how to fight. Disagreeing is a part of an honest, mutually respectful, loving relationship. A marriage with no open conflict is on very shaky ground.

For six years, friends of Basil and Yvette often laughingly referred to them as "that disgustingly cheerful couple." Basil says, "Both of us grew up in households where there was a lot of arguing, tension and drama. So, we were just trying to avoid recreating our childhood pain. Even if I disagreed with a plan Yvette came up with, I went along with it. When I made a decision first, she didn't argue, either. I guess we were both being unrealistic but it really seemed like the right thing to do."

Yvette replied, "I felt that it was wrong to assert myself when Basil made a decision that I didn't like. After all, Black men have so little power in the outside world."

BASIL: *I didn't know you were thinking like that. Does this mean you pity me? I thought you genuinely respected my opinion.*

YVETTE: *No, I didn't feel pity. I just didn't want to add to your troubles.*

COUNSELOR: *Let's come back to that. Basil, what made you decide to call me?*

BASIL: *Two weeks ago, we had some friends over for dinner and I burned everything right before they arrived. We all ended up going to an Italian restaurant around the corner. I thought the evening turned out well, but Yvette was furious because I had fallen asleep with the stove on. For the first time in our marriage she yelled at me. But it wasn't just that. What surprised me was how many things I had done over the past six years to upset her without knowing it. All of it came out and I just couldn't handle it.*

COUNSELOR: *What did you do?*

BASIL: *At first, I was in shock. I couldn't move. After she finished raving, I went down to the basement.*

YVETTE: *He stayed down there sulking for the rest of the weekend.*

BASIL: *I wasn't sulking, I was thinking about everything you said. Some of it really hurt.*

YVETTE: *I'm sorry, Basil.*

BASIL: *You know, life with you hasn't been a bed of roses either.*

YVETTE: *What is that supposed to mean?*

At this point, Basil rattled off a laundry list of grievances. Yvette was stunned.

Husbands and wives who never have disagreements cannot expect to live a level of seeming perfection for very long without developing serious neuroses. In addition, constantly ignoring or repressing hostility issues can lead to escape in drink, desertion or a romance outside the marriage, all of which make for bigger problems.

Basil and Yvette were each passive for different reasons and received marriage counseling just in time.

Basil, who was nonassertive by nature, had to learn how his passivity was a threat to the marriage and he eventually took assertiveness training to learn how to disagree without creating one of the unpleasant scenes he had witnessed in childhood.

Although Yvette's reason for her passivity was noble, she had to learn to reject what was essentially an unhealthy viewpoint. Even though she denied it at first, pity was the root cause of her inaction. A Black man who discovers that he is being coddled because of the extreme amount of racism he has to deal with on a daily basis, either becomes very hostile or starts taking advantage of his caretaker.

It took a long time to get this couple functioning properly, but it was worth it. They truly loved each other and just needed a push in the right direction to recreate a happier marriage based on equality—and minus the fear and pity.

When Constance and I disagree, I like to end up knowing where we stand. I want to settle the issue. I have no problem saying, "I'm sorry," but first, there needs to be a full discussion of what really happened. Constance just likes to throw an apology over her shoulder as she stomps upstairs to the bedroom. I'll try to talk about it later, when things are calm, but she always changes the subject. I end up hounding her to discuss what started it all, which really makes her angry. What am I supposed to do?

—Larsen

One day, when you and Constance are on good terms, broach the subject of the need for better communication between you in times of stress. Take a loving attitude and provide a safe, romantic environment (her favorite candlelit bistro?) while doing this.

As a child, Constance may have observed one of her caregivers leave the scene of conflict on a regular basis and then, returning to act as though nothing had happened. This may seem like normal behavior to her and she may genuinely not understand why you continue to pursue the matter after she has gone upstairs.

* * *

Tony felt that he was really lucky landing a classy girl like Ann. She had undergraduate and graduate degrees from prestigious universities. He had no doubts that she had better taste than he, a poor boy from the projects who had barely managed to graduate from the local city college. She was also very much in love with him, much to his surprise. He adored her. When she consulted him about furnishings for their home, he went along with everything she suggested. When they were out with friends, they both used "we" in expressing opinions about the news of the day or the meaning of life, but Tony knew that these opinions were really Ann's. He even found himself looking to her for cues as to what he should say or how he should react to various situations.

It was not Ann's fault. She urged Tony to give his true opinion on whatever she asked, and he saw that she disagreed with others with gentle grace. It was just that he believed his wife was always right because she was so smart. Five years into their marriage, they found themselves feeling somewhat estranged from each other. Nothing special was happening. They still felt in love, but somehow, something was missing for both of them.

The couples therapist they consulted noticed right away that Tony habitually deferred to Ann whenever an issue of opinion or fact came up. As this behavior persisted, the therapist found the right time to call it to their attention. Tony acknowledged his dependency on Ann's judgment and his lack of confidence if his own opinion differed from hers in any way. For her part, Ann was feeling that Tony was insubstantial. She complained that she could not grasp him and tangle with him because he would always shift his position to hers. Ann saw her husband as a shadow of a man.

Tony felt alienated. As he looked around his home, and as he heard himself talk, he could see no sign of himself. He felt inconsequential. Ann felt alienated because everything she saw expressed her own taste; she could see nothing of Tony.

The therapist coached Tony in self-assertion and helped both Ann and Tony to practice a different way or relating, including learning how to disagree and to resolve conflict. Tony could see that the pedestal on which he had kept Ann did neither of them any good. Tony and Ann appreciated each other and continued to build a more equitable, honest, substantial and gratifying relationship.

The most productive type of conflict is the win-win fight, in which the issue is resolved but both partners feel they have achieved some degree of satisfaction by entering into the conflict.

How do couples go about learning to handle differences in a win-win way? First, if you are angry or furiously determined to get your way with this one, calm down. Take a few minutes to open your mind to your mate's interests in the particular issue, and evaluate how important a role the issue plays in relation to your overall life and love together. If you decide that you overreacted and that having a fight is not worth the hassle, then let it go. Otherwise, follow the Win-Win Fight Guide.

The Win-Win Fight, Part I

When a fight starts, the biggest danger is that the initial issue gets lost and the disagreement wanders into other issues that either were raised previously or that one partner has never heard mentioned before. The hardest fighting skill to master is **Sticking to the Point.**

It is okay to express your opinions and wishes, and not run away from conflict. However, try not to accumulate hurts and angers. Unresolved conflicts can destroy any intimacy you and your spouse have managed to create. In fact, ignored or denied, hurts and angers may obediently disappear for the time being, but they will return.

Three years before they got married, Lawrence walked away from the relationship and moved in with another woman, without even saying goodbye to Denise.

Denise was distraught. She harassed Lawrence's relatives and friends until one of them gave her Lawrence's address. Denise waited on a nearby street corner until she saw Lawrence approach and then confronted him. Lawrence explained his behavior by telling Denise that he had lost his job and apartment but hadn't want to tell her. According to Lawrence, he only had moved in with the other woman because he'd needed a place to stay.

Denise moved out of her sister's house and got her own apartment to lure Lawrence back.

Now, Denise and Lawrence are married, but when Lawrence gets angry, he says things like, "This is all your fault. You dragged me back into this relationship. It was wrong. A man has to want to come back."

Lawrence dismissed the idea of marriage counseling, so Denise started individual therapy to deal with the hurt of her husband's words. She eventually faced the fact that they could not go on as a couple in this manner.

The next time Lawrence started his insulting diatribe, Denise faced him and told him to stop. She told him that he was a grown man who had to take responsibility for moving into her apartment. He had to take responsibility for having helped her plan their wedding and later, for having gone through with the marriage ceremony. Hiding behind their past problems was simply a way for him to escape when faced with something he didn't want to do or talk about.

Once Lawrence realized that his game was over, he became a real partner in the marriage, which left Denise and her therapist time to discuss issues like low self-esteem and fear of abandonment, issues which had led her to chase Lawrence in the first place.

Win-Win Fight Techniques

- ♦ Don't dig up dead issues. If it happened years ago and you already have argued over it, put it away. Past deeds cannot be undone. Making someone feel bad solves nothing. These old issues make both of you feel defensive and angry.
- ♦ Leave family members, friends, the guys at the bar, the people at work, even what the children said, out of your dispute. Your fight should be about the two of you and your relationship. Neither one of you can be held responsible for what others are or are not, or what they have or haven't done.
- ♦ Don't be afraid of your feelings, both having them and expressing them. If you erupt in anger, it is all right, as long as the eruption is only verbal.
- ♦ Avoid agreeing just to end the fight. The person who always agrees eventually discovers that he or she has been deeply denying his or her individuality. This usually leads to a sense of diminished self. Points of view not expressed, arguments avoided, choices not realized, the habit of going along to get along, all lead to suppressed frustration and rage. Only over-controlling bullies want total control over a mate, and the more that mate complies, the more trouble that mate is in for.
- ♦ Be sure you are fighting over the right thing. Don't fight about having clean shirts if you are really angry about feeling

ignored and disrespected. Try to get your facts together. The more specific you are, the better the chances for resolution. For example: When you barged into my negotiations with the automobile mechanic and took over our conversation about what was to be repaired and what the cost should be, without even letting me get a word in; and when you agreed that we would go out to the country to baby-sit for your sister without even asking if I wanted to and whether I had other plans; and when you always forget to pick up my shirts even though you say you will because it is more convenient for you to do so, I feel ignored and disrespected.

♦ Adopt the point of view that you can come to a Win-Win result, and that such a result is what you both should aim for. If you fight things out to a win-lose result, you both have lost because the loser cannot help but resent such a defeat. These defeats accumulate resentments and anger, stimulate interest in getting even, emphasize power competition, and in time, put severe strains on the marriage's harmony.

The winner in such cases does not fare much better because hard-fought wins at the expense of the one you love do lose their luster and the struggle leaves a bad taste and a resentment similar to that of your opponent's.

The Win-Win Fight, Part II

Agree on a time when both of you will be able to direct your attention to pursue the conflict calmly. Rarely is bedtime a good choice. A conflict should not be explored in such an intimate setting. If children don't allow you both to escape to an undisturbed room for as long as it takes to work things out, then get a baby-sitter, or drop the kids off at their scheduled activity or with a relative. Go to a restaurant, or the park, or sit in your car to have your talk. Try not to let life go on for more than a week before you get together for resolution. Make sure the discussion takes place when you're both feeling calm, *not* in the heat of emotion. At the point of conflict, say something like, "We can talk about this in an hour when we're both less upset."

Win-Win Fight Techniques

♦ Use statements that begin with "I" instead of "you" when

telling a mate what is bothering you. For example, "I was humiliated when you told that story about me at the party."

♦ Be aware of your body language. It is a fact that gestures, tone of voice, facial expressions and the physical stance of another human being say just as much, if not more, than the words coming from your mouth.

♦ Black men often have complained that the "sisters can always out-talk a man during an argument." This attitude is not productive and neither is a vicious "dozens" game—tossing around offensive remarks about the other person's mama, family members or friends.

♦ Listen to what your partner has to say.

♦ Eliminate from your arguing vocabulary the phrases "you always . . ."; "you never. . ."; "I'll never forgive you for . . ."; and "I hate you." And just as you must never, never threaten a naughty child with being put away if he does not behave, never, never threaten to leave your mate or get a divorce in the heat of passion. Those seeds of hate can take root. Breaking up a marriage is serious business and should only result from very rational decision making. Repeated idle threats to do so may make such a result more likely.

The Win-Win Fight, Part III

The one who has the gripe or issue has the floor first, without any interruption from the other. No explanations, corrections, or countering evidence are permitted from the listener. The listener's job is to direct his or her full attention to hearing and trying to understand what the mate is saying. The one with the complaint is to state his or her case as fully as possible. He or she is to share feelings; to articulate any facts or evidence to support his or her position; and to state what he or she wishes could happen now.

The mate should then repeat what he or she heard the spouse say, in as much detail as possible. For example, "I heard you say . . ." When finished, the complainant can calmly correct or clarify what he or she was trying to convey. Then, it is time for the mate to speak.

The Win-Win Fight, Conclusion

Now is the time to discuss corrective actions or ways of resolving the difference. Try to figure out together a solution that seems satisfactory to you both. One way of doing this is to come up with a trial plan and an agreement to review the situation after a set period of time. Decide how long the trial will last and set an unbreakable date for the evaluation of how the trial is working.

One couple we interviewed told us about their alternative plan for resolution. If they decide the issue under discussion is equally weighted on both sides, they toss a coin. The loser of the coin toss is owed a "win" for the next unresolved issue.

Whatever works for both of you is what you should seek. Each partner should emerge from an argument feeling good and satisfied with their work as a couple.

The Win-Win Fight ensures that each person has his or her say, feels listened to, has his or her experience and ideas accorded respect and guarantees that the couple works together on a solution not as partners, not opponents.

While the Win-Win Fight techniques remove some of the emotion from what should be the rational parts of the dispute, that does not mean there is no place for strong feelings. Still, when you are engaged in a dispute, don't hit below the belt or at the jugular. That means, don't aim to wound or kill. In the long run, you want to go on to a happy, long life together. Mean attacks have a way of hurting long after the issue in question has been forgotten.

If the same person finds him or herself on the losing or winning end most of the time, the couple may be in trouble. If one of you can out-talk the other, or is more adept at gathering logical arguments when you need them, or by sheer force of personality is able to overpower and get your way, you may be winning the battles but will lose the war because of the win-lose results.

When the argument is over and your partner says, "I'm sorry," make sure your mate explains exactly what he or she is sorry about so that you both are communicating and receiving the same messages. Then, figure out together what actions you can take to avoid another similar incident in the future.

A Win-Win Fight, such as the one described here, is often good for a marriage. It clears the air and promotes understanding of one's self and one's mate. It gives the couple practice in joint problem solving and reinforces each person's sense of self.

What is a Win-Win result? It is a mutually acceptable decision arrived at through thoughtful decision making by both of you and as a result of careful consideration of your facts and feelings. Both of you feel heard and understood, both of you come to agree that all things considered, what decision you arrive at is the best course for the couple. As a result of working out a conflict, you should feel closer to each other.

No matter what we do, confrontation, however infrequent, is inevitable. Accept this and try to follow the rules for fighting fair.

CHAPTER SEVENTEEN

Handling the Substance Abuser

"Dope never helped anybody sing better or play music better
or do anything better. All dope can do for you is kill you—
and kill you the long, slow, hard way."
—Billie Holiday
Lady Sings The Blues, 1956

Many legal and illegal mind altering substances have infiltrated
some of our lives. As with other serious stresses that are encountered during married life, we need to band together and support
one another when faced with a serious situation such as an addi-
cition. To encounter drug or alcohol abuse in our mate or ourselves
is an explosive challenge. You avoid a lot of trouble if you seek
help from a drug treatment specialist or program before things get
out of hand. Otherwise, you run the risk of seeing not only your
marriage, but also your life as you know it, running out like sand
through your fingers.

The situation is equally dismal if your mate is an addicted
gambler. The first resort in many of these situations is for the
mate to admonish, threaten and scold. Then there are the mate's
appeals to reason and concern for the well-being of the indulger
and the family. Then there is disgust and finally, a cut-off
point.

It is known that the more you take responsibility to rid your
spouse of an addiction, the more entrenched in the abuse both of
you become. In such situations, the mates are called co-dependents.

The prevailing wisdom is to turn the addict out of your home
and let him "hit bottom" so that he voluntarily pushes himself to

turn to a rehabilitation program. Can a marriage be saved under these conditions?

Success seems to depend on a few things, primarily on the effect of the drug or alcohol.

♦ Is the addict a mean drunk who abuses others when under the influence?
♦ Does the addict steal whatever he or she sees?
♦ Is the addict able to maintain a job?
♦ Has the addict earned the love and devotion of the family?
♦ Are the other family members sufficiently strong, patient, self-sacrificing?
♦ What pressures are being received from family members and friends?

The interplay of these and like factors makes a difference, but at best, the afflicted marriages are held together, if at all, by a very weak thread.

Drugs

The tragic results of illegal drug use—whether for kicks, emotional release or because it is "the thing to do" in some circles—has been well documented Yet people still experiment with dangerous substances in the mistaken belief that they can avoid addiction.

I started smoking reefer when I was in college. When Dick and I got married, he didn't know anything about it. He came home early one day before I could air the house out. He actually laughed because he had given up the habit years ago. We shared a joint and that was it. I promised to grow up.

I didn't realize that I was already addicted.

When he started working at home, I'd have to lie to Dick to get out of the house. I'd drive to a nearby mall and smoke in the car while trying to keep an eye out for the security people who ride the little mopeds. Dick found out and he didn't get mad. In fact, he started to join me. We both decided to quit after a friend's cousin died from a cocaine-induced heart attack. She was a wonderful caring person. Suddenly, drugs weren't fun anymore.

—Pepper

I don't know how high Barrett wants to get. She drinks like it's going out of style, snorts cocaine every time she gets paid and every time she gets a bonus from her job, she blows it at a gambling casino. I've had to make up her share of the rent more times than I care to count. Every time she cries out for help, I'm there for her. Recently, I saw a sign of improvement. Barrett started fixing up her hair and makeup. She got her resumé professionally done and found a higher paying job. The new attitude didn't last long. She showed up for work the first week but was fired by the end of the month for chronic lateness. I don't know what to do. I feel like a failure.

—Luciano

Luciano's self-esteem will plummet if he continues to blame himself for not being able to repair his wife. Right now, he is an enabler, a person who helps an addict continue on a destructive path. Only a professional can help Barrett and the only way this marriage can survive is if she really wants to get better and is willing to enter a rehab center such as Daytop or Phoenix House and work with their program. In the meantime, Luciano must take care of himself. It is a long, hard road back from addiction to the world of sobriety. The sober partner should join Al-Anon. This is a self-help group for family members of abusers of alcohol and other substances. Some drug treatment programs will advise family members on ways of contending with abusers who resist referral. Overcoming addiction is very difficult. Typically, several attempts are necessary and before recovery the addict experiences several failures, successes and relapses.

Audrey was normally sensitive and affectionate. But I could always tell if she had used cocaine because she made cruel remarks and blew up at the slightest provocation. When I married her, I had no reason to think that Audrey was a drug abuser. We were both from solid, middle class families. She was intelligent, ambitious and compassionate.

Even though I was terribly bewildered and hurt, I thank God that Audrey listened to me and went into rehab. She is going to get a second chance to live.

We'll get through this and our marriage will survive.

—Lamman

At first, Gwen did not know that Ashaki had started sniffing cocaine with his friends and she was devastated when she found out. Since he was still working and spent quality time with their five children, she decided to talk with Ashaki about, and then to ignore the situation, hoping it would go away.

Wrong.

The problem snowballed. Soon, Ashaki was always short of money and Gwen had to hide the credit cards and checkbook.

He promised to stop. Then, Gwen's pay envelope stuffed with cash disappeared. Ashaki claimed to know nothing about it.

A week later, Ashaki declared that a mugger caught him just as he was leaving the bank on payday, which explained his lack of funds.

Gwen didn't believe these lies but she kept hoping Ashaki would see her pain and straighten up. One day, she came home to find that her laptop computer and three television sets had disappeared. So had her husband. Three weeks later, he showed up looking haggard and dispirited. But it was too late. Gwen was through.

After much begging by Ashaki, Gwen agreed to reconsider the marriage on the condition that he go away to get himself together. Today, he lives in a residential treatment program with no promises from Gwen that she will resume their marriage.

Len and Toni lived together for three years before they got married. During those years, which they spent in a studio apartment on Manhattan's Upper West Side, they were happppy. About a year after their wedding, they moved to a new apartment building where they met another couple who were recreational drug users. Len and Toni began to join them.

After a while, Toni got bored with the whole scene but it was too late for Len.

He was a junkie.

For months, Toni tried to wait it out, hoping that the man she knew and loved would return. When she became pregnant, Len started going to Narcotics Anonymous for weekly meetings and it seemed like everything was going to work out.

The baby was only four months old when Len began to disappear for hours at a time. He started losing weight and Toni had to face an unpleasant truth when she found several empty vials in their bathroom.

Len was on crack.

Toni was in despair. Her family was telling her to come home and Len was promising to get clean again.

One evening, as Toni was approaching their building, it seemed as if some neighbors were avoiding her eyes and only mumbling something when she said hello. Once she opened the door to her apartment, Toni knew why. Everything of value was gone. The dinette set, their sofa, all appliances, stereo, VCR, television . . . Everything.

Toni sat on the floor of her empty house and sobbed for hours. And then she called her mother.

Len had sold everything and her neighbors, knowing the young man was desperate to buy crack, just pressed a few dollars in his palm before carrying away merchandise which had cost hundreds of dollars.

Toni refused to see Len for almost a year. She was afraid that something inside her would snap at the sight of his face and that she would kill him.

Toni was a very angry and bitter woman. Len went away to a residential treatment program. At first, she returned the letters unopened but after a few weeks, Toni's curiosity got the best of her and she began to read them.

Three years after Len sold all the family furniture, he is back with his wife and child, living in a new neighborhood.

They are happy again, just like in the old days.

Moira, 26, is an aspiring actress who waits tables in between auditions and experimental theater performances. When her husband, Curtis, found her smoking a joint backstage, their marriage began to disintegrate rapidly. Within a matter of weeks, they had separated and he was living with his sister's family. Moira didn't even try to get him back. After all, she reasoned, if Curtis could leave her over such a trivial matter, he probably didn't want to be married in the first place. It was Curtis's sister who broke the impasse by convincing her brother to go into counseling with Moira.

MOIRA: *It was a tough audience that night. The play was a comedy and my timing was perfect but that crowd wouldn't give an inch. Not one of us in the cast could pull so much as a chuckle out of them. After it was over, some of us retired backstage to unwind.*

CURTIS: *To get high on drugs you mean.*

MORIA: *Look how sordid he makes the whole thing sound.*

CURTIS: *There is no such thing as a little bit of drugs.*

MOIRA: *You wouldn't even let me explain.*

CURTIS *(bitterly): I didn't need an explanation. You roll the plant in light paper. Strike a match to it and puff away.*

COUNSELOR: *Was this the first time?*

CURTIS: *I never would have married Moira if I had known she was into drugs.*

MOIRA: *I'm not into drugs!*

COUNSELOR: *When was the first time you smoked marijuana?*

MOIRA: *About a year ago and then once again when we were touring the Midwest.*

COUNSELOR: *So, the night Curtis walked in was only your third time.*

MOIRA: *Exactly. And I've never experimented with any other drug. Not even once. I swear it.*

CURTIS: *That's three times too many as far as I'm concerned.*

COUNSELOR: *I'm sure Moira didn't know that her marriage was at risk that night.*

CURTIS: *I don't want no woman on drugs.*

MORIA *(tearfully): Damn it! I'm not on drugs and if you don't want me anymore, fine!*

COUNSELOR: *Let's slow down a minute. Curtis, were you happy in your marriage before you found Moira smoking backstage?*

CURTIS: *Yes.*

COUNSELOR: *How about you, Moira?*

MOIRA: *Yes, I was very happy and I was hurt when Curtis threw it all away over one little thing.*

COUNSELOR: *Curtis?*

CURTIS: *I have two cousins that Moira has never met because they took to the streets years ago, strung out on crack. One of them had a baby who was born deformed and died before he was eight weeks old.*

MOIRA: *I never heard about that before.*

CURTIS: *I've seen what that shit leads to and I've studiously avoided anyone or anything connected with drugs. I'm not going to change my mind.*

COUNSELOR: *Moira, after hearing this, can you understand the way Curtis reacted?*

MOIRA: *Yes, and I'm making him a promise never to experiment with any type of drug again.*

COUNSELOR: *Curtis, has Moira ever broken a promise to you or been dishonest in the years since you've known her?*

CURTIS: *I never caught her in a lie if that's what you mean, but*

I didn't know about the reefer, either. Who knows what else Moira could be hiding?

Curtis was right. Little experimentation often leads to big addiction. He was also a man who had a deep-seated and well-founded horror of drugs. The triple drug-related tragedies in his family had affected him deeply and it took months of counseling before he could view Moira again without a veil of suspicion. They ended up going back together but their ordeal had made Curtis realize that he needed to continue therapy on his own to come to terms with the grief over his lost cousins and the baby who met such a horrific end.

Every payday, Ulysses would disappear unless I met him at the check cashing place and grabbed the money before he could reach the coke dealer. One day I had to work through my lunch hour, typing an important itinerary for my boss. When I got home, it was obvious that my husband had not been there. Ulysses resurfaced two weeks later, broke and dirty. He was also unemployed because his job hadn't heard a word from him , either. If he hadn't agreed to go away for a year and get help, we'd be divorced right now. Ulysses was released a month ago. I'm taking it one day at a time.

—Marilyn

Some couples smoke or sniff cocaine together for recreation, as a preparation for sex. The mental, physical and legal risks of this choice are well known. It is a pity, probably a tragedy, but while they both indulge, it is not a marital problem between them. But if one of them becomes habituated or addicted and the other objects, this is a major and direct threat to their marriage. Many of these couples end up losing their stability, their social and financial position, their children, and also their marriage.

Nicole always had a stash of reefer on hand at bedtime. She said it did her no harm and in fact, helped her by enabling her to enjoy the sex a lot. Jomo had tried it a few times, once when he was in school and a couple of times when he and Nicole were making love. He never liked the idea, nor the effects. As time went on, he became more and more disapproving of the indulgence and more contemptuous of indulgers, including his wife. He did everything he could to turn Nicole away from the habit. She always had said that she could stop anytime she wanted to. As Jomo grew more adamant, she found herself sneaking joints at home and at work, smoking while she commuted, spending more time with friends who indulged and altogether smoking more than ever. At the same time their work slipped. Unfinished work was piled on their desks each evening and their job performance ratings plummeted.

Nicole was increasingly less reliable and Jomo far more irritable at home. When Jomo decided that he would leave to get into a drug program and she was put on notice at work, Nicole took it as a last chance to save what remained of her life. Two weeks after Jomo left, she, too, enrolled in a residential drug treatment program. By that time, all their money, jewelry and respectable friendships were gone.

Alcohol

Alcohol is America's number one drug problem. More than 18 million American are alcoholics; 85% of them refuse to seek treatment. As a result, approximately 95,000 people die of alcohol-related causes every year. If your spouse is an alcoholic, he or she faces cardiovascular disorders and cirrhosis of the liver. He or she also could kill someone else since alcohol plays a part in 50% of all driving accidents.

America has one of the highest rates of alcoholism in the world. Alcoholism is not only a problem in and of itself, but also brings many other problems with it, such as nonsupport, infidelity, abuse, lack of companionship and loss of status.

When Arnold was promoted to partner at his law firm, he was ecstatic. Now Amy could quit her job as buyer for a department store chain and stay home with their three small children. At first, Amy was hesitant. She loved her job. Yet Arnold's excitement and her mother's happiness for the children was contagious.

Amy resigned from her company and became a full-time mother.

As the years went by, Amy became frustrated and angry. At the same time, she also felt guilty for wanting to resume her career and leave her children in the care of someone else. She didn't mention her conflict to anyone. Amy found that a drink or two during the day was soothing and dissolved her irritation. After a couple of months, that "drink or two" turned into several drinks throughout the course of the day. One day, Arnold came home and was stunned to find that the children had come from school and broken a window to get into the house. Amy had passed out on the sofa and slept through the whole incident. She was snoring loudly as her husband watched in dismay from the door of the living room. Amy was an alcoholic.

Amy's drinking increased over the years and she refused to get help because she didn't believe there was a problem. Arnold thought of leaving but there were the kids to consider. They were very attached to Amy and he felt that taking them away would create more serious problems later on. Besides, he still loved his wife.

So Arnold and the kids adapted to Amy's alcoholism and life went on that way until the eldest boy started drinking, too. When Amy found empty half-pint bottles hidden in his closet, she was overwhelmed with guilt and Arnold gently supported his wife as she went to dry out so that they could help their son.

Jane was a familiar sight outside the factory on payday. She was Willie's wife and the only way for Jane to pay the rent, utility bills and buy food for the family was to lie in wait for her husband on payday and follow him to the check cashing place. After a few moments of wrangling as the two of them waited on line, Willie usually would give her enough money to run the house. Willie's coworkers felt sorry for the shabbily dressed Jane and if Willie wasn't such a great guy on the job, they would have disliked him for what his wife had to do to survive.

Willie was a wonderful man to work with, happy, good-natured and full of jokes that made the day go faster. Willie was also the type of guy who would listen to a coworker's personal problems, help if he could and never breathe a word to anyone else. For this reason, some of his colleagues helped Willie out the back door one payday so that he could get away from Jane.

Jane went home to a cold apartment, with tears rolling down her face. When the two kids asked for dinner, she gave them the last can of ravioli. They had to share it because there was no more food in the house and Jane was too proud to let her family know how badly she was living. It was 4:00 in the morning when Jane heard Willie's footsteps on the stairs and his voice bellowing an off key version of "Hold On, I'm Comin'" by Sam and Dave. She lay in her bed, rigid with fury. He fiddled with the lock for five minutes before his shaking hands could open it and then stumbled into their bedroom. He rocked back and forth on his heels. His eyes were red rimmed. "Hey good lookin'," he slurred. "What ya got cookin' "? Then he laughed at his own joke and fell face forward onto the bed.

A vein began to throb in Jane's left temple and her stomach growled hungrily. She stayed just like that all night.

The next morning, Willie's hands shook too much for him to dress himself and Jane refused to do it. Instead, she went down to the factory and spoke to the manager. She explained that Willie was an alcoholic who drank up all his paycheck and asked if she, as his wife, could pick up the check before Willie could get hold of it. The manager was sympathetic but legally, he could not turn over Willie's paycheck to his wife. As Jane turned away, something about her soft "thanks anyway," slumped shoulders, and threadbare gray coat clutched at the manager's heart.

He told her that Willie was a hard worker whom he had no intention of firing, but that Willie didn't have to know that. He was going to give Willie a warning: go to Alcoholics Anonymous after work every day, or else. He was also going to padlock the back door on payday. Jane began to smile. Knowing that she and kids were going to go hungry until the next payday, the manager gave her $30 in cash. He told her that Willie had dropped it one day in the men's room and that the manager had forgotten to return it.

They both knew better.

Since Willie was a forty-five-year-old-unskilled laborer with a junior high school education from a small town in Mississippi, the manager's warning hit him hard. He knew that he would never get another job. He started going to Alcoholics Anonymous, with Jane right beside him.

Nat was ordinarily an even-tempered, well-mannered sort of guy. But after a few drinks, his facial expression changed to a mask of fury. No one in the house was safe from his insults. Even though he never struck anyone physically, Tenija and their three little boys lived in fear of the mean drunk Nat usually became on Saturday nights.

On Sunday mornings, Nat would apologize to his family and sob pathetically. Tenija took it for about a year and realized that the situation was draining her and not doing her boys any good, either. She asked his family and her own to help. They gladly assisted.

One day, Nat come home to find a house full of concerned people who each took a turn telling him about the effects of his behavior. When the narratives were over, everyone offered their love and support but made it clear that no one was willing to tolerate his behavior any longer. Nat was truly contrite. After attending the meetings at Alcoholics Anonymous for several months, Nat confessed to Tenija that just before the family intervention, he had started to have a drink or two on his lunch hour.

He finally admitted that he had a problem and thanked his wife for her act of love.

IS YOUR SPOUSE AN ALCOHOLIC?

◆ Have you ever felt he could cut down on his drinking?
◆ Does he get annoyed when you criticize his drinking?
◆ Does he ever say he feels badly about drinking so much?
◆ Has he ever had a drink first thing in the morning to steady his nerves or to get rid of a hangover?

Has there been:

◆ A marked change in his behavior or personality?
◆ Recurring episodes of memory loss and confusion?
◆ Several occasions where he missed an appointment or stayed home from work due to drink?

If you answered YES to at least 5 of these questions, your partner may be an alcoholic.

Gambling

My mother and I had been going to Atlantic City to gamble for many years. Usually, we'd take in a show, have dinner, really make an outing of it. Shortly after Isaac and I got married, he went along with us. He had never been to a casino before and it was hard to pull him away from the slot machines. The following weekend he went back alone and blew $100. I thought it was funny until six months later when he spent our rent money trying to double it playing blackjack. I was livid and he swore he would never gamble again. As far as I know, Isaac has kept his promise.
—Lovie

Gambling is an addiction and compulsive gambling is destructive to family life. Like alcoholism, gambling is considered a disease and a most difficult one to cure. It is believed that compulsive gamblers may be as numerous as compulsive drinkers. Gambler's Anonymous (patterned after Alcoholics Anonymous) has a following of thousands.

At first, the signs are a little vague. You think that you are becoming forgetful, but you're sure you haven't seen the telephone bill come in for the past three months. Your partner works a lot of overtime and comes home restless and irritable.

After a while, you realize that things are not right. Is your partner having an affair?

You confront him and he denies that he is seeing another woman. You don't believe him. Suddenly, he tells you that he has been gambling. He is terribly sorry to have hurt you and he has learned his lesson but there is a problem.

He owes $2,000 to a loan shark.

You are now in the jaws of a shark you never saw coming. Unlike the problem drinker, who reeks with the smell of liquor, or the drug addict, whose dilated pupils usually tell the tale, the gambler has a much easier time hiding his addiction. Like a crack addict, the gambler chases the hit. Even if he has lost thousands of dollars, a person addicted to gambling will still keep playing, sure that he'll hit the big jackpot on the next try.

When Vance came along, Letia was seeking a knight in shining armor to rescue her from a life that was solitary and joyless. Vance seemed to fit the bill. He was tall, had midnight black, velvety skin and a good job at the post office. They married, had four children in six years and were very happy. Letia was working as an office manager for a Detroit construction firm and her mother was happy to watch the kids during the day. Life was good. Vance treated Letia better than any man ever had and she was deeply in love with him. Then, after ten years of marriage, Vance stopped bringing home his share of the money. Letia prayed nightly that Vance hadn't fallen into drugs. She watched fearfully and decided that his strange behavior indicated another woman in the picture. Enraged, she followed him in a friend's car and was amazed to find herself at the race track. She decided that she had picked the wrong day to follow her husband. Instead of going to see his mistress, he had gone to gamble. Letia said nothing and waited for another day. In the meantime, Letia found herself carrying more and more of the bills. One day, Vance had the nerve to ask *her for $500. That is when she confronted him and demanded to know the identity of the woman he was financing.*

Vance looked at her in amazement and swore that there was no one else. He told her that after an incredible two-year winning streak, he had started losing money on the horses and had taken so many advances against his paycheck, that he no longer had one.

Letia was relieved that Vance wasn't sleeping around. She gave him the $500, caught up the bills and told him to cut it out. Six months later, they were back in the same place. Only this time, Vance said he wasn't going to quit. He was convinced that he now had his eye on the right horse and he was expecting a huge windfall in just a few short weeks.

Letia had never heard of Gambler's Anonymous and she didn't know what to do. So, when Vance maxed out their credit cards with cash advances the next month, Letia hit him hard on the head with a frying pan. At the hospital, Vance refused to press charges and explained what he had done to the police the doctors had called. It was the police officer that told Letia and Vance about Gamblers Anonymous.

Vance returned home that night with his head swathed in white bandages and called the organization first thing in the morning.

Now, everything is all right.

A gambler truly believes that if he could just hit the big one, he could pay off his debts and quit gambling without professional help. The level of denial in this disease is extremely high.

When a gambler is unable to get anyone else to loan him money, in danger of losing his job or fears that his spouse is about to leave, he is in "The Crunch." It is during The Crunch that the gambler usually pleads for forgiveness. Of course, after he gets the forgiveness, he asks for some money to pay his debts. Once he gets the money, the gambling starts again. Sooner or later, he hits rock bottom. The pattern begins again—winning, losing, desperate and asking for help, only to start all over again.

Gambling is not an addiction that is easily cured without professional help.

Handling the Addict

A marriage cannot remain healthy if a partner suffers from any one of these terrible addictions. Recovery from each of these addictions starts when everyone around the addicted person stops helping the behavior to continue. Here is how to help end the addiction and protect your own physical and emotional health.

1. Tell your spouse how his behavior is affecting the lives of his family. Be specific. Only agree to stay in the marriage if he will get help and cooperate with you in your attempts to salvage the union.
2. Call all the creditors and find out how much money is owed and make arrangements to pay them.
3. Take your partner's name off all credit cards, bank accounts and investments.
4. Get a counselor just for yourself. You need an open, caring environment in which to deal with your own fears, hostility and disappointment.
5. Insist that your partner get professional help on either an inpatient or outpatient basis, depending on the severity of the problem, your financial resources and the available facilities in your city or state.

CHAPTER EIGHTEEN

Emotional Abuse & Domestic Violence

"Deal with yourself as an individual worthy of respect, and make everyone else deal with you the same way."
—Nikki Giovanni
Quotations in Black, 1981

Love can continue for a lifetime. The key is to see and accept your spouse for who he or she really is. This acceptance will allow you to relax within the marriage without toiling fruitlessly to change the one you love.

However, acceptance does have its limits.

Those who are ignored, constantly criticized, belittled, demeaned or attacked are victims of emotional abuse. They become just as downtrodden as someone who is physically attacked.

When Julian and I met seven years ago, I was recovering from a love affair that had ended in a very ugly manner. Julian was an unhappy man who was having trouble finding work that paid more than minimum wage. Recently, he had been thrown out by his live-in lover. He was sleeping in an office building at night.

We needed each other and clung together like shipwreck survivors.

Everything was fine for the first year and then I mentioned marriage. Julian disappeared. For days on end I frantically called the cousin he was living with. She hadn't seen him, and she grew irritated with my constant calling.

Julian had been taking some continuing education classes at our local community college so I stalked the campus. He hadn't shown up for classes and no one knew where he was.

At the time, I didn't connect my remark about matrimony to Julian's disappearance. I was convinced that he had been killed in an accident and was sick or in the morgue with no ID to let the authorities know who he was. The last time I had seen him was the week before Thanksgiving. The holidays were a nightmare. I sat in a corner and swilled rum while my relatives celebrated. One of my cousins tried to cheer me up but I could barely hear him through Julian's voice which was filling my head.

Three weeks later, Julian's cousin called. Julian had stopped by to look for his mail. Julian told her that he felt I'd given him an ultimatum, so he'd split and was now living with another woman.

My world caved in but a few months later Julian came back, saying he'd had a change of heart. We got an apartment together and lived in it for about a year before we got married.

We've been married for three years now and most of the time things are great but sometimes he makes me feel so bad.

For example, he keeps a can of air freshener on the floor on his side of the bed. Once in a while, he'll start sniffing the air when I walk in the room and then start spraying the gardenia scent as though I have an odor. I tried becoming extra vigilant about my grooming but he kept it up. Finally, I asked him about it but he dodged the question by giving me an answer that I didn't understand.

What really bothers me though are his mysterious ways. He never talks about the places he goes, his job or the people he sees. A few months ago, he stayed out all night and came home claiming he'd been in a bar nursing drinks because he'd received a warning from his supervisor and felt his job was in jeopardy.

Julian didn't apologize for the fact that I'd stayed up all night, worried sick. We didn't speak for a few days and then things went back to normal. Two months later, the same thing happened. He left for work one morning and didn't come back. For two weeks I called his job but they hadn't heard from him and I also filed a missing person report with the police department. Still nothing.

This time I was furious so I've changed the locks on my front door. When he gets home this time, I'm going to insist that we go to a marriage counselor. Julian acts like a lost little boy. I just wish I could ease the pain that is obviously floating inside him.

—Laurie

Julian first broke Laurie's heart when he left during their court-ship without being man enough to have a meaningful discussion with her beforehand. Many of his actions since the marriage have been careless and downright cruel. This most recent disappearance is outrageous (and even that is an understatement) and unaccept-able.

Laurie is deeply wounded and her emotions are battered, yet she is still concerned about *his* pain. This is a typical response from victims of emotional abuse.

Laurie and Julian's union is very unhealthy and, although they can benefit from marriage counseling, another step is required here. Julian sounds like a commitment-phobic man and he needs individual therapy to get to the root of that. In the meantime, Laurie needs to take care of herself while the two of them work to save their marriage. This means keeping up with her work, friends and hobbies and taking part in activities that she has always found pleasurable.

Neither one of you should accept emotional abuse from the other. In an often hostile world and one in which we, as African Americans, must be constantly on guard, to come home to an abusive partner is the last straw. Everyone understands that domes-tic violence involves striking a mate either with the hands or with objects. However, many people suffer for years because they don't understand exactly what constitutes emotional abuse.

Constant Deliberate Disappointment

When someone consistently and deliberately lets you down, it can be a sign of hostility toward you and the roots of that hostility can only be uncovered and handled by a professional.

Hadiyah and Jerry hadn't been married long before she made an uncomfortable discovery. Jerry had no problem making prom-ises he couldn't possibly follow through on. After each disappoint-ment, Hadiyah grew angrier. She finally started doing everything for herself and stopped asking him for anything. It took a while but he noticed and acted highly insulted. "Fine, if that's the way you want to act," he said, before storming out of the house. Hadiyah felt badly for upsetting her husband. When he returned, she apologized and things went back to normal. Months went by. Jerry would ask Hadiyah if she wanted to see a movie, only to leave her waiting in front of the theater for hours while he never showed up. He promised to call whenever he was going to be late but never did. They were supposed to spend her birthday on a Mississippi steamboat but he used the money to buy a used car, without telling her. When Hadiyah told him how disappointed she was, Jerry ignored her.

There is no way that Jerry doesn't realize he is wrong for constantly disrespecting his wife and letting her down for no good reason. The only thing Hadiyah can do in a case like this is to tell him point blank that she will not put up with his barely hidden hostility toward her anymore and demand that they seek help in the form of a pastor, therapist or mediator who can get to the root of the problem and address it. Otherwise, there is no reason for this union to continue because it is certainly not a marriage when one person is being dogged so badly.

Constant Criticism

If Bishop stayed home, Claudette asked why he was always hanging over her shoulder. If he went out, she complained that he was neglecting her. If he wore shorts, she said his legs were ugly. If he went out in the summer wearing long pants, Claudette told him how stupid it looked. Claudette routinely told Bishop that he was an idiot who would never rise about his mousy status. After a few years of being unfairly criticized by his partner, Bishop was a nervous, edgy man with little self-esteem. He turned to alcohol to find some relief which, of course, opened him up to a new type of criticism but as long as he was drunk, Bishop didn't care.

When Dorie bought a new dress, Mike told her it would be pretty if it were in a size 10 instead of a 20. If she got a new hairstyle, he wanted to know why she was trying to look young when her "fly days are long over." He made fun of her taste in front of shopkeepers, berated her in front of cashiers for being too slow and threw his dinner in the garbage on occasion, calling it tasteless and predictable. Dorie's self-esteem was at an all-time-low and Mike refused to consider counseling. So, Dorie scraped up enough money each week to see a therapist on her own. Her spirits are beginning to pick up and once they do, she will be able to make the necessary changes in her life.

Living with constant criticism causes a person to feel weak and powerless. This is not a life, it is an existence and that is not what marriage is about.

Humiliation

I discovered that Leslie and her girlfriend Mona share everything, even intimate, confidential information and stories about me and Mona's husband, Esau. At first, I thought I was imagining that Mona was smirking or laughing after Leslie and I had had bad sex or were in a financial crunch. When I realized the truth, I became too embarrassed to see Mona. I wanted to tell Esau what was going on but I didn't want to be the one to cause trouble in his marriage. I watch what I tell Leslie because everything I say or do ends up in the street.

—Jarrett

Jarrett feels humiliated by his wife and no longer trusts her and with good reason. He is right not to say anything to Esau but his own marriage will become a sham if he has to watch what he tells Leslie for the rest of his life.

When Jarrett finally told Leslie how he felt, she reacted with indignation to cover her own shame. Later, she relented and apologized but Jarrett had become suspicious. Every time Mona smiled at him, he wondered if it was a friendly smile or an "I know something about you smile." He questioned Leslie over and over, demanding to know the details of every conversation she had with Leslie. The situation became unbearable

This couple finally decided to find an apartment in a new neighborhood and Leslie learned to keep her mouth shut. Even though she is no longer in contact with Mona, it will take many years for Jarrett to trust her again.

Linette invited her mother and Clement's to a Mothers' Day luncheon at their house. Several neighbors dropped by and some friends of their teenaged children were also in the living room when Clement's mother took out a breath mint and put the package on the table so that others could help themselves. Clement picked up the mints and dropped them in Linette's lap. "You should have been the first one to go for these," he said.

Heads turned away and the room was silent as Linette rushed into the kitchen so no one could see her tears. It wasn't the first time that Clement had humiliated her in front of these people.

When a partner constantly humiliates his spouse, there are deeper forces at work The mean-spiritedness that shows on the surface only masks a deeper problem with the partner and it takes professional help to get at the root causes.

Words Hurt as Much as a Fist

Verbal abuse is used either as a form of control or manipulation. Since the victim does not realize this, she thinks she is just being too sensitive. The abusing spouse periodically alternates between cruelty and kindness. It keeps the victim in a constant state of confusion and over time, it is utterly debilitating.

My brother has had a lot of problems finding a job over the past two years. I was telling my wife, Christina, about his latest efforts one day and she said, "Just like an American Black man. Why don't his friends help him? Oh, they're probably all looking out for themselves. We don't live that way." Now, my wife is from Barbados and I had been listening to this type of thing since we started dating. She was always saying insulting things like, "American Blacks are only good at complaining" or "American Blacks don't know the value of money." On and on it went, sometimes for hours.

That day I was not in the mood to hear any of it so I asked her why she married into this culture if she felt so negatively about it. She sucked her teeth and said I was being too sensitive. By then, I was feeling really heated and I reminded her that planes leave this country for her beloved islands every day and that she could get on one right away, as far as I was concerned.

It was the first time I had ever responded to her rudeness and I can still see the look of disbelief on her face.

—Everett

Everett had learned to ignore his wife's rudeness, scorn and total disregard for his culture and feelings. He shrugged it off but it hurt somewhere deep down inside.

Most victims of verbal abuse believe that their partner would behave differently if they could somehow improve themselves. Everett was lucky. He was not a typical victim because he did not blame himself.

Susan, an attractive corporate executive, has adapted to another kind of verbal abuse. Her spouse controls the tone of their lives by refusing to talk about the mean things he says. John blames her for all the offensive incidents. If she hadn't done ABC, he wouldn't have had to hurt her feelings by saying XYZ. Susan believes him.

Lacking a basis of comparison, since she did not go through a healthy father/daughter relationship, she just sighs and decides that no marriage is perfect. Besides, John is not always like this. She feels they can get through the bad times.

With an abuser, bad times never go away without counseling or a religious conversion. This is because a verbally abusive spouse wants power or control and his need for this is so great that he requires professional help in developing empathy for another human being.

Usually, when the abused spouse realizes what is happening and starts to speak up, the controller will accuse her of "ruining the marriage" with her complaints. Remember, verbal abuse is psychological battering.

WHAT VERBAL ABUSERS USUALLY HAVE IN COMMON:

♦ They say the nastiest things when only their spouse is around to hear them.
♦ They deny that the abuse ever took place.
♦ They withhold crucial information their spouse is entitled to have.
♦ They trivialize their spouse's feelings about their words and deeds.
♦ They resort to name calling.
♦ They undermine their spouse's efforts in any arena.
♦ They criticize even the tiniest thing that the spouse does.

WHAT THE VICTIMS OF VERBAL ABUSERS USUALLY HAVE IN COMMON:

♦ They adapt to the hurtful words.
♦ They take the blame for the hurtful words.
♦ They lose their self-esteem.
♦ They defend their abuser and even try to protect him.
♦ If they do realize what is going on, they think they can change the abuser.
♦ They don't realize that verbal abuse almost always precedes physical abuse.

How to Stop Emotional Abuse

The first thing to do is realize that your perceptions are correct. Trust your feelings. You are being treated badly, no matter what your partner says.

Next, get counseling if you can afford it. If not, find someone whom you can trust (mother? sister? best friend?) and who will listen to your stories. Silence is an ally of the abuser. Breaking the silence is the first step on the road to recovery.

Talk to your partner if he or she has not become physically abusive. Insist that in order for the marriage to continue, you both have to get help. Follow through on what you say, no matter how nice the abuser behaves at that moment.

TIPS FOR VICTIMS OF EMOTIONAL ABUSE

Memorize the following tips and live by them.

♦ Living with angry, unprovoked outbursts is not a life.
♦ I have the right to be spoken to with respect at all times.
♦ I don't have to put up with name calling.
♦ I have the right to be asked instead of ordered to do something.
♦ I cannot change _____ (insert name).
♦ I cannot save this marriage without professional help.

The Road to Domestic Violence

Emotional and verbal abuse almost always leads to domestic violence. Unkind words lead to even meaner deeds and it can all end with a slap in the face or much worse. Although the media has currently chosen a Black man as its poster boy for domestic violence, the truth is that batterers come in all colors, ages, sizes and income brackets. In fact, batterers can even come in a dress.

Yes, men can certainly become victims of domestic violence, which is the case whenever they are hit, slapped or attacked in any other way by their wives. Domestic violence is not altogether a woman's problem but for simplicity's sake, we will focus on the woman as victim here with the caveat that all rules that apply to male batterers apply to their female counterparts, as well.

How do we find ourselves in the position of victim? Many of these abusive men are very attractive. They exude an energy and an aggressiveness that makes us feel safe and supported. We are flattered by their attention, including their possessiveness of us. When they suggest we dress a certain way, walk and talk a certain way, when they boss us around a little, we feel parented and loved.

Some of these men are quiet and watchful. They go along with what we want, seem easy enough to get along with, and really seem to need us. Little do we know that some of them are taking mental notes of grievances, which they are adding to a list of all their other life experiences that have hurt and enraged them.

Much of the time, it is only in retrospect that we can recall warning signs. By the end of the first year of marriage, however, we will have directly experienced a spouse's abusive potential. If on the other hand we already have encountered dominating, disrespectful behavior during the dating period, and we still persist to living together or marriage, then we may fit into one of the following categories: the over optimistic; the risk taking, the guilty; the pain dependent; or the desperate for a husband.

We are over-optimistic when we believe that once we marry a man we can iron out his rough spots. We believe that we will make him feel so loved and taken care of, he will not lose his temper with us.

The risk-taking women are prone to "giving it a chance." They decide to marry and "see what happens." Their belief is that they can always get rid of the husband if he does not shape up. Sometimes, risk takers find that it is not so easy to end a marriage with an abuser. These are the kind of men who pursue you, even stalk you, if they cannot persuade you to forgive and forget.

The guilty are women who easily feel sorry for those who seem unhappy or inadequate, because they identify with these conditions. They take on themselves the job of comforting the afflicted, even, or perhaps especially, if they must sacrifice to do so. They are likely to do their best to please their abusive husband in an effort to win him over. Since they feel guilty anyway, they believe his accusations and try to do better each time.

The pain-dependent women may believe that they deserve a miserable life as the cost of the flashes of happiness they receive in the marriage. They do not demand respect because they are not used to receiving it. Sometimes, these women are provocative and almost bring on the brutal behavior. They become locked into a mutually overstimulating pattern on which they and their husbands are dependent.

The "must-have-a-husband" woman is willing to put up with Godzilla if he will marry her. She feels measured by whether or not a man chooses her as a wife. If Mr. Right has not come along, and she fears he never will, she will settle for a person despite her doubts about him. She rationalizes or overlooks the negative signs, setting her sights instead on how wonderful she will feel as a securely married woman. Often these women suffer in silence because they are too ashamed to let even a trusted friend or family member know how badly things are going.

Take a long, hard look at yourself to see whether you fit into any of these categories. Sometimes, we do not even know that we are a potential victim.

THESE ARE THE SIGNS TO WATCH OUT FOR:

♦ He is loving for much of the time, but with little or no provocation will fly into a rage.
♦ He finds some fault with each one of your friends.
♦ He gradually discourages you from spending time with your friends.
♦ He discourages you from seeing your family.
♦ You find that you no longer entertain or are invited out.
♦ You are persistently questioned about your whereabouts and everyone you meet.
♦ He convinces you that he can manage the money you earn better than you can.
♦ He resents your asking how he spends money.
♦ You find yourself scurrying around, nervously trying to please him.
♦ He bosses you around in an increasingly rude way.

Batterers are basically bullies. The weaker you are, the bolder they become. Such men seek to isolate you and keep you dependent on them, so as to better control you. They are driven to complete domination in an effort to fill up their empty places and prove that they are indeed, whole, adequate and strong. They feel these things at the moment of wielding punishment, but the high is fleeting. Afterwards, they may experience genuine remorse. But the empty place remains, so soon they are driven to a repeat demonstration of power.

Don't make the mistake of believing that you are responsible for the abuser's punishing behavior. Most abusive men will tell you that your behavior made them react as they have. If you had not done what you did, or said what you said, or said it in the way you did or had you done what you were supposed to do, they would not have been provoked to excess. Therefore *you,* not they, caused your abuse.

Don't believe it.

It is the abuser's own need for and lack of control that has driven him to abuse and you are merely a conveniently available target.

Yes, it is acknowledged that a loving, hard-working, responsible husband can lose control when the stress is too great, or the issue at hand extraordinarily sensitive for him, or when he is under the influence of alcohol. We are not talking here about the once-in-a-lifetime lapse. We are referring to habitual behavior.

Suppose you find that you have married such a person, or better, that you *are* such a husband. It is better to be than to have a battering mate. It is almost impossible to change another adult, but with enough motivation and effort, it is possible to change yourself. If you find yourself battering, run—don't walk—to a therapist. You must seek professional help.

If you are married to a batterer, and the batterer refuses to seek professional psychological help, then you do best to leave. This advice may sound strange in a book about saving your marriage, but it is more important to save your life and your spirit. If you are economically dependent on your husband, make yourself self-dependent. In extreme cases, a battered women's shelter will give you protection and allow you time to plan for a separate life. You also need counseling to help you repair your morale and to guide you towards an independent life.

If you are both determined to save your marriage, you will

have your best chance if each or you alone are in individual therapy, and both of you, together, are in couples treatment. Domestic abuse is a serious problem that requires serious attention.

Good luck.

CHAPTER NINETEEN

Adultery

"Remember, wherever you are and whatever you do, some-one always sees you."

—Marian Anderson
Quotations in Black, 1981

Marriage can be like a dependable old car. You never think about it but you are comforted by its presence. That is, until the brakes fail, or when one of you discovers that the other has been unfaithful. Then, the car breaks down and only time will tell whether it can ever be safe enough to ride in again.

During biblical times, adulterers were punished by stoning. Today, although Americans wouldn't go that far, they do agree that adultery is wrong and realize that it destroys far too many marriages. However, opinions vary wildly on how to punish the wrongdoer. "There is less tolerance for adultery than there was a generation ago," says Frank Pittman, author of *Private Lies: Infidelity and the Betrayal of Intimacy.* "We no longer believe grown-ups should be permitted to act like children . . . We've lost patience with all the celebrities parading their affairs in front of us . . . they are people who haven't been toilet trained yet." The thrill-seekers who cause such hurt and pain just to pursue their own selfish pleasures certainly fit Frank Pittman's view of immature infants but, as we shall see, not all stories of infidelity are quite that simple.

What Type of People Cheat on Their Spouses?

We are inclined to think that only evil people cheat on their spouses and that most of those evil people are men. The truth is that nice people cheat and women cheat as often as men do. Another common theory is that only someone in a lousy marriage would cheat. Wrong again. Many people in perfectly good marriages cheat for many different reasons, which we will explore in greater detail.

In short, there is no one type of person who cheats on their spouse.

Why Do Some People Cheat on Their Spouses?

The main question that a betrayed partner asks when he or she finds out that the spouse has committed adultery is, *why?* Most of the time, lacking an answer that makes sense, the betrayed partner places the blame on herself or the person with whom her spouse had sex. The wife says things like, "If I were only twenty pounds lighter or had longer hair, this wouldn't have happened" or "that woman was always tryin' to steal somebody's man, he just fell into her trap." These type of explanations are overly simplistic and hardly ever encompass the whole, complex truth.

Normally, there are many coexisting dynamics that lead a person into infidelity, for example: a weakness in character; a painful existence; and revenge for a real or imagined hurt.

Adultery as a result of a **weakness in character** can be found in excuses such as:

- ♦ "She was just so fine that when she came onto me, I just went for it."
- ♦ "He was someone new and exciting. Ben and I have been married for so long, our conversations are stale."
- ♦ "She's the most powerful woman in the office. I figured I could advance my career."
- ♦ "It's been a long time since anyone whistled at me. It felt good to know men still find me attractive."
- ♦ "We were just casual friends. I don't know how things got so out of hand."

Adultery as a result of a **painful existence** is explained by such statements as:

♦ "Marty goes on cocaine binges. He hits the street and stays gone for weeks at a time. I just haven't found the inner strength to leave him yet."
♦ "My wife acts like I'm just a boarder in our home. She never speaks to me unless she has to and I spend most of my time alone. All she ever really wanted was a baby and a house. Now that I've provided that, my usefulness is over."
♦ "I know that technically I've committed adultery, but we were separated and he was cagey every time I mentioned getting back together."
♦ "It was nice being around someone who didn't put me down and insult me in front of other people all the time. I've found out that I'm smart, not stupid, like Karen always says."

Adultery **to achieve revenge** for a real or imagined hurt is explained by such bitter remarks as:

♦ "John's been having affairs for years; I'm not as blind as he thought."
♦ "It was the only way I could pay Elva back for making my life a living hell for the past ten years."
♦ "When we got married, he didn't tell me that there was an ex-wife and five kids in his past. I had a right to know."
♦ "He drinks up all the bill money and I have to replace it. He deserves whatever I dish out."
♦ "Everytime we get into a fight, she says she should have listened to her mother and never married me. It hurts more than she knows."

Clues That Your Partner is Having an Affair

The main clues that your spouse is involved in an extramarital relationship are hardly ever clichés like lipstick on his collar. The signs are normally a lot less obvious. Usually, one partner senses that something isn't quite right with the other. If someone is having an affair, it is hard for him to hide it completely. In fact, marriage counselors have documented some behavioral changes that indicate a spouse is having an affair.

Becoming Unapproachable: When anyone needs to keep a secret from someone with whom he lives, it is easier to do so by avoiding deep conversation or excessive intimacy.

Behaving Differently: Some reported behavioral changes include excessive vanity; unexplained absences; different sexual needs; statements that seem out of character and a pronounced change in demeanor.

Acting Vague: Becoming agitated over the simplest questions or seeming to be in a dreamlike state, thinking unspoken thoughts or a reluctance to make plans for the future.

Your Gut Feelings: If you find yourself constantly shrugging off small signs that an affair may be going on, or spend a lot of time trying to find rational explanations for events or behaviors that make no sense, this may be your best clue that your spouse is having an affair.

Don't accuse your partner of being unfaithful without proof. There could be other explanations for a spouse's strange behavior, such as money problems or an illness he has just discovered. Tell your spouse that there seems to be a problem and that it has to be addressed right away. Do this before your fears and suspicions take control and you wound your spouse by making false accusations.

When to Confront Your Spouse

There are those who have confronted their partner at the first sign of infidelity. Most people don't do that. Most people worry and weigh evidence for a long time because the reality of their life partner having sex with someone else is just too scary and painful to actually deal with. They rationalize away the facts and any corroborating data which support the notion of an affair.

We'd rather find reasons to explain away even the most obvious signs of infidelity because the alternative is just too awful. At some point, though, we run out of rationalizations and then it's decision-making time. The main question to ask yourself before confronting your partner is, "Do I really want to know?" The next questions is, "If my partner confesses to the adultery, do I intend to leave or stay?"

Unless you have given both questions many hours of thought, you are not ready to confront your spouse.

When it is no longer possible for the situation to continue as is, ask the question of your spouse directly and try to handle the answer in a responsible fashion.

Tales From the Battlefront

Esther was the last of her sisters to marry. She and Joe had grown up together. They were friends who didn't see each other as marriage partners until they were well past their teens. Even though she had known Joe all her life, Esther still felt shy on their first "date." After a six-month courtship, Joe proposed. Their families were thrilled.

The first three years were exciting and romantic. Esther worked as a nanny and Joe worked on construction sites all over South Carolina. In fact, he and his friends built the couple's house, a one story, three-bedroom structure with an eat-in kitchen, family room and a huge living room. Modest. Comfortable. Esther and Joe were happy, even though God had not sent them the children they desperately wanted.

When Esther's mama died of a sudden heart attack, Joe thought his wife would go insane with grief. After the funeral, she climbed into bed and turned her face to the wall. Esther got out of bed only to wash up and go to the bathroom. When she wasn't crying, she was absolutely silent. She lost her job. She refused to eat. This went on for six weeks. Joe finally told Esther's family how bad things were at home. The word spread. Soon, everyone in town knew about Esther's situation. They packed the little house after church the following Sunday. Men. Women. Children.

The men smoked and talked. The women cooked, quilted and gossiped. No one was whispering. The children played tag and no one tried to stop them. Just after sundown, Esther's bedroom door opened. She was dressed in her Sunday best. Her hair was combed and pinned up. Esther walked through each room in her house as Joe watched anxiously. Finally, she smiled and the tension broke. Esther spent the rest of the evening eating and talking. Joe had never heard her talk so much, but it felt good. He had his wife back.

Two years later, the company Joe worked for went out of business. They were living on their savings when Esther discovered she was pregnant. By the time Joe Jr. was born, his father was working as a janitor at the high school. It didn't pay half as much as the old job but it was work. A little girl came next. They named her Naomi, after Esther's mother.

Joe Jr. was in the fifth grade when he came home from school in tears. Another little boy was claiming to be his brother. Esther soothed her son but her body went cold. Her hands shook as they kneaded dough for the supper biscuits. She and Joe had been married for fifteen years. He had always been honest and trustworthy. Never an unkind word. Never a missed birthday or anniversary celebration. Never a raised hand or voice. He paid the bills and bought Esther whatever he could afford. Most important, they were still in love.

Joe Jr. told his story again in between bites of beef stew while Esther watched her husband's face. He wouldn't look her in the eyes.

That night, Joe cried as Esther walked around their bedroom, throwing his clothes into an open suitcase. He swore that it only had happened once and that he would never be unfaithful again. The affair had taken place years ago when the construction company left town. Joe had been more troubled than anyone realized. He had had a one-night stand with a woman who lived on the outskirts of town.

Joe moved in with his brother's family. He went to work every day and to church every Sunday. In between working and praying, Joe ignored the snickers and gossip. He simply waited for Esther to forgive him. It took two years for Joe to get back home.

For the next thirty-five years, Joe and Esther stayed married through good times and bad times. Joe Jr. grew up, married and had nine children.

Philip and I had been married for seven years and we still had hot sex every night. I'd been seeing Louie on my lunch hour for almost a month. We usually went to a hotel around the corner, scarfed down some Chinese food and made love. I was just doing it for the thrill until one day I ran into my landlord's wife while Louie and I were kissing goodbye. She never said anything but it was enough to scare me into ending my lunchtime affair with Louie.

—Loretta

Like most women, I didn't head for the church on my wedding day knowing that I would eventually cheat on my husband. I also didn't count on being bored out of my mind, either. Even though the affair has been over for over a year, I'm still afraid that my husband will find out. That would be a nightmare. He would be so hurt.

—Sadie

My wife is a good woman but Dani is just gorgeous. I'm flattered that she is even interested in a plain type of guy like me. It's amazing. Here I am, fifty years old and balding, with a mistress who could be a Jet *centerfold. In high school, the pretty girls always ignored me. The problem is that Dani has expensive tastes so I do overtime without my wife knowing about it so that I will have extra money to spend on her.*

—Abosi

I own a car dealership in Montgomery, Alabama, where my wife works as a fund-raiser for social service organizations. We also own a co-op on the upper East side of Manhattan because we visit New York frequently to visit relatives and do business. Toya and I have twin boys who are in a school for the gifted. I admit that my life with Toya is just perfect but I like the chase of seeing a desirable woman and trying to get her to fall in love with me. I already know that Toya is mine.

—Rene

My lover is a well-known married man so we have to be especially careful. Yes, I believe that marriage is an institution that should be respected, but it is his marriage not mine. My husband left me for another woman. That woman wasn't thinking about me. Why should I think about his wife?

—Jackie

I've been married for seventeen years and have had at least that many affairs. I always choose happily married women because I have no intention of leaving my wife for anyone and they can understand that. They don't bother me about spending more time or holidays with them because they aren't available, either. I have a good life.

—Anwar

A few years ago I found out that my husband was having an affair. I was devastated to the point where I considered suicide. Now, I've finally pulled myself together and am doing my thing outside the marriage. What is good for the goose is good for the gander.

—Cyndie

This woman, having suffered a terrible wound to her self-esteem, is trying to prove to herself that she is still attractive.

However, this is still trouble just waiting to happen. If her husband has reformed and finds out what is going on, the marriage is over. He will return to the woman he was having the affair with or pick up someone else. If Cyndie promised to forgive, then she should do so, unless evidence surfaces that shows her faith has been misplaced once again.

My cousin's wife saw Mark helping this woman into a cab. I didn't want to get the family involved, so I lied and pretended that it was I who had seen him. After he confessed to a one-night stand, I threw him out of the bedroom. The only reason I didn't divorce him immediately is because we have six children and it would be hard for me to support them.

—Tanya

My brother covers for me when I go to see my girlfriend. When I feel guilty about what I'm doing, it isn't the actual adultery that makes me feel bad. It's the fact that my wife is crazy about my brother and would be doubly hurt if she knew what was going on.

—Rod

Tom always made his calls from another room. If Sheila were in the kitchen, he would talk from the bedroom, and vice versa. Sheila also noticed that he spoke more softly on the calls he made than on those that came in for him. Tom also usually opened the mail for bills and took care of them. One day, while he was on one of his regular business trips, Sheila thought that she would relieve her husband by paying the bills that had come in during his absence. She noticed a series of calls to one, unfamiliar telephone number. She decided to call the number. A woman's voice was on the answering machine. Now, very suspicious, Sheila decided to try to talk to the woman. She did and they spoke for an hour. The woman had been having an affair with Sheila's husband for a year. She had not known that Tom was married. They plotted a dramatic confrontation for him when he returned from his business trip.

All affairs are discovered eventually, no matter how careful the participants. Eventually, something or someone will give you away.

When You Are the Betrayer

After that ghastly night when Leona found out about the affair, we had a terrible few months. Just when I thought things were all patched up, she starts screaming and crying one day out of the blue and we had to rehash the whole thing all over again. How many times will this happen?

—Carlos

When you have betrayed your life partner by engaging in sex with someone else, you must understand that it will take a long time for your spouse's hurt and pain to go away. It will require a lot of hard work for the marriage to survive. The wounded partner experiences shock, a sense of betrayal and indescribable pain. That partner who has been betrayed must be allowed to grieve and the betrayer usually has a problem with that simple fact. The one who has committed adultery will want to drop the subject after the discovery or confession, believing that if the topic is avoided, it will fade into the past. He or she will say something like, "We've already talked this out, why are you bringing it up again?" This is not fair and the partner who has been betrayed does not have to tolerate it.

The wounded spouse will ask you for the details, which should be discussed in a setting that includes a professional marriage counselor to avoid the possibility of domestic violence. You, on the other hand want to confess, apologize and let the matter rest. It is really just too bad if discussing the affair makes you uncomfortable. If you want to save your marriage, you'll just have to start behaving like an adult which means dealing with *all* the consequences of your actions.

Lex and Edwina had been married for six years. Lex was an auto mechanic and Edwina was a secretary. Lex was shocked when a mutual friend whispered to him that Edwina was having an affair with someone on her job. He confronted his wife, who promptly confessed. Lex was enraged and demanded to know every detail.

Edwina was too embarrassed to give him more than a sketchy outline of what had happened. She went out and got a new job, in the hope that Lex's questions would stop once she was no longer

*in contact with the other man. In spite of all this, Lex became
suspicious every time she left the house.*

*After a while, Edwina got fed up. "You've got to let it go," she
told him. Lex became withdrawn and even more hostile. Finally,
Edwina asked him to go into therapy with her. At first, he said
no, but after a few weeks he realized that without some change,
the two of them would no longer be able to live together.*

Edwina was surprised when the therapist spent several sessions
allowing Lex to ask all of his questions about the affair and having
her answer them. Of course, the first question Lex asked was,
"Why did you do it?" It was a reasonable question. Edwina's
answer was "I don't know." Lex then decided that it was something
he did or had not done. The therapist refused to allow him to
blame himself, especially since Edwina didn't have any concrete
facts to support his feelings. Edwina had to take responsibility for
her own actions.

The only way for Edwina to regain Lex's trust was to answer
his questions and quietly hang in while he vented his despair and
unhappiness. The counselor arranged a specific set of weeks for
Henry to vent. Edwina's discomfort was not taken into consideration in this instance. Her feelings were not the issue as Lex grieved
for their lost relationship. Since Lex was the injured party, Edwina
just had to deal with it and then start on the long road back.

When You Are the Wounded Partner

Adultery can destroy even the most happy marriage. Staying
married is about honesty, trust and communication. When the
partner finds out that his spouse has had sexual relations with
someone else, the foundation of the marriage is rocked. An affair
is an escape from dealing with the problems in the marriage. It is
easy to understand how a person who discovers that a spouse has
been unfaithful will feel angry, betrayed and unloved. A spouse's
unfaithfulness is a deep betrayal.

The first reaction is shock, followed quickly by knifelike pain
and almost paralyzing anger. Finally, there is grief. The marriage
cannot ever go back to the way it was. In order to stay married,
a new union must be constructed.

It does not matter how you find out that your partner has been
unfaithful. Some adulterers confess. Others wait to get caught. It
does not matter. As the betrayed partner, you will still fluctuate

between agony and fury. You will start to wonder whether the intimacy you thought you had was really there, or just your fantasy playing itself out.

Once the matter has been discussed, the betrayer will be anxious to put it in the past. You can't let that happen so quickly. You need to understand why the affair happened. Was it caused by anger, boredom, substance abuse? The underlying reason for the adultery must be addressed or true healing will never take place.

This is definitely the time for professional help. A marriage counselor can help the two of you gain insight into your problems. A marriage counselor will also help the betrayer to understand the need to take responsibility for the adultery, regardless of what excuse he or she has for it.

Kassan found that Fadi had started having one-night stands five years before, when she was pregnant with their first child. After Kassan recovered from her shock and hurt, she and Fadi decided to try and mend the fences. Fadi swore he would never stray again and Kassan wanted her marriage to work. Kassan resumed their married life but with one major difference. She insisted that Fadi wear a condom. He strenuously objected to this for many reasons, but Kassan would not be moved. Even after they got the negative results from the AIDS test that she insisted they take, she held fast. (The incubation for AIDS takes years.) She was determined to take responsibility for herself and their children by protecting herself against any disease her husband might have picked up. Despite Fadi's protests, he soon realized that if he wanted to be with Kassan, he had to wear a condom during sex. It was that simple.

According to the Center for Disease Control in Atlanta, Georgia, Non-Hispanic Blacks represent 30 percent of all reported acquired immunodeficiency syndrome (AIDS) cases in the United States, but make up only 12 percent of the U.S. poplulation. While the total number of reported AIDS cases historically has been highest among whites, racial/ethnic minority groups in the United States have always been overtly represented in proportion to population size, and the numbers continue to grow.

Everyone has a right to self-defense. The AIDS virus is a killer and if you suspect that your spouse (male or female) has been fooling around, common sense demands that you protect yourself. This is clearly a delicate and difficult situation. Perhaps reading this section together can open up a frank discussion between you and your mate if this is an issue between you.

Deciding Whether to Stay

The question of whether to leave or stay is not a simple one. The first test it presents is the commitment to your marriage. If you have been betrayed, you must ask yourself the following questions:

♦ Are you more committed to your marriage than to getting revenge for the hurt?
♦ Are you truly able to put the whole episode behind you? Or will the blow to your security and your rage make your lives miserable?
♦ Do you believe that your mate is capable of stopping this behavior?
♦ Do you understand that just "putting it behind you" will not work over the long haul?
♦ Are you willing to seek the help you both need to make the long journey back to some degree of trust?
♦ Are you both willing to see a marriage counselor for a long period of time?

Don't think that you have an obligation to work on breaking up your marriage. Many men and women react to such a discovery by turning their attention to revitalizing their marriage and renewing their attention to their relationship with their mate.

The Long Road Back

Can that breach of trust be rebuilt? My answer is that it can, if both parties sincerely want to clean up the mess and if they are willing to work at it over a long period of time. Their efforts will be successful only if they observe the following principles:

1. The person who has committed adultery must be willing to accept a high degree of accountability. A certain amount of freedom must be voluntarily surrendered. In the beginning, this means telling where you've been, how long you were there and what you were doing there.
2. The person who was the "victim" of an affair must be willing

to take some risks. You simply cannot rebuild trust if you are never willing to trust. You must let go of the natural instinct to build a prison without walls against the spouse whose infidelity has hurt you. Is there a possibility that you might get hurt again? Absolutely. But if you're not willing to run that risk, you will not be able to salvage the relationship.

3. Forgiveness is like medicine. It takes more than one dose. When two people decide to work on cleaning up the mess, they want to put the past behind them and go on with their lives. It is easy to verbalize a willingness to forgive. But you have only verbalized your goal. The hurt will resurface many times. Each time it resurfaces, you must mentally declare your intention to forgive. If you do it enough times, the occasions of emotional pain will become fewer and farther between.

No one should expect to clean up the debris overnight. In most cases, it will take a period of years to rebuild the relationship, but if you persevere, your marriage will eventually be stronger than it was before the storm came through.

CHAPTER TWENTY

When Depression Sets In

"The problem with depression is that it can become general-
ized to encompass your entire existence."
—Dr. Craig K. Polite
Children of the Dream, 1992

Everyone feels sad, bad or stressed out from time to time. It's
called the blues and although the blues are painful, they are not
the same as clinical depression.

Depression is a dreadful disease which can also be fatal. Esti-
mates vary, but indications are that about 15% of the U.S. population—one man in ten and one woman in five—will have a serious
depression at some time in their lives, usually before they hit their
forties.

When trying to decide whether a person simply has the blues
or is clinically depressed, professionals look to the duration and
frequency of physical distresses for which no particular cause can
be found; how many different symptoms there are at a given time;
the family history; and current events in the person's life.

Obviously, when someone is very sad all the time, can't hold
a job or go to work, even takes to bed and closes off from people,
it is not so difficult to make the diagnosis of depression. But do
not depend on that picture to suspect depression in others or in
yourself. It is not particularly unusual to mask our depression with
extraordinary good humor, even unrelenting hilarity, or unceasing
activity. On the other hand, a lot of people find that they are
uninterested in many of the things they used to find enjoyable.

SYMPTOMS OF DEPRESSION

♦ Disturbance in sleep habits and patterns.
♦ A sense of hopelessness.
♦ Feelings of inadequacy or irritation.
♦ Impatience.
♦ Chronic rage.
♦ Poor appetite or overeating.
♦ Poor concentration.
♦ Difficulty making decisions.

Although depression is a serious illness, it is treatable with psychological counseling and, sometimes, with medication. As a race, we tend not to seek counseling for symptoms of depression. Some of our attitudes toward the medical establishment have already been discussed and, to many of us, the idea of paying good money to talk about what is wrong with our lives is wasteful and self-indulgent.

Black men, especially, tend to be downright resistant to seeking counseling or psychotherapy when they find themselves stuck in life. Somehow, it seems more manly to struggle along, no matter how unsatisfactorily, rather than to admit the need for some help. Men express all kinds of objections, namely, that they should be strong enough to take care of their own feelings; otherwise, it would mean they were crazy. Even women often reject seeking help because they feel it would be a betrayal to talk to a stranger about family members, or that it is wrong to confide in an outsider. Many people fear learning that there is something terribly wrong with them, and that a therapist will discover that rotten core.

We believe that nobody can really understand us, especially a therapist who might be the wrong color, or thinks he or she is better than we are because of their schooling and different life. It is too much money, too much trouble, we won't get anything out of it. There are all kinds of "reasons" why not to seek outside help. Mostly we are afraid of the unknown.

Women are almost twice as likely as men to become depressed. How much of this is due to hormonal differences, the way women's emotions are linked to their intellectual reactivity, and/or social pressures has not been determined, and perhaps never will be, but there is little dispute that women are more likely to suffer from depression than are men. In addition, women are very likely simply to endure their suffering. But the more we internalize our anger, the more likely it is that we may turn that anger against ourselves and become depressed. Even though Black women are seen as tough survivors, we still suffer from depression.

Peaches began to feel overwhelmed by her life. Little by little, she began to let things go. First, she stopped making the beds and refused to pick up the disorder of living. Then, rather than prepare the attractive meals in which she had taken so much pride, she started to make dinners come out of cans. Too exhausted to get up, and unable to face another day at work Peaches took many days of absence. She was fired. Then, she really let herself go. Her hair went untended, she skipped showers, she refused to change her clothes. Paul grew alarmed. It was obvious that Peaches was very depressed.

Some experts theorize that Black professionals are particularly at risk for depression because this class has higher expectations than other African Americans. No matter what the person's social standing, depression causes that person to stop functioning as he normally does for a significant period of time. The depressed spouse may lose interest or pleasure in most of his normal activities. Good news cheers him up only for a very short time, if at all. The depressed spouse will knock himself and have negative thoughts about the future. His concentration may be poor. As it gets worse and untreated, the person starts to feel helpless and worthless. Thoughts of suicide are not uncommon.

Depression is a very serious disease and should not be taken lightly. Depressed people should not be blamed or told to "cheer up." Depression is a disease they cannot control.

DEPRESSION

Depression requires three things:

a problem;
a lack of faith in your ability to resolve the problem;
an inability to live with the problem.

Eliminate one and you weaken the others.

Hubie always had a hair-trigger temper. But now it seemed that even a breeze threw him into a rage. He constantly found fault with Debra. When she went against his expectations he would yell and then stop speaking to her for weeks. The children avoided him, and increasingly his friends did, too. Some friends and relatives told Debra that Hubie was suffering a mid-life crisis and that he would get over it, some year. They told her to put up with his behavior and wait. Others advised her to leave him. But Debra decided that she would try to save her marriage. She knew she could not just passively endure Hubie's behavior. She also knew that giving him back what he dished out, withdrawing or escalating the conflict would not improve the situation.

Debra decided to convince Hubie to consult their family physician. Since their sex life had all but disappeared, she used that as a reason to persue professional help. She was surprised that Hubie agreed so readily. He realized that things with him were not going right and thought maybe he could get a tonic to help him out. After the examination and the results of the tests were in, the doctor suggested that Hubie consult a psychologist. He believed Hubie had an underlying case of depression. In the meantime, he prescribed an antidepressant.

Do not try to talk a depressed person out of his gloom. It does not help and often makes things worse. The talker gets frustrated, the listener feels equally frustrated, guilty and probably more depressed. The best approach for the mate is to listen and to encourage her husband to talk about his feelings. Don't be too sympathetic, don't be dismissive, don't coddle, don't scold, don't point out the illogic or untruth of their assertions, don't be too cheery, don't act too worried. Just try to be understanding. Psychotropic medication relieves pain and suffering. The newer medications have few or no side effects. Psychotherapy gets below the surface for more lasting change. They are best in combination.

Without a doubt, the best way to seek to improve your life, and surely to defeat depression, is through psychotherapy. But it may well be unnecessary for you to work with a psychologist, social worker or psychiatrist. They can remain as a last resort. A family member or friend, especially an older person who has experienced and weathered the various storms of life, may be the guide you need. Pastors are trained and experienced in giving counsel. Sometimes you can think things through with each other. If you decide to do this, there are some rules. The task for the healthy partner is to listen actively but not to psychologize. Psychologizing means offering reasons for why another person is doing, feeling, reacting the way he or she is. A mate helps by providing an accepting ear and encouraging the depressed person to search out loud for memories and experiences that throw light on his or her feelings. The depressed persons needs to come to her own answers. From her mate, she needs understanding, not answers, no matter how brilliant. Remember, from time to time all of us need to step back to look at our situation and to find help in dealing with it.

It is important to make no major decisions while you are depressed. The condition makes everything seem bleak and hopeless and when you are depressed, your judgment is clouded. Certainly, do not act our your negative feelings towards other people, especially your mate. Don't quit your job or leave your marriage. You might be projecting your view of yourself as inadequate or inferior, which you will use to justify and fan the negative flames of your anger. Remember, it is very difficult to live with a depressed person, so your mate might be dealing with her own anger. Both of you need support and comfort. Turn toward each other, not against each other, as a matter of "for better or worse, in sickness and in health."

WHEN IT'S TIME TO GET HELP

♦ You have trouble concentrating to complete work or studies.
♦ You experience a significant change in your appetite, sleep or sex drive.
♦ You suffer from uncontrollable crying spells.
♦ You have uncontrollable thoughts of harming yourself.
♦ You have severe mood swings.

Thomas was never happy in the "corporate straitjacket." He believed that Black men were never treated fairly, were never recognized when they did well, were never accepted, but just tolerated, barely. He had rather high-level jobs in several corporations for about ten years, then decided that he would go into business for himself. Before he left his last job he fell in love with a coworker, whom he later married.

Thomas's wife, Bernice, thrived in the corporate world. She rose rapidly, became an officer, and at a young age became responsible for many departments in a multinational enterprise. It seemed that the more Bernice rose, the more the weak economy jeopardized Thomas's business until it tottered on bankruptcy.

Thomas became very discouraged, opened his business later and later each day, and seemed to be doing less and less to promote his work. At the same time there was increasing dissension between Thomas and Bernice. They fought a lot, criticized each other sharply, and stopped speaking to each other for long periods of time.

Bernice saw Thomas as lazy and incompetent. Thomas saw Bernice as an Uncle Tom drone. He had negative income, hers was in the six figures. He demanded that he control the spending of the money. She submitted to what she considered his bullying, but surrendered with resentment.

The treatment of this couple revealed that Thomas was suffering from a clinical depression. He had no energy, no hope for achieving the success that he felt was incumbent upon him, and was deeply envious of Bernice. As his depression was acknowledged, and he was able to release his facade of bravado to share his pain, Bernice was able to relate to his suffering and stop blaming him for his inactivity.

A combination of therapy and medication helped Thomas to overcome his depression. He was enabled to stop comparing himself to Bernice, or even to his internalized, socially conditioned view that the man had to be the more adequate, more successful, boss of the marriage. He thought through his own options and preferences. He and Bernice acknowledged the racism with which he had to contend in the work world, and the fact that he was not temperamentally suited to cope with it in a constructive way. He decided to remain with the business but to renew energetic promotion and follow-through in order to revitalize it. Thomas was able to stop blaming the economy, Bernice, the customers, conditions, and even himself. Instead he began to strategize to overcome obstacles.

Bernice's understanding of Thomas's emotional problems did not abate her rage about their financial arrangement. She thought that she should pay her own way but not a penny more. Depression or no depression, Thomas needed to pay his own way. And she definitely resented the way he put down her achievements while he lived off them. When she began to recognize the inherent sexism in her attitude, she considered the complexity involved in their sharing the ups and downs of their life together. Now she was carrying the financial load; at another time, he might. If she were a man she would not resent paying their way. Why not do so as a woman? Thomas and Bernice adopted the perspective of a lifetime over which things would even out. As their defensiveness was reduced, there was room for positive affection and cooperation. They learned to respect each other's struggles, to give each other positive feedback, to give and accept help from each other. They learned that there was more to their relationship than jobs or money. They recognized ways of nurturing what was enduring, and de-emphasizing what was temporary and superficial. Bernice learned to accept Thomas as a whole person, with his strengths and shortcomings. She learned to support him instead of criticize him, and Thomas, in turn, was freed to recognize and give credit to his wife's accomplishments.

Thomas, who had revealed his misgivings about his own adequacy, developed his self-acceptance and a recognition of his real assets achieved despite the negative social pressures to which poor, African American boys are subjected while they grow up in the ghetto. Thus, by strengthening their acceptance of self and spouse, Bernice and Thomas reinforced their commitment to each other and to their marriage. Their dynamic changed from one of criticism and confrontation to one of positive and more loving interaction.

There are some lifestyle habits that prevent, remedy, or help mild depression from getting worse. It has been found that a daily routine of at least 30 minutes of vigorous exercise and 20 minutes of meditation is a combination that lifts depression. Add to that a focus on some area of interest to you—your work; a hobby; an outside activity; a social cause; a young person who needs mentoring; an older or ill person who needs friendship; or anything else that turns you on. And be sure that you get enough sleep and that you eat healthy. Spiritual nourishment is also a major help.

Psychotherapy comes with no guarantees. You must choose the therapist who feels right for you. First, get recommendations from someone you trust, or investigate the neighborhood mental health clinics which are low cost or accept Medicaid. No matter to whom or where you go, do not hesitate to discuss with the doctor or therapist any questions and concerns you have about your treatment. Your involvement is an important part of the recovery process.

CHAPTER TWENTY-ONE

When One of You Is Sick

"I need somebody to come and get me."
—Mary McLeod Behume

In many wedding ceremonies, the couple pledge themselves to each other in sickness and in health. Often, that isn't an easy promise to keep. Illness is not welcome. It frightens us at our deepest levels. It confronts us with our mortality, which for most of our life we try to ignore. It reminds us that we have more to do, more to give, more to gain, and it drives us to despair and/or rage if we think we may not have the time or capacity to achieve these goals. If our spouse is the one who is seriously ill, the illness awakens deep-seated fears of abandonment. It puts the lie to our wish of omnipotence which while all goes well, we convince ourselves we have.

It is deeply painful to watch our loved one suffer or to endure our own suffering. But serious illness gives us the opportunity to really express our love and togetherness, both as giver and receiver. It can forge a bond that will never be broken.

As we have seen, staying married even when you both are physically and mentally healthy takes a lot of work. A serious illness however, may pose such a strain on a union that it becomes not only work but a real struggle to hold the marriage together.

The trips to doctors, the examinations and tests, the waiting for results, remembering to take the medicines, keeping up with the countless bills, the relying on others to help us out . . . It is all a damn nuisance, to say the least.

In fact, it may be necessary to remind ourselves frequently of that "sickness and health" part of our marriage vow.

The ability to cope with the lengthy illness of a spouse varies greatly from person to person. Many factors enter into the situation.

♦ Gender is an issue. Men feel far more helpless when faced with chronic illness.
♦ Experience with illness. If you have never known a very sick person, at times feelings of revulsion probably will overwhelm you. If you did know someone who was very ill and that person died, the fear of another death can feel strangling.
♦ Money. Unless you and your spouse are very well off, your lifestyle can change for the worse in a very short time due to medical bills and the loss of one paycheck.

All of these factors and many more will determine how you and your spouse deal with a chronic illness. Obviously, if you have the support and help of family and friends, things will be a lot easier, but you should also consider one of the many support groups that are linked with many serious illnesses. They can help immeasurably with emotional sustenance, as well as an information base for financial assistance.

Our past and expected relationship with our mate also comes into play when illness strikes, as does our degree of social and family support or pressure, and the age group we fall into. How long we have been married also matters. Our particular personality and outlook on life are significant, as well as that of our partner.

The gender difference leads more women to a nursing role, for which some may be ill-suited. The more resentful they feel, the more guilty they become. On the other hand, many women feel truly fulfilled by being able to care for a loved one, no matter the cost to themselves.

Marie's groom suffered a massive stroke one month after their wedding. She was 23, he was 30. He was left unable to speak, could walk only with extreme difficulty, then not at all, could not feed himself nor take care of his toileting. He was very confused, having lost much of his reasoning power, bodily control and essential humanity. Thirty years later, Marie was still lovingly taking care of her husband on her own while she taught school for their living. Marie neither sought nor received help.

When Marie casually disclosed this situation to the psychologist who served her school, the psychologist set about convincing Marie that she was entitled to occasional relief periods and the help of family, friends and neighbors. The enthusiastic responsiveness of family members to such requests surprised Marie. They had not offered for fear of offending Marie who seemed to take such pride in her self-sufficiency. Once she opened herself to outside help, Marie began to learn of community resources available to her and her husband. One program, a respite day care or several days and nights "camp" for the handicapped, allowed her first weekend vacation in thirty years. As she gave herself permission to avail herself of this help, Marie found not only a revitalized life, but also renewed dedication to her husband.

Whether it is built into the species or has been socialized in, women are the nurturers, the ones who are much more inclined to care for the ill. Obviously, many men are tender care providers, and are more willing and capable than many women, but these men are the exception.

Wives and mothers perform the nursing, both day and night, of their children, their husbands, their own parents and even their husbands' parents. It is mostly taken for granted that they do so. Mothers who sit up with sick children night after night and who nurse their husbands through minor and major illnesses are often neither thanked nor helped.

When men are thrust in the role of caretaker, however, they receive praise and casseroles and many offers of help. When husbands finally recognize that it is as difficult for the wife to caretake as it would be for them, they will learn to give their wives moral and physical support and thanks. We all need recognition and encouragement, even women who feel impelled and are gratified to perform according to their sense of womanly responsibility. If you are a woman, allow yourself the freedom to make a choice. Perhaps your husband or your mother or someone you hire is better able to carry out long-term nursing duties. It is not a failure for you to choose not to be the caretaker. It is certainly not a failure for you to choose not to do everything by yourself. Accept help, even request and arrange for it.

If you are a husband, see that your wife, who is in a caretaker position, receives your help and recognition and also that your friends and extended family rally to her support.

Walt's mother had an agonizing, long battle with cancer before she succumbed when Walt was eight years of age. When Eva,

Walt's wife found a suspicious lump on her breast, Walt panicked. When it was found to be malignant, he bolted. He did not visit his wife in the hospital and was distant when she returned home after a lumpectomy. Eva was deeply hurt by his behavior and soon the couple were so alienated that separation seemed to be the only course.

Luckily, Eva's oncologist concerned herself with the psychological state of her patients. When she found out about Eva's situation at home, she summoned Walt to Eva's next visit and demanded that they meet with her colleague, a health psychologist. It did not take long for Walt's fear of illness in general, and of cancer, in particular to be revealed. Their sessions led to mutual understanding of his earlier trauma to his wife's situation. With the help of counseling, Walt realized that his mother's plight differed from Eva's and that at this time of life, he differed from an eight-year-old, dependent child. This work enabled the marriage to survive Eva's illness and subsequent cancer treatment.

Most couples can come together to deal with an acute illness. They can mobilize their energies to handle the care required and are frequently too distressed even to think about anything except recovery for the ill mate. Chronic illnesses seem to cause more trouble, especially if its repercussions can be managed only with difficulty. Marian's arthritis slowed her down so much that Pete had to walk at a snail's pace when he walked with her. Hilda slowly but steadily lost her eyesight to diabetes and glaucoma. Jim's prostate surgery left him incontinent and unable to achieve an erection. Jim is now confined to a wheelchair; Hilda is on dialysis.

Chronic disabling conditions in yourself or your mate require you to make definite changes in your view of each other. If you demand that you and your mate be the same as always, except with a new limitation to work around, you will face constant frustration. Instead, you must prepare to reframe your relationship and revise your expectations of your mate and of yourself. You have important work to do.

When she was diagnosed with breast cancer at thirty years old, Danyela Parkson was a high school math teacher who also tutored "at-risk teenagers" after school hours. After her mastectomy, Danyela found that her husband, Turhan, was having trouble coping with her illness. He was never unkind and always went out of his way to help her adjust. But since she was feeling unsure about her future, she needed him to understand her uncertainty and fear. As Danyela tried to make Turhan understand, he became more and more frustrated. Luckily for their marriage, Danyela's gynecologist convinced her to join a Breast Cancer Survivor's Support Group.

Danyela started meeting once a week with breast cancer survivors from around her city. The women were from different races and classes, united in their common need to share their concerns and receive vital information from health professionals who came to speak to them. "I was there to learn and enjoy the fellowship," said Danyela. Danyela continued attending the meetings for a year and she learned a lot from the other survivors. She and Turhan (who showed up a few times, himself) learned to cope with her illness while strengthening their marriage.

First, both of you should find all the information that you can on the particular condition or illness from which you or your mate suffer. Read about it, ask many questions of your doctors and appropriate others, and use the Internet if you have access to it. Contact the support groups that have formed for most disabling conditions, for example, The Lupus Society, The Arthritis Foundation, The Lighthouse for the Blind, and the like. Become authoritative experts on the condition. Thus equipped, both of you should collaborate to become managers of your condition and its treatment, definitely not its suffering victims.

Then, develop a plan of living, independent of the way you used to do things. This new plan should maximize the capabilities of the person with the illness, should account for all that needs to be taken care of in the home and should be mutually satisfactory.

Family members, immediate and extended, and friends should be considered resources who can help out. Be sure to provide for recreation and fun in your new way of living. Divide your responsibilities as equitably as possible, taking into consideration what each is now better able to do. Build in lots of private time for the caretaker.

Find out how you can use community programs like rehabilitation services or Cancer Care. Emphasize all that is good, positive, loving and fun in your relationship and in yourselves. Figure out how best to help each other keep a positive outlook and make the best of each day.

Then, have a series of open and honest talks with each other about how you feel about the illness, the disabling condition, your new life plans, these new arrangements, and what you hope for from yourself and from your mate. Listen to yourself, and listen to your mate. Each of you try to understand your own feelings and beliefs and try to communicate them clearly. Keep these sessions part of your routine.

Every month or so, when anything special comes up, sit down together and share your view of the event and your experience of what is going on in your lives. Remember to be open, direct and loving.

If we have enjoyed many years of a positive relationship with our spouse, we probably will be more willing to adapt to the necessary changes necessitated by his or her illness. If our relationship was already on the brink of disaster, then a severe illness may be the last straw. This is a good reason to keep your relationship close and positive so that it can survive the storms.

Other things being equal, you will probably have more trouble coping with chronic, disabling illness if you are young than if you are older, perhaps because chronic illnesses are less expected and therefore deemed less acceptable during our twenties and thirties perhaps because we have had little experience at those ages coping with disappointment and bad luck. However, the younger you are—again, other things being equal—the more flexible you may be, the more energy you may have to invest in recovery and perhaps the greater your belief in your ability to overcome everything.

The older you are, the longer you probably have had to build loyalty to each other and the need for one another. A pragmatic acceptance of what life has to offer seems to be easier to achieve with the wisdom gained over the years. The older we get, the more we expect that illness will come to one of us, so that not rising to the occasion becomes unthinkable.

If we are patient and accepting and have a strong sense of self, we will have inner resources we can rely on to help us survive our own or our spouses' illnesses. We will find ways to compensate for what is lost, and build new gratification from the current challenges. If we are generally impatient, have a strong need to be recognized by others as successful, find ourselves seeking approval from the outside world or if we are naturally somewhat depressed or find it hard to change or to feel out of control of all that is going on around us, then it will be more difficult to cope with severe or chronic illness in ourselves or in our mates.

Do not wait until you find that you must escape altogether from the situation and your mate. Go to your pastor or a trusted relative or friend and talk about your feelings. Or seek professional help from a psychologist or social worker. You have little to gain by burdening your mate with this personality-driven exasperation with a situation that cannot be changed. Work on yourself, because you can change. You will be a better person for the work and your marriage will be saved.

CHAPTER TWENTY-TWO

Growing Old Together

"Even with all my wrinkles, I am beautiful!"
—Bessie Delaney
Having Our Say, 1993

When I first got married 25 years ago, my idea of love was having a husband who bought me flowers, rubbed my feet, sat down to dinner with me every night and held me as I drifted off to sleep. Yes, I knew there would be rough times but I believed that my new husband and I would simply glide through them, hand in hand. I know now that that was a romantic fantasy. Real love is listening to the same jokes year after year but not wanting to be anywhere else but right there at his side. Real love is knowing that he would do the same. Real love is knowing, even during disagreements, that the man in front of you is truly your best friend.

—Rosemarie

She reads gory murder mysteries. I prefer biographies. She laughs at "The Honeymooners" I find "Martin" hilarious. It doesn't matter. We read together. We watch each other's shows. We just want to be in the same room, growing old together like we've been doing for the past fifteen years.

—James

We used to just let our tempers flare and say whatever was on our minds. Now, after forty years, we know better than to hurt each other like that. I know where he is strong and he knows where I'm weak. We stay away from areas which might cause a pointless argument that doesn't add anything to our marriage. Anyway, I never say that Leo and I are growing old together. What is old anyway? We're starting to get involved in more activities and having a lot more fun. We're not getting old together. We're getting better together.

—Elaine

There are not too many "old" couples these days. It is not that we are not living longer, and that the years do not pile up, but more that we don't look old, act old or feel old.

Years ago, people accepted being old after they reached the age of forty. They started to wear clothes for the old, shoes for the old and acted old, too.

Now, it's hard to find those formless, styleless dresses, cotton stockings and lace-up shoes that proclaimed to the world you had reached the age of sexless wisdom. We stay young longer now and married people retain their youth and vitality longer. Women often retain the spring in their step into their eighties and beyond.

Why is this? By and large it is because long-married couples in compatible matches are reasonably content with their lives, and provide a central core of care and support for each other. If there are children and grandchildren, they add more loving contact to a support network. One of the conditions that has been found to contribute to longevity of marriage is an involved, supportive network of caring people as part of the couple's life. Other factors include having an optimistic attitude about life, performing meaningful work within our ability and interest levels and being able to love one or more people, including one's mate, of course.

If you are getting on in years or plan to, and you expect and want to do so within your happy enough marriage 'til death do you part, here are some guides that should help.

Social support. No matter how carefully we plan our lives, and how carefully we try to protect ourselves and our loved ones, there will always be mishaps, setbacks, perhaps catastrophes that occur willy-nilly. Illness, deaths, job loss, arrests or drug involvements for our children are the kinds of pressures that you may encounter along the way. These problems require the help of people outside the couple. When you can turn to a group of people you know and trust and who will rally around you both, the result is less strain on your relationship and less pressure on each of you. Surround yourself with people you like. Remember to be open to include younger people as friends. It is very dismal to see your small group of friends die off one by one, leaving you alone and wondering why.

Enjoy the grandchildren. Studies have found that African American grandmothers are more actively involved in the lives of their grandchildren than are the grandmothers in other groups. Unfortunately, more and more of these grandmothers are being given total responsibility for the children of parents who are incapable of raising them. That is a problem for another book. But for the older couple to be actively involved with their grandchildren is an opportunity to see the world unfold through fresh eyes and to enjoy the children's growing up without the worries they bore when bringing up their own children. At least, not the same worries. A close relationship with your grandchildren enriches your life. Tell them your stories, cook your favorite foods for them, show them your skills, listen to their stories, triumphs and complaints, listen to music together, provide them with the loving support and family heritage that can be offered only by you.

No more empty nest syndrome. Thirty years ago, we used to hear of parents who became despondent when their last child left home, if only to go to college. It was called the empty nest syndrome. Presumably, husbands and wives found that they had nothing in common to talk about anymore, were bored with each other, found little interest in sex and turned their sights away from each other. That was the time that men walked away from their long-term wives and into the arms of a much younger woman. The wives turned to depression, refuge in alcohol, or to greater demands on their children's attention.

The empty nest syndrome is rarely mentioned today, because it is rarely found. The TV ideal wife did not work outside of her home and built her life around the care of her children, husband and home. When she was faced with no children to fuss over, no one to eat her fancy meals, no laundry and household disorder to occupy her, and no outside involvements that meant much, she faced emptiness. She felt increasingly useless, clung to her husband too much for his comfort and without shared interest in the children, the couple found that they had little in common. The basic problem in these situations was caused by the fact that the couple had wrapped their lives around their children's. To be so child-centered that you find that the children's needs not only your primary but your only concern is dangerous . If the children come before your husband or wife in every way; if you find that your conversations are only about the children; if they interrupt your conversations with adults and you comply by turning your attention to them; if they can sleep in your bed when they want to and they mostly want to; if your menus are about their preferences only; if you resent spending money on anyone but them; if every vacation outing or entertainment is according to the children's desires or your view of their educational needs—then you are dangerously child-centered.

This is burdensome for the children. Children feel too much in control to feel safe, and therefore, cannot depend on their parents' wisdom and protection. They develop a false sense of the world that ill prepares them to get along in the outside world of adults and peers. They become over-dependent on their parents and in general, do not develop emotionally with a sense of competence. Excessive doting is not to their benefit and it takes away any strength from the foundation of your marriage. The shell that is left when the children leave does not withstand the removal of its central core. When the children go, the marriage collapses. Even when the children do not leave home after their education, the marriages still break up because the common bond of raising the children has ended.

If you find yourself in this child-centered mode, reread this book to enliven your marital life. Do not misconstrue any of what we say as advocating child neglect. Children do best as part of a mutually caring, mutually nurturing family structure where *everyone* counts. They learn that their contributions are important and appreciated, and they learn how to value and appreciate others as well as themselves. Two parents who care for each other and for the children provide security. One over-attentive parent and one who is left out provides an insecure, anxious base. Two over-attentive parents causes the child to wonder why he needs so much attention. While few African American women had and have the luxury of staying home and burying themselves in the lives of their children, many of us translate our perception of the dangers surrounding them to a fierce over-protectiveness or to compensatory over-involvement with our children because of unaddressed dissatisfactions with our husbands. Some fathers try to realize, through their children, their own unfulfilled dreams, or to see that their children have all the love and attention that was lacking in their lives. The excessive extremes of these patterns cause us to neglect our marriage and that causes the trouble.

We have many opportunities to make our marriage even more

exciting and fun after we have launched the children. For one thing, we have more time to devote to it, not only because the children are now on their own, but also because we may not be working as hard to "make it." We might even be retired so that we have even more emotional space for our mate and our life together.

This is the time to plan together to explore all the things you always wanted to explore but did not have the time to do. Classical music concerts, jazz, museums, visiting parks, subscribing to a science magazine, trying out different foods, taking a course for the public, going dancing and all the rest. These activities are interesting, make *you* interesting, brighten your life and give you lots to talk about.

Dress up and go out on dates. Why can't Friday or Saturday night be your night to go out? When you were courting, one or both of those nights probably were. And take vacations. If you cannot afford to go away, make a weekend or even a week your vacation at home. Follow the vacation routine and do things that would characterize a vacation in your city. Help each other stay in that mode. It could be lots of fun.

Has sex become humdrum and infrequent? During menopause and after, many women feel more sexual than ever. Allow yourself to be turned on. Men may need a little extra stimulation. Go for it! Look through *The Joy of Sex* and try out the different positions. Talk love talk. Make noise. You have the house to yourself. You can give and get massages and choose fondling each other as an activity for the day, rather than as a prelude to sex. Don't forget to take time for all the foreplay you need. If impotence or painful intercourse is a problem, don't hesitate to seek medical help. There are a number of medications that help restore erections and many treatments for thinning vaginas. Take advantage of medical progress. But remember, you can have gratifying sex without traditional intercourse. Mouths, tongues, fingers are all erogenous zones. Experiment. Talk about what feels good. Guide your partner to the best sensations for you, and enjoy his or her guiding you in the same way. Never criticize. Just seek pleasure and enjoy giving it. You be responsible for your delights. Don't delegate that responsibility to your mate. Finally, the habit of a hug and a kiss in the kitchen and holding hands every chance you get can accent your renewed romance all day, every day.

You have been married a long time. That makes you survivors, winners. You know each other's quirks, habits, sensitivities. You are accustomed to being together. You have given and received much from each other and with your ability to commit, you have found the strength to weather the storms that tear so many couples apart. Still, you may have neglected your friendship. Now is the time to renew your friendship by treating each other as best friends. All that goes into having and being a best friend should be directed to each other. Best friend, romantic partner, life mate . . . The best is yet to come.

PART FIVE:

Career Conflicts

CHAPTER TWENTY-THREE

The Fast Track

"The ultimate of being successful is the luxury of giving your-
self the time to do what you want to do."
—Leontyne Price
Newsday, February 1, 1976

Work is supposed to enable you to enjoy your life. It is not life
itself. Life is composed of time. None of us has an unlimited amount
of this precious commodity. If both of you are working on the fast
track, slow down just a little and work on the marriage. Some
couples can't enjoy their own nuptials for fear of disrupting their
careers. For men and women on the fast track who have large,
formal weddings, returning to work after the honeymoon is often
a relief. Suzanne, a 31-year-old public relations executive told us:

*"I'm so happy that my wedding is over because all the plan-
ning took me away from too much of my work. Now that
life has returned to normal, I'm thinking about taking on
some new clients and setting higher performance goals for
myself."*

Her husband, Dan, a 36-year-old motivational speaker announced
happily:

*"My lecture agent says that this is going to be a great year
for me. He has sixteen cities lined up already and I'm spending
the next few weeks working on a new presentation."*

Just because a man and woman are successful in their chosen fields, does not mean that they can stay married. Many people are obsessed with the strategic moves they need to make to advance their careers to the extent that their marriages take second place in their lives. When both people are super-involved in their work, like Suzanne and Dan, there aren't too many disagreements about the lack of time one has for the other. However, when one person is super-involved in his career and the other takes a more moderate view, misunderstandings and hurt feelings are usually the result.

Analda, a psychiatric nurse, married Barry McClain when he had just finished law school and was starting out with a prestigious firm. She had heard that beginning lawyers worked long hours but she had no idea that that meant spending most of her time alone, even on weekends. She started thinking about divorce after they had been married only three years. "I figured that since I was alone all the time anyway, it might as well be made official. Even when Barry was home, all he talked about was work. Which partner was getting which case. Who thought they were going to make partner and didn't. Which court decisions had been the most surprising. I mean, the list just went on and on." They ended up in counseling.

COUNSELOR: *Barry, do you understand what Analda is complaining about?*

BARRY: *Listen, this isn't just about me. I work hard for both of us.*

ANALDA: *Even when the firm gives you time off, you won't take it. That's not for us. You've just become obsessed with that job.*

BARRY: *I'm dedicated to my work right now. It won't be this way forever.*

COUNSELOR: *How much longer do you think Analda will have to spend so much of her time alone?*

BARRY: *Another five years at most.*

ANALDA: *Five years! You must be crazy!*

COUNSELOR: *Is that your choice or a company requirement?*

BARRY: *Well, it is pretty much my choice. I'm learning a lot and I can move up faster if I just stick to my game plan.*

COUNSELOR: *How is your relationship with Analda when you do have time at home?*

BARRY: *Okay, I guess.*

COUNSELOR: *Guess?*

BARRY: *I don't mind being at home, but sometimes Analda just won't give me any space.*

ANALDA: *That's because you're rarely at home. When you do find the time, I want us to talk and be close.*

BARRY: *What she really means is that she wants to crawl all over me and I really can't stand it. Especially when she starts asking for sex.*

COUNSELOR: *So, I think it is fair to say that maybe you spend so much time at work because you wish things at home were different and that Analda sticks to you when you do find time to go home because she misses you. This excessive closeness makes you want to take off again? Then the whole vicious circle begins again.*

BARRY: *I haven't thought about it like that.*

It is obvious that Barry felt suffocated by Analda and used his career as an excuse to avoid her. Their treatment took a different turn after this revelation, and they began to focus more on basic compatibility issues. As of this writing, they are still working things out.

Even when neither of you is a workaholic, obligations to your respective companies can make it hard to carve out some leisure time together. Sometimes, one partner is exhausted or just not available. This is why many fast-track couples end up having separate social lives. Although it is important to have some alone time, don't let this become a habit.

Donna and Henry came into couples' therapy as an almost perfunctory, last gesture before calling an end to their marriage. They had been married for six years, and described at least four of those years as unhappy. Since they married, they had both become increasingly involved with their jobs. Things reached the point where they didn't have a meaningful conversation for weeks at a time. They pretended that everything was okay. Both of them kept up cheerful facades. Henry was slated to make vice president in a few months so he grew extremely morose and irritable when the therapist suggested that they both take some time off from work. Donna understood his feelings because she had some of the same emotions. Nevertheless, she succeeded in cheering him up and they both agreed that they should make an attempt to save the marriage.

During their marriage treatment they came to realize that they still loved each other. They actually had to get to know each other once more and were saddened to discover how much closer they were to friends, coworkers and other outsiders.

When Donna told Henry that she wanted to share her successes with him in the future, he understood. He discovered that he wanted the same thing, too. They both left therapy with renewed patience and optimism.

They took a three-week vacation together. It was good for both of them and wonderful for the marriage.

Jacqueline and Victor both had high profile careers which meant long hours and extensive travel for both of them. They were able to make decisions collectively and had respect for each other's professional lives. Jacqueline and Victor knew how to pursue their separate careers and then get together to laughingly share their experiences. They both had a sense of humor and never let things get too heavy between them. Best of all, they actually enjoyed talking to each other, which is one of the foundations of a good marriage.

Jacqueline and Victor have found the right balance between love and work. Although they are steadily climbing upward, both feel that their marriage comes first and they are determined to stay together and not take life too seriously.

Mick and Glory's problem was that they defined success by their job titles and material possessions. When both of them were downsized, they had no identities at all. They couldn't think of anything to talk about aside from worrying about what their friends must be thinking of their fall from grace. They wandered around their home, touching objects they didn't want to part with. They were like ships passing in the night.

Their marriage counselor helped Mick and Glory learn to delegate some of their work once they both found new jobs and stop taking themselves so seriously. It took more than a year but they both developed hobbies and reconnected with family. They were on the right track when they finally learned that success shouldn't be measured by the title or position you acquire, but rather, by the obstacles you overcome and the full life you have created for yourself.

CHAPTER TWENTY-FOUR

White Collar/Blue Collar Liaisons

"Sticks in a bundle are unbreakable."
—Kenyan proverb

I had just passed my 38th birthday when I began to panic. All my girlfriends had found husbands while the only man that seemed interested in me was Kevin. Kevin's mother and mine had grown up together. He was two years older than me and we were both only children. Kevin's mother had been hoping for years that our relationship would go beyond "just friends." I never considered a romance with Kevin until my "gonna be an old maid" panic set in. Suddenly, Kevin didn't seem so bad. He was tall, handsome, reliable and quiet. He didn't drink or smoke and had his own car and apartment. Plus, he'd had a crush on me since childhood. So, I ignored my mother, who had hoped to see me married to a professional man and ended up at the altar holding the arm of a driver for UPS. Kevin wanted a big wedding but I insisted that the guest list be limited to family because I had lied to my friends and coworkers. They thought he was an executive. I had worked hard for my M.B.A. and was doing well in my job in marketing for an international cosmetics company. I knew that the truth about Kevin was bound to come out if my associates were mingling with Kevin's friends at a wedding reception. I didn't want to hurt Kevin's feelings by telling him all this, so I just said our day should be "private." Kevin turned out to be really smart but he had no ambition. I convinced him to enroll in a nearby community college. He quit after the first semester because "he was too tired for classes after driving the truck all day." On one of his birthdays, I gave him a book called Success Without College. *He read it and didn't do any of the exercises. I finally told my close friends the truth about Kevin and they were very supportive of me but whenever I had company, he would shut himself in the bedroom and I had to beg him to come out. By our third anniversary, Kevin and I were both tired of each other and thinking about divorce.*

—Betty

According to a 1994 report by the *Wall Street Journal,* the number of black female professionals grew at an astonishing rate between 1982 and 1992 and they currently number almost 200,000. However, the number of black male professionals has declined, because corporations find African American women less threatening and prefer to hire them over an African American male. Black women know that there are not enough professional husbands to satisfy the demand. As a result, some of them decide to marry a blue collar man. Unfortunately, many of these women intend "to change the situation" once they are married.

"Change the man after you marry him." Women have been trying to do this in one way or another since the beginning of time. It almost always fails. They also find that it is next to impossible to re-raise an adult. Serious effort to improve, reform, rescue or otherwise change the person we married almost inevitably leads to frustration or disaster, and just about never to the desired changes.

When we consider how we become the person we are, we realize that it is a long and complex process with an unpredictable outcome. We are born with a genetic predisposition to temperament, to body build and biological function, to the way our mind works and perhaps to our basic pattern of likes and dislikes.

Countless studies of identical twins, especially of those raised apart, even those separated at birth, show that they are very much alike at any given age. Forty-year-old twins meeting for the first time find for example, that both smoke pipes, play chess, win at tennis, play the violin and are teachers. Apparently, they are born with these inclinations.

Our parenting, especially during our first three years, is especially important in shaping who we are as adults. The more loving, consistent and appropriately supportive that care, the more secure and confident the child. If the child is sufficiently fortunate to be surrounded with accepting approval, a stimulating environment and opportunities to demonstrate and develop social and academic competence, she develops a strong sense of self. What she learns about the world, what she is rewarded for or punished about, the opportunities and barriers in her way, the friends she chooses, the world events that occur during her lifetime—these things and more interact with her original genetic heritage to form the person she is when she marries.

Yes, we continue to develop until the day we die. In adulthood, accumulated life experiences or we, ourselves, can change us to some degree, but rarely can wives or husbands change us in any significant way. By the time we reach maturity, we mostly know who we are. And for better and for worse, we like and are loyal to our person. We don't take lightly efforts to invalidate who we are by trying to make us different, even in areas that we actually would like to change.

What about the other side? By the time we marry, we usually have developed a picture of our ideal mate. This ideal is formed from what we have observed our opposite sex parent to be or what our same sex parent has implied or told us to look for in a mate.

Betty was concerned because she felt that her husband was not working hard enough to make their marriage succeed. She wanted him to earn a college degree in order to qualify for a white collar job. She thought that she was very supportive to him by repeatedly telling him that he had the ability to accomplish these goals, and even assuring him that she was happy to pay for their expenses while he pursued these opportunities.

Kevin believed that he was already working hard enough for their marriage. He said he brought home steady pay which demonstrated that he was man enough and responsible. He tried to please her but he was who he was and could not and would not try to be a different person. He wondered why Betty had married him if she was so dissatisfied about him. He also said that it was getting to be less and less tolerable to feel that Betty was ashamed of him before her snobbish friends.

As their work proceeded, it became clear that Betty did indeed reject the person she had married. She had seen him as raw material to be brushed up and polished to be more like the men in her circle who had rejected her as wife material. She wanted Kevin's devotion and loyalty, his unselfish consideration of her needs and wishes, and also his inherent dignity and pride. She wanted all that plus a self-presentation that met the approval of her friends and colleagues and that fulfilled her fantasies about the ideal husband and perfect father of her children.

By the conclusion of their marriage therapy, they both had discovered a key factor for marital success—acceptance. Betty struggled through the wounds to her self-esteem by her sense of not being considered good enough to be chosen by those she admired, as well as by all the failings an ambitious person has experienced by the age of forty. She learned to reclaim her sense of adequacy. In so doing, she released Kevin from carrying that burden. She also had to struggle with her responsibility for the happiness of her mother. As the only child, she had always worked hard to fulfill her mother's expectations. She earned the best grades, did her chores faithfully, went far in school and was a professional success. It was important to her to give back to her mother by seeing to her happiness. A good marriage was part of what she owed her mother and she wanted to give that to her, as well. The therapy helped her to understand that the best gift to her mother would be her own happiness, with or without a mate.

Kevin was able to acknowledge his idealization of Betty, which had led to two problems. Kevin accepted whatever Betty said as unassailable and therefore every "suggestion" by her was experienced as an attack on his adequacy, with an in-hand threat to leave him if he did not comply. He had reacted with protective defensiveness, muted rage expressed by overcompensating, approval seeking behaviors. He learned that if he took what Betty said more at face value than as an indictment of his worth, he could explore the ideas, express his feelings and make up his own mind. The couples' treatment provided opportunities for Betty and Kevin to practice a more democratic interaction style, leading to less anger and frustration for both of them.

By the end of the couples' treatment, Betty rediscovered her appreciation of Kevin's many positive qualities and her basic love and respect for him. She was less inclined to try to change him. Kevin was reassured by Betty's feelings. He also decided that it was not to his discredit to aim for advancement in his job, but that he need not do so only by returning to school. They both agreed on a basic lifestyle for the near future, became truly supportive of each other and more loving and close.

If you love and respect your husband, here are some ways to show it:

1. **Don't allow your friends and relatives to put him down.**

   A lot of women believe that when they hang out with the girls, everything said is left in the room. Suppose you fall out with one of these ladies. She can make sure he finds out "how you and everyone else really feel about him." He will feel really hurt by the gossip and resent you for his humiliation.

2. **Don't hide him.**

Many sisters don't mind sleeping blue collar but they don't plan to take these husbands to corporate events or any other place where there is a chance of his meeting someone from the office. Believe me, he knows why you cheerfully "let him off the hook" after receiving an upscale invitation.

3. **Don't talk down to him.**

When you talk to a man as though he is illiterate, it will make him defend his wounded pride by hurting you in any way he can.

4. **Don't make up stories about him.**

When the two of you are around your associates, avoid saying things like, "Oh, Tom may be a carpenter now but that's just because he's studying for the bar." A scene like this can't help but tell a man that you can't stand who he is.

5. **Don't expect him to pay half of everything.**

If you're making $100,000 a year and your husband brings home $300 a week, how can he contribute the same amount of money that you do to the household and leisure time activities?

6. **Don't talk about your job all the time.**

An affluent black woman has probably scaled many brick walls to succeed. It is only natural and right that she take pride in her accomplishments. But put yourself in his place. Concentrate on finding activities that you both can enjoy and talk about later.

When A Man Becomes Threatened By His Wife's Financial Success

Unfortunately, a blue collar husband may begin to feel threatened if his wife's salary continues to climb rapidly after the wedding. He may become acutely embarrassed by his own status and fearful that you will become attracted to another man in your professional circle. Once the husband feels that you have outgrown him and might leave the marriage, he will just give up on his sensitivity training and start acting out. Many times his behavior becomes excessively macho. This can be very hard to deal with and professional counseling is definitely needed so that the marriage can continue in a healthy fashion.

A Brother Talks About His Wife's Macho Job

I have been married for 23 years. For the past sixteen years, my wife has been a cop. She has been successful in moving up the ranks to captain and may eventually become the first African American police chief in our medium-sized city! She is extremely happy with what she does and I could not be more happy and proud of her accomplishments. When we were married I was committed to support her in reaching her career goals, whatever path she chose. It has proven to be the best decision I ever made in our relationship. I remember when many of my male friends asked me, "Why are you letting your wife become a cop?" I was dumbfounded. How was I going to tell another functioning adult what she could not do? My wife would not have allowed me to dictate to her what her career or other life choices should be. I knew that.

Woman Blue Collar/Man White Collar

Colette, aged thirty is a Railroad Clerk for the New York City Transit Authority. She is good at her job and happy with her high school education. Colette is extremely attractive and is constantly approached for dates by coworkers and subway riders alike but she is faithful to her husband.

Grant, aged thirty-four is an advertising agency account executive. He has an MBA from New York University but was not a very happy man until he met Colette three years ago. The couple had just celebrated their first wedding anniversary when an exasperated Grant insisted that they start marriage counseling.

COUNSELOR: *Grant, tell us why you wanted to come here.*

GRANT: *Colette and I spend far too much time arguing about women I have to interact with in order to do my job. I'm tired of it.*

COLETTE: *These women are calling my house. I don't like it and I don't know any other females who would put up with it, either.*

GRANT: *This is not about your girlfriends. It is about my career. The jobs that your girlfriends' husbands have don't require calls at home.*

COLETTE: *So, what are you trying to say? That you're better than them?*

GRANT: *No. That my job is different from theirs. Anyway, the project that I'm working on will be over in a few weeks and the calls will stop.*

COLETTE: *Then tell me why you don't get calls from businessmen? How come every time I pick up the phone, it is a woman?*

GRANT: *First of all, you're making it sound like our phone rings continuously. The total number of business-related calls that I got at home last month was ten.*

COLETTE: *Fine. How many of those ten calls were from women?*

GRANT: *I don't know but it really doesn't matter if it was one call or all ten. You have got to trust me.*

COUNSELOR: *Let's talk about trust for a moment. Colette?*

COLETTE: *I trust him but I don't want these women to think I'm some kind of fool.*

COUNSELOR: *So, you're actually worried about what these women think of you?*

COLETTE: *Now you're confusing me.*

COUNSELOR: *Sorry.*

COLETTE: *I'm worried that Grant might start cheating on me.*

GRANT: *And you think putting a stop to my calls will prevent that?*

COLETTE: *No, but the two of you won't make your plans on my phone.*

GRANT: *Our phone.*

COLETTE: *Whatever.*

COUNSELOR: *Colette, why do you think Grant wants another woman in his life?*

COLETTE: *Because he's not satisfied with the one he has.*

GRANT: *What are you talking about?*

COLETTE: *You criticized the way I talk, how I dress and even how I eat. You must be comparing me to somebody.*

It turned out that Colette and Grant had attended a company dinner a few months before. Grant, concerned that she might not be making a good impression in front of his boss, started searching the room and comparing Colette's outfit, mannerisms and demeanor to those of the other women in the room. Colette did not realize that this was just a general comparison. She was under the mistaken impression that there was one particular woman he was interested in. This set off a chain reaction which came to a head over the phone calls. Grant and Colette agreed that they needed to relearn the importance of honest communication.

Rex shows a profound disregard for my professional abilities. I'm proud of what I have accomplished and I know Rex is just putting on a front when he puts me down. It is just a way of making himself feel better. But If find myself holding back on the job. If I get another promotion, it could cost me my marriage.
—Hilda

Hilda is doing herself a terrible disservice. She has to be allowed to grow as far as her talents will take her. She and Rex have decided to get professional help.

The key to making white collar/blue collar liaisons work is acceptance and "we" not "me" thinking. Many couples have found lasting and fulfilling love in these type of marriages.
So can you.

CHAPTER TWENTY-FIVE

Long-Distance Love

"Before you marry keep both eyes open; after marriage shut one."

—Jamaican proverb

After Rupert Sandifer lost his job due to company cutbacks, he was unemployed for almost six months. It seemed like no one in Boston needed another stock analyst. Desperate, Rupert started interviewing in New York City and quickly landed a position paying nearly twice his old salary. Myrle, however, did not want to quit her teaching job or pull their teenaged sons out of a school where they were both doing well. Rupert took the job anyway and theirs became a commuter marriage. "It's been tough on my family," says Rupert "but the market is tough right now, even for Blacks with a college degree. We have to go where the jobs are."

We are living in a time of backlash against Black progress and affirmative action is dead. African Americans have survived backlash before. We will overcome this episode, as well. In the meantime, it is becoming even harder than normal for African Americans to get a job, regardless of our qualifications. Moves up the corporate ladder and into the boardroom are rare. In the current climate, when a promotion, bonus or job offer are at stake, not too many of us are willing to turn down an opportunity because it is in another state.

In the meantime, the spouse also has a job that he or she cares about. Often, we have children who should not be uprooted by frequent moves. Frequently what results is a committed couple living apart. They may see each other as frequently as every week-end, or as rarely as once a month. These arrangements put a lot of stress on a marriage.

SURVIVING THE LONG-DISTANCE MARRIAGE

Tip: The wife is away. No, this is not the time to call old girlfriends to see how they're doing. Not the time for a second bachelor's party, either. How about fixing some of those things around the house that you've been promising to fix?

Jealousy & Suspicion

Florence is a road manager for a hot rhythm & blues act. She is one of the few women in a profession dominated almost entirely by men. Her husband, Antonio, is head of the computer trouble-shooting department at a large financial company on Wall Street. Florence has her eye on a singer whom she is trying to groom for stardom so that she can move into personal artist management. The singer is tall, broad-shouldered and pretty-boy handsome. He also has a charisma that Florence hopes will reach across the stage and land in the lap of an audience of adoring females.

Florence is astute enough to realize that her protégé has issues that probably began because he was abandoned by his mother. He requires a lot of nurturing and she is there to give it to him.

Henry believes that Florence has been faithful but he is wonder-ing how long that can last. Every time she comes home from the road, he wants to hear about her experiences in minute and excruciating detail. Sometimes, she needs to clear her head and think about what her latest experiences all mean before having a conversation about them. And she becomes crabby when he presses. "Every time I try to tell my husband that I don't cheat on him when I'm out of town, he makes me feel guilty. It is really beginning to bother me. I really hate it when he starts signifying. He makes little snide remarks that get under my skin. I don't know how serious Antonio is when he starts making infidelity jokes."

Sometimes, Florence just lets the signifying roll of her back. At other times when she is under pressure, Florence will respond sarcastically, which provokes an argument between them. Antonio said, "I know my wife has never cheated on me but I'm sure that men are throwing themselves at her in these strange cities. And why can't she leave the hotel phone numbers for me to contact her?" As Florence realized, trying to communicate with someone under a cloud of suspicion is very difficult. If she does try to talk as soon as she gets home, as evidence of her fidelity, Antonio will feel that she is trying to salve her conscience. If she ignores his comments, Antonio's suspicions simply grow. She can't win either way.

A position like this leaves even the best union unprotected. It is not irrational to wonder what the other half is doing. But it can make the one who travels feel resentful. This is not unusual among couples who spend a great deal of time apart. The only way to handle this situation is to face it head-on. Both parties need to be open in airing their concerns and fears. Right now, there is too much being left unsaid. Florence and Antonio aren't really communicating at all. Before starting the talk, each person should make a written list of his or her issues. This way, the discussion can stay focused without deteriorating into an argument. Antonio needs to stop the infidelity jokes. Florence should allow Antonio to telephone at any time and she should promise to return the calls as soon as she can. What Antonio really wants is reassurance. Florence could say something like, "I'm still yours baby. I'll tell you all about the trip after a nap and a shower."

Virginia was appointed to a high-level position heading an important government agency. Her headquarters were in Washington, D.C. Wilson wanted to move there with her but they decided that such a move for him would not be practical. They could not sell their house in Long Island, he had no job prospects in Washington's tight job market and Virginia's job was a political appointment that had no guarantees of lasting beyond the current term of office. She found a small apartment and settled into the routine of working for extended hours during the week and commuting home on Friday afternoons. She found that she felt free to spend as much time as she needed at her office. It was a relief not to have to worry about getting home early enough to cook dinner. Virginia realized that she was a workaholic but she enjoyed what she did and was well-rewarded for it.

Wilson missed Virginia. The fact that they agreed that she would call him every night before she went to bed helped. He was reassured that she was safe. They had long telephone conversations that kept each other up on their day-to-day lives. He often won-

dered why he was never interested in having such conversations before she left.

SURVIVING THE LONG-DISTANCE MARRIAGE

Tip: The husband is away. This is not the time for male bashing sessions with your girlfriends. It is not an opportunity for you to raid his closet and throw out all the clothes that you don't like. How about videotaping his favorite sports team at play to send him by overnight mail?

There is no way a mate can convince a jealous spouse of his faithfulness. Whatever he says can be heard as suspicious. If he does not present a plea of innocence, it is heard as an admission of guilt. If he protests vehemently, it is heard as a cover-up. This is a lose-lose argument. If you are inclined to be insecure in your marriage and have a tendency to be jealous, try to recognize that your alternatives are few. If you get no admissions, either you will have to hire a private detective or find some other way of spying on your husband or wife.

Or, you can relax and trust.

Just because your mate spends nights away from home in your commuter marriage, does not mean that a third party is entering the picture. Too much jealousy can ruin an otherwise good marriage.

SURVIVING THE LONG-DISTANCE MARRIAGE

Tip: Use your traveling home time to shed the tensions of your work. Arrive home refreshed. Pay attention to your family. Enjoy them. Leave your work in a closed briefcase.

When Dwight is away on business, I telephone him a lot and then I log how much time it takes him to call me back.

—Petra

Petra thinks she is checking up on me by making these incessant telephone calls to me while I'm away. It's silly because I could be with a woman and interrupt our conversation to take Petra's call. The calls just interrupt me and are embarrassing.

—Dwight

After Dwight voiced his frustration, Petra admitted that when he is away on trips, her girlfriends fill her head with stories of male infidelity. And they love to tease her about her naïveté. Finally, she put a stop to it by warning them that she would ask them to leave as soon as the jokes started about men who play around on business trips. She was serious. They knew it and they stopped.

The stay-at-home partner should keep busy with an exciting life. Focus your attention on making productive use of your time when your mate is away. And pay attention to enjoying intimacy when the two of you are together. Don't waste your time imagining things that upset you. Just sitting around worrying would not prevent your worst nightmare from coming true, so why bother? Drop this emotional burden.

Sometimes, the at-home mate believes that the traveling spouse is having a wonderful, glamorous time while away. This is especially true when the travel or assignment is in an exciting city. Dinners on company expense accounts, fancy hotels, meetings with important people, getting respect because of image and position . . . Home seems very dull in contrast.

Dennie heard this often from her husband, Vin. She noticed his increasing resentment of her trips, even though they were a necessary part of her job. His questions about her trips always seemed to have an edge. They talked about these reactions and he admitted that he was somewhat envious of her. He also worried that she might be comparing him to the men she met and finding him lacking. She tried to assure him that this was not the case. She hated having to eat dinner either in her hotel room or alone in a restaurant. Often she skipped dinner and made do with some peanuts or a candy bar. The flying was uncomfortable, airports a hassle, negotiating the foreign languages was frustrating. As a woman, she had to push so as not to be ignored. The men she met were far from interesting to her and besides, they hardly ever made eye contact with her. She was too exhausted by the time night came to do little but talk to him on the phone, feel lonesome and fall asleep.

When time for the next trip came, she asked Vin to come with her. He was delighted. Dennie had a lot more fun because Vin was there, but he also had to admit that the whole experience was a lot less glamorous than he had imagined. The result of this is Vin's undiluted joy in welcoming Dennie when she returns from her business trips. He feels better about her work and gives her a lot of credit for enduring so much boring, company-related travel.

SURVIVING THE LONG-DISTANCE MARRIAGE

Some More Tips:

♦ Take your spouse's concerns seriously. Don't ridicule them.
♦ Talk over all the problems. Remember, if one of you has a problem, both of you have a problem.
♦ Do what you can to demystify your life away from home.

There are many long-term marriages that have sustained years of separation because of employment demands. Some couples cannot get together even monthly because of distance and expense. Yet they remain bonded and loyal to each other. Such marriages involve mates who are individually independent, resourceful and positive in outlook. They are firmly committed to their marriage and to their mate. They are not distractible, but habitually focused on their priority issues. They are flexible, self-directed and are more rather than less secure about themselves.

Separations within marriage present plenty of challenge to keep things together. Make the effort, because long-distance love can work.

PART SIX:

Money Matters

CHAPTER TWENTY-SIX

The Spender vs. The Saver

"Save money and money will save you."
—Jamaican proverb

As we've said repeatedly throughout this book, two people bring two different backgrounds, life experiences and ways of living to every aspect of their new life together. The way you view and handle money is undoubtedly unique to you. Money is a potentially explosive issue and the leading cause of conflict among couples, especially during the first years of marriage. These conflicts can lead to big disappointments and hurtful confrontations. Money disputes are so harmful that they can lead to divorce court. How to spend your money is an extremely loaded issue.

If you and your husband are over thirty and have been working and spending your own money for years as single individuals, it is even harder to learn how to consult with someone else on financial matters. After all, you have been accustomed to spending your own hard-earned money however you saw fit.

How to spend the money should not be a control issue. Decisions should be based on which methods of spending and saving will help you as a couple reach the goals the two of you have set—together. This means that it doesn't matter whether the husband and wife earn the same amount or one makes more than the other. Your mutual goals are all that count. Here are just a few of the issues that must be discussed and basic decisions that need to be made if the goals that the two of you have decided on are to stand a good chance of being reached:

♦ Should you have a joint account where all the funds are comingled, or do you prefer separate accounts for individual spending and a savings account for mutual goals?
♦ Who will sit down and actually write the checks each month?
♦ How much will it cost to reach a major goal (such as saving the down payment on a house) and where should that money be stored?
♦ How will you handle extra money (such as job bonuses) that comes in the house?
♦ Will the two of you have weekly spending allowances? What will that amount cover and when is it okay to dip into the accounts for more?

An important source of trouble for any marriage is conflict over money management. Of course, there is a major marriage threat if neither of you knows how to manage the family income, or there simply is not enough money, no matter how skilled the management. But disagreement about spending and saving is worse and there is little or no likelihood that you will find yourselves closer as a result of unresolved trouble.

The reason that conflict over money use can be so destructive is that in this society, money has come to represent the most elemental of survival forces. Self-esteem, respect, power, generosity, love, deprivation, success, failure, acceptance, rejection and security are just some of the forces that the idea and the use of money represent. That is a heavy load. Depending on how powerful the energy connected to one or more of these forces, the more inflamed the conflict between husband and wife when they seriously differ about money matters.

It is all very complicated. If we are prevented from handling money so as to feel good and safe around issues such as deprivation and acceptance, we become deeply afraid. We become equally intolerant of our mate's money behavior, if his behavior would make us feel anxious and unsafe were we to adopt it. If we believe our mate is pushing us into money behaviors that make us feel insecure and imperiled, or handles money him or herself in these ways, we may become too upset to tolerate both the situation and our mate. If our mate has the same degree of negative passion about our way of handling money, we are in for double the trouble. All of this left to run its course leads to a broken marriage.

Couples argue a lot about money. This is good, if the arguing brings your ideas about money and your behaviors relating to money closer together, or if it makes you more accepting of each other's money habits. As we know, when couples argue wisely, they work out a win-win resolution. But sometimes the differences are too far apart, or the feelings are too entrenched to settle for less than total victory for you and total surrender for your mate. Then what?

Jill considered herself a champion shopper. She knew where to find the bargains for any type of item. She knew what brand was better for what and where you could get it wholesale. Jill loved to shop. And she did a lot of it. Herbert recoiled at the idea of buying anything unless it was absolutely essential. Somehow, he considered attractive merchandise to be a lure to trick the gullible to prevent their attaining wealth. He had no respect for those who could not resist the call of materialism. Before they married, he considered Jill's spending and buying a peculiar but somewhat amusing little habit.

After they married and had pooled their income, he found himself becoming less tolerant and finally furious about what he saw as wasteful weakness. Jill found herself sneaking in any new purchase, discarding paper bags before she arrived home, pulling off price tags and otherwise trying not to aggravate Herb. She also found herself becoming angrier and angrier.

They loved each other and did not want to be angry with each other or worse, so they sought help when they could not work things out on their own. They were asked to present their cases. Herb spoke of the need of African Americans to save and invest rather than remain dependent and deprived because of foolish self-indulgences. He sounded very intellectual, very self-righteous. Jill was also self-righteous but very emotional. With tears streaming she protested that she worked every day, earned a good salary and was entitled to spend the little that she did to keep their home attractive and herself as presentable as she was before they married. She hated the way he was with his out-of-style clothes and his cheap ways. She felt so unloved. At this Herb also was moved to tears as he proclaimed that he did love her so very much.

It was evident that their passion had deeper roots than disagreement about budget. As it turned out, both Jill and Herb were the oldest of many siblings of families headed by single mothers. Both families had survived on welfare, and both Herb and Jill were humiliated by that fact. Both were determined to live a better life. They'd worked hard in school, were awarded scholarships for college, and were now living a middle-class life. But they differed in their reactions to their early lives. Herb vowed that he would never, ever be poor again. He did not mind living poor, but he abhorred the notion of *being* poor. So he tended to hoard, to be afraid to spend, to be driven to work, earn and save. Whenever he saw Jill with a purchase he had visions of depleted reserves, bankruptcy, poverty and humiliation. On the other hand, Jill sought to erase the memories of deprivation. Her humiliation had been in having to wear worn out hand-me-downs and Salvation Army shoes that never fit; in never being able to buy a record or a soda; and in being the butt of schoolmates' jokes. She vowed that she would never again be the object of pity because of her poverty. Whenever she bought something she was excited by her ability to do so. Whenever she gave away last year's clothing, replacing it with something new and stylish, she felt triumphant.

Jill and Herbert's spending styles were defensive. Jill defended herself from the hurt of deprivation. Herb defended against the hurt of inferiority represented by lack of money. When Jill spent for what Herb considered unnecessary items, he felt threatened by a plunge back into those earlier hard times. When Jill was stopped from buying what she wanted, she also was threatened by those old familiar feelings that she never wanted to feel again. They had the same basic feelings and fears, but different ways of dealing with them. Their rigidity and their passion about their behaviors indicated that they were dealing with irrational reactions to their shared reality. When they discovered the emotional roots of that shared past, it became less powerful. As a result, they could work out their differences.

This uncovering of how their behavior represented the repair of earlier, painful life circumstances allowed both Herb and Jill to loosen if not cut the ties between their earlier deprivations and their current situation. Thus enabled, they could be more understanding of each other's coping styles. They became more flexible in their thinking, resulting in a harmonious resolution of their spending differences. Their sharing of their previously partially buried memories of their early lives also brought each of them relief and greater closeness and intimacy.

Petunia grew up poor and likes to put away every penny. Her personal nightmare is that she will end up struggling for food or shoes again. Petunia still has relatives living in the ghettoes. She is terribly afraid of slipping up and landing back there. Nelson grew up comfortably middle-class and while he is no spendthrift, Petunia's penny pinching makes him irritable.

Nelson has to try to put himself in Petunia's shoes and walk around in them a bit. If Petunia does not want to talk about her childhood, Nelson can read books on growing up in poverty and try to imagine the horror of being hungry and having nothing to eat. This will make him more sensitive to his wife's plight. Seeing her husband making efforts to understand her past will make Petunia more willing to listen to his point of view. His concern helps build Petunia's trust and affection for him.

Brainstorm solutions to the problem. You are partners, not adversaries. If both of you feel that you have worked on the plan together, then each will have a vested interest in seeing that the plan works.

Muriel and Jack had other problems. Muriel was an adored only child who was given everything she wanted and more. Her husband had to earn everything he got, not necessarily because of financial difficulties in his family, but because his strict parents believed that was the right way to raise him. Muriel never learned to deny herself; Jack never permitted himself to indulge. Their differences were over learned attitudes and habits. Muriel's love of self and capacity to enjoy were traits that had attracted Jack in the first place. Muriel was also attracted by what she considered Jack's strength and wisdom as evidenced, she thought, by his capability in managing his money. Although they made almost equal salaries, when they married, Muriel not only had almost no savings, but also had considerable debt. Jack, on the other hand, had lots of investments and a co-op apartment, too. Muriel did not want to go as far as Jack did with his controls over budget restrictions, but she wanted to learn restraint from him. Jack did not admire his tightness and preferred to join Muriel in her capacity to feel freer to enjoy.

This couple was able to apply themselves to working out a family spending plan that was somewhat more generous with funds for incidentals than Jack would have chosen, and that alloted more for savings than Muriel was accustomed to allot. They agreed to help each other remain true to this budget, and they did.

Whenever a couple sits down to talk about anything, there is always the question of who is going to win. Both parties are interested in being right. Each party intends to prove he or she is right.

At best, couples help each other reach agreed upon family goals for spending and saving. They try to understand each other's attitudes and feelings, and accept each other's right to be who they are. They avoid finger pointing and criticism, even if they differ. They accept their differences. They try to avoid the common pitfall of assuming parent-child roles. (The parent scolds, teaches, directs and punishes. The child complies without agreeing, rebels, wheedles, has tantrums, pouts and depends on the parent to set limits.) The couple stays in their adult-to-adult mode, realistically assesses their financial situation and their own strengths and weaknesses, and comes to a rational agreement about how they will manage. They are not afraid to change things that do not work out. If they find that they cannot deal with each other about these matters without temper, disgust or stalemate, they seek help. They know that this usually means that more is at stake for one or both partner than money alone.

Money just seems to fly out of Brianna's hands. She doesn't even look for bargains. If Brianna sees something we need or want, she just peels the dollars off and marches home with the item. Shopping around for the best price never occurs to her

—Randy

As long as one of them is shrewd about money, financial disaster is avoidable. Before each major purchase, Randy and Brianna could decide on the highest price they are willing to pay and write that amount down for Brianna to take with her to the store. Or, they could shop around for "the best price" together.

Remember, Black men and women have always married for emotional reasons rather than financial—or, the need for a woman to be supported. In this way, our marriages have always been different from those of the dominate culture.

The Logistics

Each of you have different feelings about money and how to handle it. The key is to decide on the financial goals each of you have. Combine these goals into one plan and realistically look at how those goals can be accomplished. Listen to each plan without interrupting, eye rolling or sighing. Such behavior will only make the other partner angry. Here is where empathy comes in.

Most Black families live paycheck to paycheck. There is no cushion of inherited wealth and, most of the time, extended family members don't have enough to loan. Most of us are also first-generation college graduates and professionals, so money is important to us, both literally and symbolically. The agreement you reach together about how to earn enough money—and how to use it—may be vital to keeping harmony in your marriage. Money is a very powerful subject and we all have different attitudes about it.

If ignored, these differences become land mines that can blow up the best of marriages.

CHAPTER TWENTY-SEVEN

When There Isn't Enough Money

"Humor is laughing at what you haven't got when you ought to have it."

—Langston Hughes
The Book of Negro Humor, 1966

Lack of money and the anxiety associated with that lack can be a primary source of stress in marriage. According to the 1993 Census report, one in ten Black men, aged 16–64 years, was not active in the labor market. Some of these men were in the underground economy. Others were too discouraged to keep on trying. Not surprisingly, this number is twice as high as the one for white men.

A far more common scenario is that both members of the couple are working but simply don't earn enough to make ends meet.

Whatever the case, lack of money can produce feelings of inferiority, guilt, helplessness, even anger and the loss of a job is a serious blow to the marriage. It is no wonder that every time the unemployment rates rise, so do the number of divorces. If you are one of the African American couples who are disappointed in your sex role expectations (for example, if you are a man who can't earn enough to be considered the breadwinner) and find yourself poor, you are especially challenged.

It takes deliberate effort on the part of both of you to hold things together. Being poor in this materialistic society, which in so many ways seems determined to humiliate and even punish the poor—compounded by being targeted for humiliation and punishment on the basis of race—makes it easy to be full of rage and defeat. Domestic violence, child neglect and abuse, depression, abandonment, physical illness and debilitation are not confined to but certainly flourish under these circumstances.

We never have any extra money. Every cent that Silas and I earn is already accounted for before we cash our checks. It is a terrible way to live. I've started looking for a better-paying secretarial job but Silas won't even try to better himself. He works as a messenger and only earns minimum wage. On the weekends, I stare into the TV set while he plays basketball across the street with his buddies. At night, he joins me and we watch TV together. There is no way we can afford to go out.

—Lee

Lee has taken the first step, which is to seek a new job. Silas is probably afraid to venture beyond what he knows. With no job skills, he may feel that browsing the help-wanted ads is a pointless exercise. Silas needs to spend his weekends in the local public library. Most libraries have sections where you can find books that will tell you how to prepare for civil service tests or turn a personal interest or hobby into a cash-generating enterprise. The library also offers occupational handbooks which describe thousands of jobs and tell you how to go about training for them.

In the meantime, something must be done to relieve the terrible, marriage-destroying pressure on a couple like Lee and Silas. Here are two ideas:

1. Buy a deck of cards and some soft drinks and invite people over to play Bid Whist or another game. Ask each person to bring a different dish or dessert. Thank each guest as they arrive, point them towards the game area and take the food into the kitchen. Take some of each dish and put it into the freezer right away. At the end of the evening, you and your spouse will have:

   ♦ enjoyed an evening together;
   ♦ plenty to laugh and talk about;
   ♦ enough food to last about two weeks.

Do not buy any groceries for the next two weeks. Put the cash that you saved in a bank account or put it toward resume paper, stamps and whatever else you need in your job search.

2. Baby-sit children on Saturdays when their parents are busy running errands. The two of you should handle the kids

together and casually mention to their parents that you are looking for a new or second job. Use half of the money the parents pay you to have some inexpensive fun together, such as visiting a museum. Use the other half to pay for the job search.

Many professional couples never have enough money, either. Reva and Woodrow are a good example. Their standard of living rose with their income until they, too, are barely making ends meet.

When Reva and I got married four years ago, our total combined annual income was $75,000 . We felt rich. Since she already owned her own home, we moved into her place. It was a three-bedroom starter house in a fairly decent neighborhood. Both of us had paid off our student loans and other debts before the wedding so we had a lot of cash just sitting around.

We decided to upgrade our lifestyles.

First, there was the work on the house. Reva wanted a second bathroom and I wanted a deck. After that was done, we started buying African art and other memorabilia. It was a lot of fun. We met other couples who were into collecting and now we have friends across the country and even a few overseas. It's wonderful.

Right after we went through our art phase, I got a big promotion and a $10,000 raise. We thought about having a baby but then decided that there was a lot more that we still wanted to do. We did start saving but we also began receiving offers of credit that we didn't even ask for. We took advantage of everything that came in the mail.

We now own a timeshare in Florida, another house that we are renting to Reva's cousin, two cars and several rooms of new furniture.

Reva's company downsized a few months ago and she was one of the unlucky employees who was let go. Right after that, she was in a car accident and hasn't been well enough to look for another job.

The bills come in faster than I can pay them. There is never enough money to do anything except pay the creditors.

—Woodrow

Woodrow and Reva's plight is not unusual. It is what typically happens when people abuse credit and live above their means.

Fortunately, their problems are a lot easier to fix than those of Silas and Lee. Here's how:

1. If it is possible to sell the extra house and timeshare, this should be done immediately.
2. If the couple lives in an area where public transportation is available, both cars should also be sold. If not, at least get rid of one.

All the money from the sales should be used to pay off the credit cards.

3. Next, the couple should investigate every possible way for Reva to earn money from home. Perhaps she could do proposal writing using a laptop. How about phone consultations in her professional area of expertise?
4. Finally, a few pieces of art and memorabilia should be sold to pay most or all of the furniture bills.

The Time to Talk About Money

Pick a suitable time to talk about money. Suitable is not when the bills are piled high on the table in front of you and the budget is already tight. At such a time, emotions are running high and nerves are stretched to capacity. You are both more prone to outbursts and saying things that you don't mean because of the combination of stress that comes from living on a lean income and having bills that you don't know how to pay staring you in the face. A more favorable occasion would be when you're thinking about making a major purchase or when one of you has received a raise. Discuss your short-term goals, long-term goals and how much money you need to accomplish them. Postpone starting a family until you have a firm footing. Put something aside, even if it is only $10 a week. It may not sound like much but it grows quickly and eliminates that sense of desperation inside you.

Distinguish Between Need and Want

We are inundated daily with advertisements that exhort us to spend, spend, spend. If you haven't already learned to distinguish between need and want, now is a good time to learn. Wants come from relatives, friends, neighbors and advertisements. Each of these sources has or promotes products guaranteed to make you feel happier, more successful, sexier or better looking.

If you are trying to improve your financial status, buy only what you really need and stay away from purchases that simply give you a false sense of status, such as $100 sneakers with some celebrity's name on them.

Remember to always put a little money aside each in case of layoffs or illness. If you plan to have children, prepare for that, too.

A Bigger Paycheck Doesn't Mean Control of Your Spouse

No matter who earns the most money, or even if one of you is not working at all, the two of you must work out a financial plan that you both agree on. Don't use the size of your spouse's paycheck to measure his or her worth and never use it as a weapon in an argument. You are equal partners and no one should have more power in a marriage just because of a larger paycheck.

A Final Word of Caution

Be very careful to support each other emotionally during financially difficult times. When there isn't enough money, the man starts losing confidence in the marriage. African American husbands can very quickly start to question their continued ability to provide for their families. History has shown us that he frequently has walked away as the last vestige of personal control and out of sadness for his inability to provide. When two people truly love each other, this is the ultimate tragedy.

Fifty Ways to Make Your Marriage Last

1. Go out for a Sunday afternoon brunch.
2. Go on a ski vacation even if neither one of you knows how to ski.
3. Go the movies.
4. Go to the annual Black Enterprise networking conference.
5. Have a picnic.
6. Go to the children's zoo (without the kids).
7. Take a long hot bath together.
8. Go out for pizza.
9. Attend the Ebony Fashion Fair.
10. Take erotic photos of each other.
11. Go to the Mardi Gras in New Orleans.
12. Spend the night in your local hotel.
13. Get up early and watch the sunrise.
14. Host a barbecue and invite all the neighbors.
15. Attend the National Black Expo in your city.
16. Show each other your high school yearbook.
17. Rent a bicycle built for two and take a nice long ride.
18. Bake a cake.
19. Read Walter Mosely's books aloud to each other.
20. Collect and listen to old Black comedy albums (e.g. Jackie "Moms" Madly, Ray Moore, Redd Foxx, Richard Pryor, Wild Man Steve, etc.).
21. Look at your wedding album.
22. Rent pornographic videos.
23. Play Monopoly.
24. Play cards.
25. Go to the library.

26. Spend a weekend in Las Vegas.
27. Visit an art gallery.
28. Learn to play pool.
29. Go jogging.
30. Join a bowling league.
31. Join a gym.
32. Give each other a massage.
33. Have a Spike Lee Film Festival and invite all your friends.
34. Write love letters to each other.
35. Try a new sexual position.
36. Rent *Claudine*, starring James Earl Jones & Diahann Carroll.
37. Watch your wedding video.
38. Wash each other's hair.
39. Take a cruise.
40. Help one welfare mother get a job.
41. Call each other at work.
42. Teach an illiterate person to read.
43. Find shelter for a homeless family.
44. Help one person register to vote.
45. Take courses in African American history.
46. Write letters to your media describing positive events in your neighborhood.
47. Campaign for an up-and-coming politician who represents African American interests.
48. Decorate the Christmas tree.
49. Celebrate Kwaanza and invite both your families.
50. See a marriage counselor.

Resources

Suggested Reading

Basic Black: Home Training for Modern Times, by Karen Grigsby Bates & Karen Elyse Hudson (Doubleday, 1996)

Children of the Dream, by Audrey Edwards & Dr. Craig K. Polite (Doubleday, 1992)

555 Ways to Earn Extra Money, by Jay Conrad Levinson (Owl Books, 1991)

Good Health for African Americans, by Barbara M. Dixon, Rd., LDN (Crown, 1994)

Having Your Baby: A Guide for African American Women, by Hilda Hutcherson, M.D. with Margaret Williams (One World/ Ballantine, 1997)

How to Love a Black Man, by Dr. Ronn Elmore (Warner, 1996)

What Makes the Great Great, by Dennis P. Kimbro, Ph.D. (Doubleday, 1990)

Win the Job, by Jeffrey G. Allen (John Wiley & Sons, 1990)

Organizations

American Institute of Stress
124 Park Avenue
Yonkers, NY 10703

Cocaine Anonymous
6125 Washington Blvd. Suite 202
Los Angeles, CA 90230
Hotline: 1-800-COCAINE

Institute of Black Chemical Dependency
2614 Nicollet Avenue South
Minneapolis, MN 55408
(612) 871-7878

National Institute of Mental Health
Public Inquiries
5600 Fishers Lane, Room 15C-05
Rockville, MD 20857

Strengthening the Black Family
1509 Tierney Circle
Raleigh, NC 27610
(919) 834-8862
(919) 834-7141

On-Line Information

Africa Online	http://www.africaonline.com
African American Museum	http://www.artnoir.com/aama.html
BET Holdings	http://www.betnetworks.com
Black News Network	http://www.bin.com
Britannica Online	http://www.eb.com
CareerPath	http://careerpath.com
Debt Counselors of America	http:/dca.org
Internet for Kids	http:www.internet-for-kids.com
Jazz Online	http://www.jazzonin.com
Job Hunt	http://www.job-hunt.org
Job Search	http://www.lib.umich.edu/chdocs/employment
Marriage and Family Therapy	http://www.echo-on.net/~mmjw
MCA Home Entertainment Playroom	http://www.mca.com/home/playroom
NetNoir	http://www.netnoir@aol.com
Shoestring Travel	http://www.stratpub.com
United States Black On-Line	http://www.usbol.com
Universal Black Pages	http://gatech.edu/bgsa/blackpages.html

Rites of Passage Programs

Baltimore Rites of Passage Kollective
3645 Cottage Avenue
Baltimore, MD 21215
(410) 462-1494

Concerned Black Men, Inc.
1511 K Street NW Suite 1100
Washington, DC 20005
(202) 783-5414

HAWK Federation
175 Filbert Street Suite 202
Oakland, CA 94607
(510) 836-3245

West Dallas Community Centers, Inc.
8200 Brookriver Drive Suite N704
Dallas, TX 75247
(214) 634-7691

Bibliography

Books

Aldridge, Delores P. *Focusing: Black Male-Female Relationships.* Third World Press, 1991.

Barbach, Lonnie and Geisinger, David L. *Going the Distance: Finding & Keeping Lifelong Love.* Plume, 1993.

Blumstein, P., and Schwartz, P. *American Couples.* William Morrow, 1983.

Boyd, Julia A., Ph.D. *In the Company of My Sisters: Black Women and Self-Esteem.* Dutton, 1993.

Cosby, Bill. *Love and Marriage.* Doubleday, 1989.

Cose, Ellis. *A Man's World.* Harper Collins, New York, 1995.

Davis, Dr. Larry E. *Black and Single.* Noble Press, 1993.

Diggs, Anita Doreen. *Talking Drums.* St. Martin's Press, 1995.

Diop, Dr. Cheikh. *The Cultural Unity of Black Africa.* Third World Press, 1990.

Duncan, Barry L., Psy.D. and Joseph W. Rock, Psy.D. *Overcoming Relationship Impasses.* Insight Books, 1991.

Forward, Susan and Craig Buck. *Money Demons: Keep Them from Sabotaging Your Relationship.* Bantam Books, 1994.

Fraser, George. *Success Runs in Our Race.* William Morrow, 1994.

Gates, Henry Louis, Jr. *Thirteen Ways of Looking at a Black Man.* Random House, 1997.

Hopson, Derek S. and Darlene Powell Hopson. *Friends, Lovers and Soulmates.* Simon & Schuster, 1994.

Hutchinson, Earl Ofari, Ph.D. *Black Fatherhood: The Guide to Male Parenting.* Impact Publications, 1992.

Jhally, Sut and Justin Lewis. *Enlightened Racism: The Cosby Show,*

Audiences, and the Myth of the American Dream. Westview Press, 1992.

Kimbro, Dennis. *Daily Motivations for African Americans.* Fawcett Columbine, 1993.

Madhubuti, Haki R. *Black Men: Obsolete, Single, Dangerous.* Third World Press, 1990.

McMillan, Terry. *Waiting to Exhale.* Viking, 1992.

Page, Susan. *Now That I'm Married, Why Isn't Everything Perfect.* Dell, 1994.

Pinkney, Alphonso. *The Myth of Black Progress.* Cambridge University Press, 1984.

Staples, Robert and Leanor Boulin Johnson. *Black Families at the Crossroads.* Jossey-Bass, 1993.

Thomas, John L. *Beginning Your Marriage.* ACTA Publications, 1987.

Tucker, M. Belinda & Claudia Mitchell Kernan. *The Decline in Marriage among African Americans.* Russell Sage Foundation, 1995.

Welsing, Dr. Frances Cress. *The Isis Papers.* Third World Press, 1995.

Wiley, Ralph. *What Black People Should Do Now.* One World/ Ballantine, 1993.

Winters, Paul A. *Race Relations.* Greenhaven Press, 1996.

Woodson, Carter G. *The Mis-Education of the Negro.* Africa World Press, 1990.

Woodson, Robert L. *On the Road to Economic Freedom: An Agenda for Black Progress.* Regnery Gateway, 1987.

Articles

Bernay, Beryl. "Black Families Rediscover Sag Harbor." *The New York Times,* September 20, 1992.

Bosanko, Deborah. "The Kinder, Gentler, Richer American." *American Demographics,* January 1995.

Boucher, David. "There's Plenty of Time at Home for Work." *The New York Times,* November 20, 1994.

Brodsky, Elaine. "The Other Woman: Confessions of a Woman Married to a Man Married to His Business." *Inc.,* September 1988.

Carmody, Deirdre. "The Media Business: An Enduring Voice for Black Women." *The New York Times,* January 23, 1995.

Chapelle, Tony. "Profile: A Pioneer Who's Skeptical of Minority Brokerages." The *New York Times*, September 18, 1994.

Cohen, Roger. "Once Welcomed, Black Artists Return to an Indifferent France." The *New York Times*, February 7, 1994.

Cook, Anthony. "Betrayed by Her Loving Husband." *Money*, July 1993.

Crispell, Diane. "Marital Bust." *American Demographics*, June 1994.

Dewitt, Karen. "Two Black Lawyers' Crazy Idea that Worked." The *New York Times*, January 28, 1994.

Dolan, Ken and Daria Dolan. "Follow These Ruses to Avoid Family Fights over Money." *Money*, July 1993.

Hoffman, Saul D. and Greg J. Duncan. "The Effect of Incomes, Wages and AFDC Benefits on Marital Disruption." *Journal of Human Resources*, Winter 1995.

Jones, Charisse. "Reassessing a Dream." The *New York Times*, April 10, 1994.

Jukes, Jill and Ruthan Rosenberg. "I've Been Fired Too! The Spouse's Reaction." *Business Quarterly*, Autumn 1991.

Leavy, Walter. "50 Years of Black Love in Movies." *Ebony*, February 1995.

Lippert, Barbara. "Fire and Ice." *Brandweek*, November 7, 1994.

Norment, Lynn. "Why Some Marriages Last and Last . . . and Last." *Ebony*, February 1995.

Randolph, Laura B. "Browning the Suburbs." *Ebony*, January 1992.

Richardson, Lynda. "Minority Students Languish in Special Education System." The *New York Times*, April 6, 1994.

Roberts, Sam. "Black Women Graduates Outpace Male Counterparts." The *New York Times*, October 31, 1994.

Ruffin, Frances E. "Yours, Mine and Ours." *Black Enterprise*, March 1986.

Shellenbarger, Sue. "Work & Family." *Wall Street Journal*, June 29, 1994.

Siesel, Nancy. "Blacks in the Suburbs: Lonely, Puzzled and Unsure of Oneself." The *New York Times*, March 17, 1994.

Staples, Brent. "The End of the Movement." The *New York Times*, September 4, 1994.

Williams, Lena. "At Home with Camille O. Cosby: A Private Woman, A Public Cause." The *New York Times*, December 15, 1994.

Wynter, Leon E. "Business & Race." *Wall Street Journal*, December 21, 1994.

About the Authors

Anita Doreen Diggs is the author of *Success at Work: A Guide for African Americans*, *The African American Resource Guide* and *Talking Drums*. She is a member of the American Society of Journalists & Authors, Black Women in Publishing, The Go On Girl Book Club and The Authors Guild.

Vera S. Paster, Ph.D. is a Professor in the Doctoral Program in Clinical Psychology at the City University of New York. She has also been a marital and couples therapist in private practice for twenty-seven years. Dr. Paster was once honored with an appointment to President Jimmy Carter's Commission on Mental Health, the Primary Prevention Task Group.